SCOTLAND

SCOTLAND

NIGEL BLUNDELL

PARKGATE
BOOKS

ACKNOWLEDGMENTS

The Publishers and the Author would like to thank in particular three organisations, whose assistance has made this book such a dramatic exposition of Scotland's glories, past and present. For research and for the generous use of photographs, we express our extreme gratitude to Historic Scotland, the National Trust for Scotland and the Scottish Tourist Board. Also to be thanked are Gavin Booth for photo research in Edinburgh; Iain Thomson for writing Chapters 17 to 22 and 24; Doug McIvor for writing Chapter 23; David Lyons for the photographs illustrating the poetry on pages 182-211; Simon Clay for the Chapter 23 whisky bottle photography; the Illustrated London News Picture Library for the photographs on pages 161, 164, 165 and 167; and Image Bank for the photograph on page 160.

Photograph Page 2: *Kilchurn Castle, Loch Awe.*
Photograph Page 3: *Dun CarlOway Broch, Isle of Lewis.*

First published in 1998 by
PRC Publishing Ltd,
Kiln House, 210 New Kings Road, London SW6 4NZ

This edition published in 1998 by
Parkgate Books Ltd
Kiln House
210 New Kings Road
London SW6 4NZ
Great Britain

© 1998 PRC Publishing Ltd

British Library Cataloguing in Publication Data:
A catalogue record for this book is available from the British Library.

ISBN 1 85585 014 1

Printed and bound in China

Reprinted 1999

Contents

INTRODUCTION

INTRODUCTION

Scotland is a beautiful country, and in this book we shall discover how the terrain and its geographical features shaped the history and the lives of its peoples. But who are these people, the Scots? Why are they so different from their neighbours to the south, and why do people all over the world cling avidly to their Scottish ancestry?

Scotland is really a country of many peoples, the Lowland Scot of Anglo-Saxon stock, the Gaelic Highlander to the north and west, and the Orkney and Shetland Islanders of Norse origin. Over the centuries these people were wary of each other but through a series of conflicts and bloody battles they eventually began to recognize themselves as one nation.

Scotland covers an area of 7.2 million hectares (30,000 square miles) which constitutes more than a third of the area of Great Britain. The country lies between 55-60° north, with central Scotland being on the same latitude as Moscow. The northernmost part of Scotland — the Shetland Islands — is closer to the Arctic Circle than to the south of England, with mainland Ireland being a mere 20km (12 miles) away at its nearest point. The Scottish western seaboard stretches for 416km (260 miles) as the crow flies — but this becomes 3,200km (2,000 miles) if all the coastal indentations are followed. The country also incorporates nearly 800 islands.

With an intricate coastline more than 9,654km (6,000 miles) in length, the ebb and flow of powerful tides and a great upwelling and mixing of ocean currents on the continental shelf to the west of the Outer Hebrides, Scotland's coastal waters are among the richest in the world. In spite of its northerly latitude, Scotland enjoys comparatively warm seas due to the influence of the North Atlantic Drift — a comparatively warm stream of water originating all the way across the Atlantic in the Gulf of Mexico. In the winter the seas around western Scotland are frequently warmer than the land, giving an equable climate despite the northerly latitude. Because of the geography of the country, some 80 percent of Scotland's surface is classified as moor, rough pasture, or otherwise uncultivable ground.

The turbulent history of Scotland reveals it to be a country of persistent conflict, and although never fully conquered, it was almost constantly under siege. In the Highlands there were the early feuds between the clans; the incursion of the Gaels or Scots into the south-west brought them into frequent confrontation with the Picts. In the first half of the first millennium the lowland peoples had to deal with the Romans, whilst towards the end of the millennium, the Northern and Western Isles were invaded by the Norsemen — the Vikings. The beginning of the second millennium saw the Normans' attempts to conquer the land and later, of course, came the bloody conflicts with the 'auld enemy', the English. For more than 1,500 years Scotland hardly knew a decade of peace.

The wars and conflicts which defined the course of Scottish history are well chronicled, but this book attempts to show the richness and diversity of a culture that includes far more than just battlefield heroics, however valiant or in vain these might have

been. Indeed, as much of the stirring prose and poetry of Scotland relates to the rugged beauty and splendour of the geography as it does to the exhilarating victories and despairing defeats of its armies. The physical beauty of the land can touch the heart, every bit as much as a sad lament mourning the loss of heroes in battle. From the Atlantic storm-lashed Western Isles, through the purple heather-clad Highlands, to the miles of golden sandy beaches of the north-east coast one can see why Scotland is a country worth fighting for. Anyone who has been 'over the sea to Skye', sat in the wooded glades on the banks of the Dee, or strolled along the shores of the 'bonny banks' of Loch Lomond knows the mysterious allure of this place.

The former Scottish counties have been disbanded and the country is now instead divided into nine 'Regions': Dumfries & Galloway, Strathclyde, Central, Highland & Islands, Grampian, Tayside, Fife, Lothian and Borders. For the purpose of setting the scene for the historical events that follow, Scotland can roughly be divided into four geographical areas — the Northern Isles, the Western Isles, the Highlands and the central Lowlands and Borders.

The Northern Isles comprise the islands of Shetland and Orkney. According to geologists, Shetland is the mountainous area of the pre-Ice Age Scottish/Scandinavian continent. Over the course of millions of years, this vast area was gradually eroded by rivers as well as the sea, and the weight of the ice under which the land lay during the various Ice Ages caused it to sink until all that was left of what was once part of the European continent, was Shetland. Orkney is situated just 10km (6 miles), at the nearest point, from the extreme north of mainland Scotland, but is separated by one of the most turbulent stretches of water in the British Isles — the Pentland Firth. The islands have, over long periods of time, experienced many changes in sea level and even as recently as the end of the last Ice Age were joined to mainland Scotland. The Northern Isles contain some of Scotland's most remote inhabited islands, which still proudly retain their strong Norse heritage, and are now adjusting to an influx of oilmen with all the trappings of exploration and exploitation — Scotland's very own 'Klondike'.

The Western Isles evoke stirring images of beauty, mystery, and romance, which have long attracted visitors to their shores. Visions of these inaccessible outposts have been kept alive by poets and balladeers singing of shipwrecks, ancient kings, and saints; the Skye Boat Song romantically tells of Bonnie Prince Charlie, and thousands of pilgrims visit Iona every year to attend the sacred sites of St. Columba. These islands — with a way of life completely at one with nature — offer an escape from the more hectic mainland.

Previous Page: *The Torridon area includes some fine mountains. Liathach is 3,456ft and Beinn Alligin some 3,232ft.*

Right: *A stunning view of the two Buachailles from Glen Etive.*

The visitor will never forget the storm-lashed rocks and the myriad swooping sea birds with their plaintive cries, or the brilliant summer sunsets. Each island has its own geographical distinction and there is an incredible diversity between them. The Isle of Arran, in the Firth of Clyde, with its rugged mountains rising to 874m (2,866ft) at Goat Fell, is often called 'Scotland in miniature' for its variety of rocks, hills, glens, and lochs.

Between Edinburgh and England, in the south-eastern corner of Scotland, the rolling fields are surrounded on three sides by high hills and moors, and the frequently wild North Sea on the other. Through the fertile valleys and meadows the majestic waters of the Rivers Tweed, Teviot, Yarrow and Ettrick flow. Of the region's area, covering 466,200 hectares (1,800 sq miles), almost half of it rises above 305m (1,000ft) high.

Geographically the Highlands are all the lands and islands north of the Highland Boundary Fault, an irregular south-west to north-east geological rift from Helensburgh in the west to Stonehaven in the north. Yet much of the land north of this notional line is flat in the extreme — Caithness and Buchan for example. Scotland's highest villages, Leadhills and Wanlockhead, are actually in the Lowlands, in Dumfries & Galloway. The great mountain ranges that give the Highlands their name lie to the centre and west of the region; the east coast (with the exception of the odd spectacular mountain) is predominantly flat.

There are only a few major centres of population in the region; the great mass of Highlanders still live in villages and their economy is founded largely on agriculture, tourism and the harvest of the sea. The Highlands are predominantly treeless, but much of

Highland Perthshire abounds in fine woodland. Crofting is the definitive land use of the Highlands, but the east Highlands see agriculture in the form of vast, managed farms. This area with its turbulent history of clan feuds and fierce battles contains the sites of the infamous massacre at Glencoe and the fateful battle at Culloden.

The Great Glen is a 97km (60-mile) long giant cleft that cuts diagonally through the heart of Scotland from Fort William north-west to Inverness. The glen was created more than 200 million years ago by a massive shift in the earth's crust. Telford's Caledonian Canal runs its length linking a series of lochs including, near the northern end of the Great Glen, the mysterious Loch Ness with its black deep water. The loch is 40km (25 miles) long and barely 3km (2 miles) across at its widest point. At its greatest depth it is over 305m (1,000ft) deep and the dark color of the water comes from the many peat-stained rivers and streams that flow into the loch. Britain's highest peak, Ben Nevis at 1,344m (4,408ft), lies near the western end of the Great Glen.

The history of the Scottish peoples begins in the Northern Isles, with the hunter-gatherers of the Mesolithic Age (around 7,000 BC), through the Neolithic farmers (c7,000-2,000 BC), the Bronze Age (2,000-600 BC), to the Iron Age (600 BC-AD 500). The exact origins of these people is unknown, although what is almost certain is that they were Celts. Historians generally agree that they were a part of a stream of minor migrations from Europe to the British Isles which took place in the first millennium BC. The Celts were certainly a warrior race with colonial ambitions but it seems likely that their colonisation happened peacefully over hundreds, if not thousands, of years. Knowledge of the early history of Scotland is inevitably very sketchy but a great deal was learnt by the uncovering of the Iron Age village, Jarlshof, in the 19th century near the southern tip of Shetland. This is one of the most important archaeological sites in Britain, as it shows the development of civilisation from the earliest times through to the medieval age.

The beginning of the first millennium saw the Romans invade the British Isles and, though it is possible that Roman fleets sailed as far north as Shetland Isles, there is little to show in the Highlands or Islands of their influence. It is in the Lowland plains and moors that we find evidence of the southern European invaders. In 121 AD, the Emperor Hadrian visited Britain and ordered the building of his famous eponymous wall as a deterrent to the raiding parties of the factionalised Scottish lowland tribes. Parts of the wall can still be seen standing between the estuaries of the Solway and the Tyne. By 400 AD troubles at home caused the Roman

legions to be recalled from Britain to defend their homeland, and ultimately Rome herself, from the Goths. 30 years later not only Scotland, but the whole of Britain had been completely abandoned and roman civilisation was left to disintegrate.

Towards the end of the millennium Scotland had some new visitors with strong colonial ambitions — the Vikings. The Shetland Isles were a mere two days sailing by longship from the fjords of the Norsemen's homelands and within the next hundred years, they became an important base for the Viking raiding and migration sea routes 'west over the sea' to Britain, Iceland, Greenland and almost certainly North America. Lamlash Bay, on the island of Arran, was one of the best natural harbours in the Western Isles. Furthermore it was close to the shipping routes the Vikings used to sail to their more southern territories and, for a while, formed part of the Norse Kingdom of Man and Sudreyjar. In the latter half of the 9th century a Viking earldom was established in Orkney. Scandinavian rule in Orkney and Shetland lasted 600 years until the mid-15th century and there are still lingering loyalties with the Viking influence remarkably prevalent in the northern isles. Norwegian

Above Left: *A reconstruction of an early farming settlement.*

Bottom Left: *Bronze Age man built many stone circles although their precise purpose is unknown — there are splendid examples at Brodgar and Stennes in Orkney and Callanish in Lewis.*

Above: *Night in a west coast cave dwelling.*

Right: *Mesolithic hunting in south Edinburgh.*

Constitution Day is still celebrated in Kirkwall, while Lerwick remembers its Norse heritage when it holds the midwinter festival known as 'Up Helly Aa'.

The beginning of the second millennium saw the Norman invasion of England which coincided with a time in Scottish history when the people, under the rule of Duncan, King of Strathclyde (1034-1040), were coming together as one nation for the first time. The borders of this ancient kingdom differed very little to those of today. When Edward I, the 'scourge of Scotland', came to the English throne at the end of the 13th century, it marked the beginning of centuries of serious conflict between the English and the Scots. Edward invaded Scotland, but in 1297 the great Scottish hero William Wallace overthrew the English in a famous victory at Stirling Bridge and took occupancy of Stirling Castle for a time.

A year later, in a battle at Falkirk, Edward I wrought his revenge and a final surrender of the Scots seemed inevitable when their champion Wallace was captured and put to death in London, in 1305, by direct order of the English king. It was left to Robert the Bruce to recover the kingdom and the battle which followed against Edward II is arguably the most important conflict ever to have taken place on Scottish soil. Bruce's stirring words 'Now's the time, and now's the hour, and Scotland shall be free' and the ensuing victory at 'Blar Allt a Bhain-chnuie' or the Battle at the Burn of Bannock on 23-24 June 1314 was to win independence and assure Robert the Bruce the status of national hero.

Two centuries later appeared the romantic figure of Mary Queen of Scots (1542-1587) who is, without question, the most renowned female figure in Scottish history. It was during her reign that the new religion, Protestantism, took a grip in lowland Scotland, which in turn led to ensuing religious rivalries which would eventually culminate in the disaster of Culloden some 200 years later. Mary was forced to abdicate in favour of her son, christened Charles James, and this proved to be a momentous event in both Scottish and English history. In 1603, on the death of Elizabeth I of England, James VI of Scotland was proclaimed King James I of England, Scotland, France and Ireland. He called his dual kingdoms of England and Scotland by a new name — Great Britain — which he had to force an unwilling English Parliament to use. Ruling the Scots from London would prove difficult and a century of warfare — and two 'Pretenders' to the Scottish throne — would see such horrors as the massacre at Glencoe and the slaughter ofn ther clans at Culloden. The subsequent 'Clearances' of the 19th century would end the traditional Highland clan lifestyle for ever.

The history of the Scottish peoples in the 19th and 20th century was one of constant change as they took full and considerable part in first the Industrial Revolution, and then in the expansion, development, consolidation, and rule of the British Empire. Scotland has always produced more than its fair share of influential architects and engineers: burt has also been influential in the field of the arts —particularly poetry — with a number of world famous writers including, of course, Scotland's favorite son Robbie Burns. By comparing these works with later writings it becomes obvious how much the Scottish language has changed. However, the immortal memory of Robert Burns lives on with the worldwide festivities of Burns Night every 25 January. Other Scottish festivals are celebrated around the globe — and not just by Scots and their descendants: the Highland Games are held annually in North

Above: *Bonnie Prince Charlie stands on top of Glenfinnan Monument overlooking Loch Shiel as a tribute to the clansmen who fought for his cause. It was erected in 1815 by Alexander Macdonald of Glenaladale.*

Right: *In true Scottish baronial style, Crathes Castle in Aberdeenshire was built in the latter half of the 16th century on land originally granted to the Burnett family by King Robert the Bruce in 1323. Prominent features of its gardens are the topiary yew hedges dating from 1702.*

America, Africa and the Antipodes, as well as Scotland even, horror upon horror, in the sassanach south.

The chapters that follow do not claim to be an exhaustive account of the social and economic history of Scotland, but rather a glimpse of the nature of the geography and people of this beautiful country. It is hoped that those who know the country and those yet to visit might gain a different perspective of the nature of the land by an understanding of the nature of the people. It is true that the country was under perpetual siege for nearly one and a half thousand years but the spirit of the people has prevailed and any visitor can be guaranteed a warm and generous welcome and excellent hospitality.

PART 1:
THE LAND

1 Geology and Geography

The popular perception of the landscape of Scotland gleaned from picture postcards and the lids of shortcake tins is one of heather-clad mountains and deep brooding lochs. The landscape certainly possesses these in abundance but there is so much more. The rolling moorlands, vast woodlands and the gently flowing waters of the majestic River Tweed in the Borders all contrast vividly with the stark, rugged beauty of the Highland peaks; while the shallow estuary of the Solway Firth with its sandy beaches, bordering England in the south-west, is almost a different country from the Atlantic storm-lashed wildness of the Hebrides further up the western seaboard.

Most tourists who enter Scotland from the M6 (in other words, from the south) tend to press on northwards as far as possible before stopping. In so doing they miss the pleasant woodland and the whitewashed farmsteads set in the green rolling hills of the Borders. The estuary of the Solway Firth provides sandy beaches and most of the sleepy little towns of Dumfries & Galloway date from the 18th century. It is often cited that Tomintoul is the highest village in the Highlands of Scotland, but here in the Lowlands, Wanlockhead at 421m (1,380ft) above sea level, is the highest village in all Scotland. Along with its neighbouring village Leadhills, it was a centre for lead mining until earlier this century.

The vast area now known as Strathclyde incorporates many of the old counties including Ayrshire, Renfrewshire, Lanarkshire, Buteshire and Argyll, to say nothing of the great city of Glasgow. The region can reasonably claim to feature practically everything Scotland has to offer: sandy beaches in Ayrshire, the farmlands of Lanark, the bustling throngs of a modern city in Glasgow, and the mountains, lochs and firths to the north and west. The small village of Alloway on the outskirts of Ayr is the birthplace of one of Scotland's favourite sons, Robert Burns, and is consequently today a thriving tourist centre.

Central is the uninspiring name which has been given to a part of Scotland that used to ring with names such as Stirlingshire, Clackmannanshire and Kinross. This scenic region is steeped in the history of Scotland with its famous battles and royal castles. The bridge over the River Forth in Stirling was built in 1415 and you can still walk over it following in the footsteps of every king of Scotland from James I to Charles II — on the other hand the Stirling Bridge where William Wallace won his famous victory was made of wood and has long since disappeared. On a clear day a view from the ramparts of Stirling Castle will take in Ben Lomond, the Trossachs, Loch Katrine and the extraordinary flat plain of the Forth Valley. In the industrial and richly historical town of Falkirk were the famous Carron Iron Works which, from 1760, made Carronades — the guns for Nelson's ships.

The Highland & Islands is the region most foreign tourists will most readily picture when they think of Scotland. It does, after all, have the highest mountains and the deepest lochs and is infused with the history of the clans. Beside Loch Leven lies the brooding Glencoe, which witnessed the infamous slaughter of members of the MacDonald clan, the bleakness of the area is emphasised by the lack of trees or even heather. Crossing the Ballachulish Bridge and heading north along the banks of Loch Linnhe in the Lochaber district of Scotland's Highland Region we come to Fort William and Ben Nevis (1,344m/4,408ft), the highest mountain in the British Isles. A five-mile long footpath, starting near Fort William, leads to the summit of the mountain.

Ben is the Scottish term for mountain, from the Gaelic beann — 'peak'. A drive up the A82, the length of the Great Glen, from the Ballachulish Bridge to Inverness will afford mountain and loch scenery of awe inspiring splendor. In the north-east of the region lies the Black Isle, so named not because of its colour, but because it is rarely whitened with snow. The rich red soil grows the finest oats with which to make porridge — along with haggis, undoubtedly Scotland's most famous dish.

The Isle of Skye is arguably the most romantic and best known of the Western Isles. It is known as the 'Cloudy Isle' and certainly the Cuillins, the island's main hills, are often shrouded in mist — which is not surprising considering they stand over 915m (3,000ft) high. The island will forever be linked with Bonnie Prince Charlie's flight after the disaster at Culloden and the role Flora Macdonald played in his escape. The Royal Hotel at Portree now stands on the site of an inn where they bade their last farewells. Further south lies the little island of Iona where 48 Scottish monarchs lie interred in the burial ground known as the Ridge of Kings. This regal cemetery's occupants include the 9th century Kenneth MacAlpin, Macbeth, and his victim Duncan, as well as four Irish kings and a further eight from Norway. The pink granite cathedral is the focus of thousands of pilgrims who visit Iona every year to pay homage at the site where St. Columba settled to launch his great missionary exercise in the 6th century.

The tiny island of Staffa is known world-wide for the scenic wonder of Fingal's Cave which inspired the young Mendelssohn to write his overture The Hebrides. Outside the Hebrides, the islands of Shetland and Orkney include some of Britain's most remote inhabited islands. Nowadays the airport at Sumburgh, at the southern tip of Mainland Shetland, is busy all year round handling a high volume of oil-industry traffic.

The Grampian Region with its salmon rivers, the magnificent Dee, Don, Spey and Ythan to name but a few, is an angler's paradise. The northern coastal plain boasts fine agricultural land and the region has areas of outstanding scenic splendour with its heather, conifer forests, and, of course, the Grampian hills to the

Previous Page: *Looking west the snow-capped peaks of Liathach: at left Mullach an Rathain, on the right Spidean a'Choire reflected in the mirror-calm Loch Clair.*

Right: *Map of Scotland, showing major cities and geographical features.*

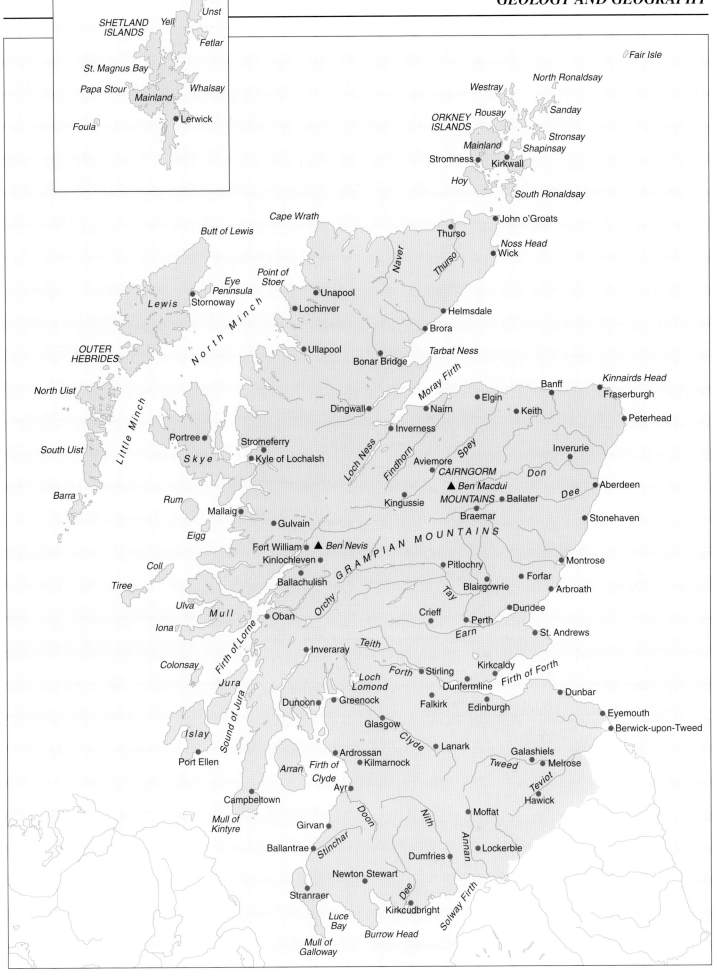

Herma Ness

SHETLAND
ISLANDS
Unst
Yell
Fetlar

St. Magnus Bay
Papa Stour
Whalsay
Mainland

Foula
Lerwick

Fair Isle

North Ronaldsay
Westray
Rousay
Sanday
ORKNEY
ISLANDS
Stronsay
Mainland
Shapinsay
Stromness
Kirkwall
Hoy
South Ronaldsay

Cape Wrath
John o'Groats
Butt of Lewis
Thurso
Noss Head
Wick

Point of
Stoer
Eye
Peninsula
Unapool
Helmsdale
Lewis
Stornoway
Lochinver
Brora

OUTER
HEBRIDES
Ullapool
Tarbat Ness
Bonar Bridge

North Minch
Moray Firth
Kinnairds Head
Banff
Fraserburgh
North Uist
Dingwall
Elgin
Keith
Peterhead
Nairn
Little Minch
Inverness
Inverurie
Portree
Stromeferry
Spey
Aberdeen
South Uist
Skye
Kyle of Lochalsh
Loch Ness
Findhorn
Aviemore
CAIRNGORM
Don
Dee
Barra
Ben Macdui
Rum
MOUNTAINS
Ballater
Mallaig
Kingussie
Stonehaven
Gulvain
Braemar
Eigg
GRAMPIAN MOUNTAINS
Fort William
Ben Nevis
Coll
Kinlochleven
Pitlochry
Montrose
Tiree
Ballachulish
Forfar
Ulva
Orchy
Blairgowrie
Arbroath
Mull
Oban
Tay
Dundee
Iona
Firth of Lorne
Crieff
Perth
Earn
St. Andrews
Inveraray
Teith
Colonsay
Forth
Stirling
Kirkcaldy
Jura
Loch
Lomond
Dunfermline
Firth of Forth
Dunbar
Dunoon
Greenock
Falkirk
Edinburgh
Eyemouth
Glasgow
Clyde
Lanark
Berwick-upon-Tweed
Islay
Ardrossan
Galashiels
Kilmarnock
Tweed
Melrose
Port Ellen
Arran
Firth of
Clyde
Ayr
Teviot
Campbeltown
Doon
Hawick
Mull of
Kintyre
Girvan
Nith
Moffat
Ballantrae
Stinchar
Annan
Lockerbie
Dumfries
Newton Stewart
Stranraer
Dee
Solway Firth
Kirkcudbright
Luce
Bay
Burrow Head
Mull of
Galloway

TORRIDON

Torridon, in Ross & Cromarty, epitomises the grandeur and wildness of the Highlands. It includes some of Scotland's finest mountain scenery, including towering Liathach (1,053m/3,456ft) — the 'Grey One'. The spectacular 7km (4.5 miles) ridge of Liathach has two main peaks — Spidean a' Choire Leith (Peak of the Grey Corrie) and Mullaich an Rathain (Summit of the Row of Pinnacles) - and between them the narrow, exposed ridge of Am Fasarinen. The other two of the big three Torridonian mountains are Beinn Alligin (985m/3,313ft). They are of red sandstone some 750 million years old; the tops are of white quartzite some 150 million years 'younger'.

There are 277 mountains in Scotland whose peaks rise above 3,000ft (compared, to only eight English). They were first catalogued by Sir Hugh Munro and 'bagging' them all has become a challenge to which many hillwalkers aspire. Liathach's two peaks account for two of them: Beinn Eighe and Beinn Alligin two more. But these ancient, steep-sided hills can be tricky even for experienced climbers in winter when conditions can change rapidly as these pictures show.

Below: *In the middle of the year, glowering under a cloudy sky, Liathach has just a hint of snow at the peak.*

Right: *Liathach seen across Loch Clair on a clear winter's day perfect for walking. Beinn Eighe is to the right.*

Below Right: *From the slopes of Beinn Eighe just in the snow, the scudding clouds hide most of Liathach as the weather starts to come in.*

south. On the east coast stands the historic 'Granite City' of Aberdeen, the region's capital.

The north coast of Aberdeenshire, Banffshire, and Morayshire, with its little fishing villages, have some of the most scenic beaches in Britain. 'How far is't to Forres?' Banquo asks Macbeth as the three witches are brewing up. Forres is towards the western end of the Morayshire coast and there's no sign of a blasted heath — only pleasant green fields, pine woods, and distant views of the mighty Grampians. The majestic River Dee with its royal connections enters the North Sea at Aberdeen after its journey from the Grampians. The River Don, not so famous as the Dee but just as beautiful upstream, also enters the sea at Aberdeen and, in the old part of the city, the oldest medieval bridge in Scotland — the Auld Brig o'Balgownie — crosses a deep salmon pool.

Along with Grampian, Tayside, which includes Angus and most of Perthshire, boasts some of the finest scenery in Scotland as well as some of the richest agricultural land. The holiday resort of Arbroath is also an east coast fishing port located in Tayside, north of the region's capital Dundee, and is known for its 'smokies' — haddock smoked over wood-chip fires. The red sandstone ruins of Arbroath Abbey date from 1178 and it was here, in 1320, that the Declaration of Arbroath asserting Scotland's independence from England was made.

The River Tay with its catchment area of 518,000 hectares (2,000 square miles) has the heaviest flow of any river in Great Britain and is a most attractive as well as valuable resource to the region. Its waters have been harnessed for hydro-electric power — however fish ladders have been built to assist the salmon making their way upstream so they can still get back to their traditional spawning grounds. Over 60,000 salmon are caught annually by commercial fishermen and sporting anglers. The River Tay has for long been famous for its production of fine freshwater pearls, but the mussel population which provided these gems is now in decline due to overfishing and pollution.

The original scheme of the planners who divided Scotland into its new regions was to lump Fife together with Lothian. A hundred or so years ago this would have been completely untenable as the Firth of Forth was, to all intents, like an ocean between them. A sense of history did, however, prevail and the two regions remain separate entities. Fife is a farming region with a rich historic past, although these days it also contains most of Scotland's coalfields. Falkland Castle — a former royal palace — was built in 1539 and, along with its famous golf course, the town of St. Andrews has the oldest university in Scotland.

Edinburgh, the elegant 'Athens of the North' and capital of Lothian, is linked to Fife by the Forth Rail and Road Bridges. Seated magisterially in the Firth of Forth, off the north Berwick coast, is the Bass Rock with its sheer rise to a height of 107m (350ft). The rock is home to every type of British seabird, and gannets with wing-spans of 2m (6ft) can be observed. On top of the cliffs are seven acres of grass where sheep used to graze. It may be that the grass manured by millions of seabirds has a special quality and Bass mutton was widely sought after as a delicacy.

With its rolling moorlands and hills to the west, and woodlands, rivers and good grazing land to the east, historically the Borders is the most fought-over land in Scotland. Today it produces some of the best knitwear and tweed in the world, fine horses and superb salmon fishing.

The Major Cities of Scotland

Glasgow

Sitting beside the mighty River Clyde, Glasgow is Scotland's largest city and the administrative centre of the Strathclyde Region. The city prospered and grew after Scotland's union with England in 1707, especially through the lucrative trade in New World tobacco and sugar. Glasgow continued to expand during the Industrial Revolution but, by the end of the 19th century, its fortunes declined and areas such as the Gorbals became notorious for their poverty-stricken and crime-riven slums. Sauchiehall Street in the heart of the city became renowned for its music halls at the beginning of the 20th century, and the Glasgow School of Art is one of several buildings in the city designed by the influential Art Nouveau architect and designer Charles Rennie Mackintosh.

Manufacturing now accounts for fewer than one job in five and only two of the yards from Glasgow's proud shipbuilding days remain, but whisky distilling continues to be an important local industry. On the outskirts of Glasgow, Pollock Country Park houses the Burrell Collection, a wealthy shipowner's eclectic art collection with 8,000 objects from many cultures, including ancient civilizations. Celtic and Rangers are the two leading city soccer (football) clubs: together they are known as the 'Old Firm' and there is extreme rivalry between the Catholic supporters of Celtic and the Protestant supporters of Rangers.

Edinburgh

Named after Edwin, King of Northumbria in the 7th century, Edinburgh is the capital and second largest city in Scotland. Situated on the Firth of Forth, Edinburgh is also the administrative centre for the Lothian Region. The renowned Firth is an estuary of the River Forth and an inlet of the North Sea with Edinburgh's main port Leith and the Rosyth naval base on its banks. The Firth is crossed by the world famous Forth Rail Bridge, opened in 1890, and the 1964 Forth Road Bridge. As a young lad I remember crossing the famous old rail bridge on my way north to holidays in Aberdeen and throwing a penny from the train window: it was considered lucky if the penny managed to find its way into the Firth without striking the girders of the bridge.

The backbone of Edinburgh's Old Town is the Royal Mile which runs from Edinburgh Castle to the Palace of Holyroodhouse. Some medieval buildings survive in the Old Town, while the Georgian New Town is noted for its fine neo-Classical architecture. The castle dates from the 12th century and overlooks Princes Street, the New Towns principal thoroughfare. The world famous Annual Edinburgh International Festival of Music and Drama, with its renowned 'fringe,' is held in late August and early September.

A stunning panoramic view of the city can be seen from Arthur's Seat, the stump of an extinct volcano which is now the site of a public park. This dramatic landmark stands 823ft high, has no connection with the fabled English King Arthur, but is more likely associated with the 6th century Prince Arthur of Strathclyde.

See the chapter at the end of this section: Jewel of Scotland.

Aberdeen

The third largest city and the largest fishing port in Scotland, Aberdeen is the administrative centre for the Grampian Region. It lies on the east coast between the mouths of the Rivers Dee and Don; *aber* is the Gaelic word for 'river mouth.' Aberdeen is known as the 'Granite City' as this local stone is predominantly used in the buildings. It has also much more romantically been called the 'Silver City,' an effect caused after rain when the sun glints off the shiny speckles of quartz in the granite creating a dazzling spectacle when observed from the surrounding hills. Aberdeen has benefited economically from the North Sea oil boom, and the city has become very prosperous, with house prices shooting up when the oil began to flow in the 1970s.

Dundee

Situated on the north side of the Firth of Tay, Dundee is the administrative centre for the Tayside Region of east Scotland and the country's fourth largest city. The city is linked to the south side of the Firth by rail over the Tay Bridge—rebuilt in 1888—and by a road bridge opened in 1966. The rebuilt railway bridge replaced the one involved in the infamous Tay Bridge disaster of 1879 when a train plunged off the bridge into the icy waters below with the loss of over 100 lives. Engineering, shipbuilding and servicing the North Sea oil rigs are important local industries today, while traditional Dundee products include the three 'Js' - jam, jute, and journalism. Marmalade has been made here since 1797 and in the 19th century Dundee was the centre for the manufacturing of jute products. The city was the birthplace of much-loved children's comics such as the Beano and the Dandy.

Inverness

Often referred to as the 'capital' of the Highlands, Inverness is the northernmost major city of Scotland. The city stands at the head of the Moray Firth and at the entrance of the Caledonian Canal which connects Scotland's east and west coasts through the lochs and Telford canal of the Great Glen.

Perth

The only other city of any size in Scotland Perth lies beside the River Tay in the Tayside Region. The Scottish parliament met there on occasions and it was the home of many Scottish kings. John Knox launched the Scottish Reformation from the pulpit of St. John's Kirk here in 1559.

Rich geology

It is easy to look at Scotland's massively impressive mountains, glens, and lochs and suppose that they have been there for ever, but the scenery is just the latest phase of a series of colossal geological transformations. Scotland was formed from separate parts of the earth's crust that have gradually been drifting into place for hundreds of millions of years. In fact Scotland has more varieties of rock within its boundaries than many larger countries. This geological richness occurred because large geological sheets of the planet—each with its own variety of rocks—gradually converged and fused into one rocky plate along the fault lines still seen in Scotland today. The blocks which make up the Grampian Mountains and the northern Highlands are distinct geological sheets which slid in along lines of weakness like the Great Glen Fault, colliding and fusing together 450 million years ago. These

fault lines are still active in Scotland and quite capable of causing earthquakes as the huge sheets of rock still inexorably grind past each other.

It is worth looking at the geology of Scotland, not only to understand how its breathtaking scenery evolved, but also to see its effect on the lives of the human communities who live there. The underlying geology of the country has determined the agricultural present, but the rocks and minerals also shaped the industrial past. It was the abundance of coal and shale-oil deposits below the central belt that literally fuelled the Industrial Revolution in Scotland. In more recent times, of course, the North Sea oil finds have shaped the lives of much of the population. Aberdeen in particular has experienced an 'oil rush' similar to the gold rushes of North America in the last century and the traditional fishing industry is giving way to the oil man.

The last ice age played a major part in moulding and sculpting the landscape, and directing and redirecting the flow of rivers and lochs to give us the scenery of Scotland we know today. The underlying structure of the country was, however, determined by a much earlier geological history. The distinctive appearance of separate parts of the country is due to the character of the underlying rocks.

In the north-west Highlands the slablike splendour of the pink Torridian sandstones give a soft, rolling landscape, while on the Isle of Lewis, in the Hebrides, we find Lewisian gneiss, one of the oldest and toughest rocks to be found anywhere on the earth. This rock was formed 2,500 million years ago under immense pressure, at a depth of 12 miles beneath the crust of the planet. This gneiss is the very foundation of all the rocks which have been pushed upwards to the surface through a distance twice the height of Mt. Everest. These rocks broke through to the surface at least 1,000 million years ago. The pink sandstones of the Torridon region in Wester Ross were deposited on top of the gneiss by ancient rivers flowing across the landscape at that time. The mountains of Torridon were carved from beds of this sandstone by 'recent' glaciers flowing within the last 25,000 years and, as these glaciers scoured down thousands of feet to create the valleys, the Lewisian gneiss lying underneath was exposed.

North out of Glasgow, on the A82, in what is now Strathclyde, lie the Trossachs and Loch Lomond, the largest fresh water lake in Britain, some 23 miles long and up to five miles wide containing 30 islets. Although barely out of the Glasgow conurbation, this is deep Rob Roy country, one of the most controversial figures in Scottish history—depending on differing points of view—either a Gaelic Robin Hood, or a brigand and a thief with no fixed loyalties.

It is hard to believe that Loch Lomond, with its 'bonny, bonny banks,' was created a mere 10,000 years ago at the very end of the last ice age. A colossal ice sheet ground relentlessly south, gouging out the rocky trench of Loch Lomond to a depth of 656ft below sea level. As the glaciers retreated, piles of rubble were left from the rocks that had been embedded in the ice. These piles of glacial rubble show that the glaciers stopped just short of Dunblane.

Along with the effects of glaciation, volcanic activity also played a big part in shaping Scotland's scenery. The Cairngorms in the Grampian region were created by volcanic activity some 400 million years ago. The volcanoes erupted and filled the inside of a huge mountain range with lava. The original mountains have long since gone and all that remains is a glacial granite plug—the plateau of the high Cairngorms. One of Scotland's most famous salmon fishing rivers, the Spey, rises in the Cairngorms and as it flows northwards to enter Spey Bay in the Moray Firth it passes through an area which produces some of the finest single malt whiskies in Scotland.

In the west the landscape of the island of Mull was made up of beds of lava rock—over 590ft thick—which had poured from giant volcanoes over millions of years. One of Scotland's scenic wonders Fingal's Cave and the basalt columns of Staffa, just west of Mull in the Inner Hebrides, were formed by this same intense volcanic activity in the region. Fingal's Cave is 66ft high and 227ft deep, and its hexagonal black, block basalt formations create a spectacular forest of columns, some 36ft tall. The cave is named after Finn MacCaul, a hero of Celtic folklore who is also supposed to have built the Giant's Causeway—a collection of some 40,000 basalt columns on the north-east coast of Antrim, in Ireland—which was once connected to Fingal's Cave.

The power that can shift great continents and build mountains is driven by the immense volcanic forces operating deep beneath the earth's crust. It is probable that the sites of modern Glasgow and Edinburgh were deluged by vast lava flows. Scotland's most famous volcano, Arthur's Seat—standing 823ft high—dominates the landscape of central Edinburgh. The volcano actually rose from the tropical seas of the Equator some 340 million years ago and since that time the whole continental plate on which Scotland sits has drifted north, carrying Arthur's Seat along with it.

260 million years ago deserts, similar to those of California's Death Valley, once covered much of Scotland. New red sandstone beds of rock were formed from the sanddunes of this 260-million-year old desert. The gallery housing the precious Burrell Collection, in Pollock Park, Glasgow, is an architectural work of art in its own right. This edifice of glass, light, and space is made from stone blocks cut from the new red sandstone beds of Scotland. Quarries producing new red sandstone in the Dumfries area have been worked for more than a century, and the one at Locharbriggs is still working the stone, though much of the new red sandstone used in Glasgow's distinctive buildings came from a now defunct deep quarry at Mauchline, near Ayr.

Beneath the strata of new red sandstone and the lava beds lies a second layer of red sandstone rocks, much older than the new red sandstones of the Burrell Collection. The 'old red sandstone' was formed some 400 million years ago. In this geological period—very early on in the story of life on earth—the land was dry desert, entirely lacking rain forests and tropical swamps. There must, however, have been some water as the rocks of the 'old red' period were laid down in river beds. These sedimentary rocks gave rise to the very fertile soils which can be found in places such as Strathmore, the Laigh of Moray, Caithness, and Orkney.

Inevitably this dramatic and ancient landscape has shaped the lives of Scots men and women. Down the centuries for many of them it has been a struggle, fighting the land and the elements to create a living for their families. Scottish history, too, has been driven and shaped by the land itself, by turns uniting and separating her people and in the process creating a fascinating past full of incident and romance, blood and tears.

Right: *The weird and wonderful island of Staffa — from the Norse* stafr-ey *meaning pillar — in the Hebrides, rises to a maximum of 135 feet above sea level and covers only 71 acres.*

The scene of the infamous massacre of Glencoe: the landscape is gloomy and forbidding even in the bright sunshine.

STAFFA

The romantic and uninhabited island of Staffa lies seven miles west of Mull and six miles northeast of Iona. About half a mile long by a quater of a mile wide, the 71-acre island is famous for its basaltic formations.

In fact Staffa was created at the same time and by the same volcanic activity as the Giant's Causeway on the north coast of Ireland. Celtic legend would have it that the causeway was built by the giant Fionn MacCaul who was know to the Scots as Fingal, and it is probable that the best know resultant feature of Staffa — Fingal's Cave — is named after him.

Immortalised by Mendelssohn in his celebrated *Hebrides* *Overture*, the cluster columns and seemingly man-made symmetry give the cave a cathedral-like majesty. Other famous visitors to the cave since its 'discovery' in 1772 by Sir Joseph Banks and a boat of scientists on their way to Iceland, have included Queen Victoria and Prince Albert, artist J.M.W. Turner, and poets and writers Keats, Wordsworth, Tennyson, Robert Louis Stevenson, Jules Verne and Sir Walter Scott.

Interestingly there is a town called Staffa on the shore of Lake Zurich. It was founded by one of Iona's monks who obviously had been struck by the sight of the island!

Below: *The structure of the closely packed hexagonal columns of basalt on Staffa is obvious in this photograph; they are formed by cooling within in lava flows*

ARRAN

During the Viking period, initiated in the area by a raid on Kintyre in AD 797, not only the Northern and Western Isles of Scotland but also the Isle of Man and much of Ireland came under Norse control. Arran, close to the shipping route between Norway and her subject kingdoms further south, and having in Lamlash Bay one of the best natural harbours in the west of Scotland, became an important base. For the time it formed part of the Norse kingdom the Man and Sudreyjar, the name 'Sudreyjar' denoting the whole of the Western Isles.

In 1156 Somerled, a chief of mixed Scottish and Norse descent, established a breakaway kingdom in the Isles, corresponding in area to the kingdom of Dalriada established by the Scots when they first came from Ireland. The 'kingdom' of the Isles was already being fragmented and absorbed into the neighbouring kingdom of Scotland when, in 1266, three years after the battle of Largs, Norway sold all the Western Isles to Scotland.

Right: *Glenashdale Falls plummet spectacularly 100ft down a lava sill.*

Below: *Standing stone on Arran's Machrie Moore.*

ST KILDA

Owned by the National Trust for Scotland, St Kilda, the most westerly of the main islands of the Outer Hebrides, lies 65km (41 miles) off North Uist open to the full force of the Atlantic. The pounding St Kilda has received from the oceanic breakers has led to substantial erosion and so the creation of stacks — and near vertical cliffs rising 1,000ft or more from the waves below. Inhabited until 1930, today there are only few people — the occasional (and strictly controlled) tourists or the soldiers at the early warning radar installation atop Mullach Mor (361m/1,184ft).

What St Kilda boasts is a half the British total of Puffins, possibly as many as 40 per cent of the world's gannets and sizeable colonies of fulmars, Storm Petrels and Manx Shearwaters. Sheep left behind when the islanders departed have gone wild and survive in varying, seasonal quantities.

Above and Left: *Views of St Kilda village and walls.*

Right: *Stac Lee rises sheer from the Atlantic.*

2 Jewel of Scotland

In this story of Ancient Scotland, we have skirted around the abiding jewel in her crown: Edinburgh, the capital, the centre of government, the living heart of the nation's history.

The past is still a vibrant, living reality in the city of Edinburgh. Here is the focus for discovering how people throughout the centuries lived and worked in a city and its surrounding countryside. Edinburgh is famous the world over for its magnificent architecture and there is every style from every age. Here stand royal apartments and stately homes filled with antiques, artifacts and tales of intrigue and glory. The footsteps of the celebrated and infamous can be followed along Europe's most historic street, the Royal Mile. And at the end of the Royal Mile lie the Scottish crown jewels — the so-called 'Honours of Scotland' — which have been kept safe for centuries within the protective walls of Edinburgh Castle. This massive edifice, through its every stone, tells the history of the nation of which it is an emblem.

Edinburgh Castle stands boldly atop a dramatic outcrop of volcanic rock born more than 340 million years ago following a violent eruption deep in the earth's crust. Man may first have stood on the Castle Rock about 8,000 years ago when Stone Age hunters and gatherers appeared in the densely-wooded and boggy landscape.

However, its story as a place of permanent human habitation stretches back a 'mere' 3,000 years, to the late Bronze Age. Recent excavations have uncovered evidence for a settlement of round houses on the rock dating to the late Bronze Age (about 900 BC).

It was evidently a thriving hilltop settlement when Roman soldiers marched by in the 1st century AD and returned during the second, by which date the empire had established its most northerly frontier, the Antonine Wall (built in AD 142-3), to the west of Edinburgh. Archaeologists have found a wealth of Roman material, suggesting close contact between the Roman military and the native Votadini tribe.

But the first recorded mention of a town on the present-day site is not until shortly before AD 600, by which time the Votadini tribe had come to be known as the Gododdin. The war band of the Gododdin was gathered with its king, Mynyddog Mwynfawr, on

Above: *Sunset over Edinburgh Castle — palace, treasury, refuge and prison for Scottish monarchs from the 11th century when Malcolm III built the first wooden fortress.*

Below: *The castle's dominating position on its 80m (270ft) rock above Edinburgh gave it enormous strategic importance throughout the years.*

Above Right: *In the distance, the castle can be seen across Princes Street gardens and the railway line. At right the fume-blackened Scott memorial and Princes Street.*

Below Right: *A similar view at dusk looking over busy Princes Street towards the castle. The Scottish Baronial clock tower of the North British hotel flies the Cross of St Andrew.*

Castle Rock — or Din Eidyn, 'the stronghold of Eidyn', as it was then known. In the taper-lit hall the 300 men with the bard Andiron pledged themselves in drink to die in the service of their lord. And all but a few did die, on a raid into the territories of the Angles in about AD 600, at Catraeth (Catterick in Yorkshire). Retreating to their tribal lands, the Gododdin were pursued by the Angles. Din Eidyn was besieged and taken in 638, and the place seems then to have received the English name, Edinburgh, which it has kept ever since.

By 1000 AD Edinburgh had become an important fortress. In 1018 King Malcolm II defeated the English at the Battle of Carham and firmly secured for Scotland the territory between the Firth of Forth and the River Tweed. A royal castle at Edinburgh first emerges at the end of that century.

In 1093 Queen Margaret, seriously ill in Edinburgh Castle, returned to her chamber from Mass to be told of the killing of her husband, King Malcolm III, by the English at the Battle of

Alnwick. The news caused her death and her body was taken out of the castle through the western postern gate and buried in Dunfermline Abbey, Fife.

By the reign of Malcolm and Margaret's youngest son, King David I (1124-53), the rocky summit was a thriving royal castle, serving as a court residence, as a storehouse, as the headquarters of the town's sheriff and as a prison. David was probably responsible for the earliest surviving building on the Castle Rock: the little Romanesque chapel later dedicated to his mother, who was canonised as St Margaret in 1250.

With the exception of St Margaret's Chapel, nothing survives of the early royal castle. The reason, as ever, was the conflict between Scotland and her power-hungry southern neighbour.

In 1296 King Edward I of England invaded and Edinburgh Castle soon fell into his hands. But after his death in 1307 the English grasp on Scotland weakened, and in 1314 a night attack led by Robert the Bruce's forces recaptured the castle. It was a daring plan which involved 30 hand-picked men making the seemingly impossible ascent of the north precipice and taking the garrison by surprise. Bruce immediately ordered the dismantling of the defences to prevent reoccupation by the English. Shortly after, Bruce's army routed the English at Bannockburn.

After Bruce's death and his succession by his son David II in 1329, hostilities again broke out and in 1335 the castle once more fell into English hands. Major repairs were carried out but these proved ineffective against another storybook assault by the Scots, in 1341. A raiding party, disguised as merchants bringing supplies to the garrison, managed to drop its loads at the castle gates, so preventing their closure. A larger force hidden nearby rushed to join them and the castle was taken. Most of the English garrison had their throats cut or their heads chopped off and their bodies thrown over the crags.

In 1356 King David returned to Scotland from a 10-year captivity in England and straightaway set about rebuilding his castle at Edinburgh. A massive, L-shaped tower house rose about 30m (100ft) above the eastern crags. Subsequently named David's Tower, it was intended as a secure royal lodging as well as the main defence towards the burgh. It was battered by cannon during the so-called Lang Siege of 1571-3 and it survives only as a ruin, entombed within the Half-Moon Battery which replaced it as the chief defence on the eastern side of the castle.

King David died in 1371 without seeing his great tower completed. It was left to his successor King Robert II, the first Stewart monarch, to continue the rebuilding work. In 1433 work began on a new Great Chamber for King James I. This building, intended to complement the restricted accommodation within David's Tower, may still remain, albeit greatly altered, in the two 17th century rooms in the present palace now called the 'King's Dining Room' and its anteroom. It was either in the Great Chamber or in the hall in David's Tower that one of the most dastardly episodes in the castle's history took place — the 'Black Dinner' of 1440.

King James II had succeeded his murdered father, King James I, in 1437. A youngster, he was in the care of Sir William Crichton, Keeper of Edinburgh Castle, who used his powerful position in a spectacular political assassination of his political rivals, the Douglas family. Crichton invited the Earl of Douglas, a teenager himself, and his younger brother to dine with the king in the castle. The two guests were greeted:

'With great joy and gladness. [They] banqueted royally with all delicacies that could be got [and] after great cheer was made at the dinner and the courses taken away [Crichton] presented a bull's head before the earl which was a sign and token of condemnation to death.'

The young king protested at this outrage but to no effect. The Douglases were taken to an adjacent chamber, summarily tried on a trumped-up charge treason and beheaded in the castle courtyard.

In 1457 King James II, now ruling in person, was given a present of two giant siege guns (called 'bombards') by his uncle-by-marriage, Philip the Good, Duke of Burgundy. One of the guns survives in the castle vaults. This is *Mons Meg*, made at Mons, in present-day Belgium. Weighing over 6,040kg (6 tons), it could fire gunstones weighing 150kg (330lb) a full 3.2km (2 miles).

Throughout the Middle Ages, as we can see, Edinburgh had boasted one of the major castles of the kingdom and its story is very much the story of Scotland. Outside the castle, Edinburgh already existed as a royal burgh, but not the most important or the largest in Scotland. Only in the later half of the 15th century, during the reign of King James III from 1460-88, could it be called the capital city of the country. At that time — and for centuries afterwards — it was a dirty, smelly, often plague-ridden town, chronically short of fresh water and prey to vagabonds and villains both in the streets and tenements and in the offices of local government. Its inhabitants would throw open their windows to the fetid air only to empty their chamberpots into the streets below with a cry of 'Gardyloo!' — a corruption of the French *garde l'eau*, or 'mind the water'.

No wonder that, under James III, efforts were made to convert Edinburgh Castle into a relatively clean and safe sanctuary; indeed into a renaissance palace. The castle was replanned with, as its focal point, a new courtyard, now called Crown Square, around which was placed the principal royal accommodation. The creation of Crown Square was a huge task involving the construction of massive stone vaults over the whole of the basalt rock platform sloping southwards from St Mary's Church. The Palace and St Mary's Church already stood along the east and north sides of the new courtyard. Along the west side was placed the Gunhouse, where the royal artillery was displayed. The south side was occupied by the Great Hall, the principal banqueting and reception room. This greatly restored but still impressive building was probably completed late in the reign of King James IV (1488-1513).

By the time of King James's death, on the bloody battlefield of Flodden, Edinburgh Castle was the principal royal castle in the realm. It was a formidable fortress, a royal place, the chief arsenal, a treasury for the crown jewels, the repository of the national archives, the residence of several officers of state including the treasurer, and a state prison.

As a prison it was not entirely escape proof as Alexander, the Duke of Albany and King James III's brother, proved in 1479. After killing his guards, Albany lowered himself down the rock on a rope tied to his window. His companion slipped and injured himself, but Albany carried him to the port of Leith and freedom.

The castle on the rock was never the most comfortable or healthy of royal residences. In the 13th century, King Alexander III's young queen, Margaret, described it as a 'sad and solitary place, without greenery and, because of its nearness to the sea, unwholesome' — a reference to the thick sea mist which still

Above: *Edinburgh Castle and the old town.*

envelops the castle from time to time. Nevertheless, it was the fore-most castle of the land and in 1566 was chosen as the place where Mary Queen of Scots should give birth to her first and only child: Prince James, the infant who in time would unite the crowns of Scotland and England as King James VI of Scotland and I of England.

She did not languish in the castle longer than she could help, however, because a newer and more pleasant royal household was being developed just down the road, at the far end of the Royal Mile. The Palace of Holyroodhouse, which to this day is the offi-cial residence in Scotland of the reigning British monarch, was begun in the early 16th century by enlarging a guesthouse of the nearby abbey. The interiors which have modern visitors marvel-ling, however, were added later, most in the 1670s by the architect Sir William Bruce but many earlier decorations were commis-sioned by Charles II. They include the extraordinary Royal Portrait Gallery, with 110 Scottish kings and queens painted in 'large royal postures' by a single artist, George de Witt, between 1684 and 1686.

Leading from the picture gallery are the Audience Chamber and the private apartments of Mary Queen Of Scots — scene of one of the best documented murders in history, when Mary's favourite, Rizzio, was stabbed to death by her husband Darnley's accom-plices. And although, for reasons of state, she was persuaded to have her son, James VI of Scotland, born in Edinburgh Castle, it was at Holyrood that he learned that he was also to become James I of England, the monarch of two kingdoms.

When Mary was forced to abdicate, there were still those in Scotland who continued to support her cause. Amongst them was Sir William Kirkcaldy of Grange, Keeper of Edinburgh Castle. By the summer of 1571 he was defiantly holding the fortress against the regent governing on behalf of the infant King James. A rather desultory siege of the castle continued for well over a year (hence its name: the Lang Siege) until in 1573 Regent Morton sought help from Queen Elizabeth I of England. An English agent reported that 'there is no mining that can prevail in this rock but only battery with ordnance to beat down the walls'.

Heavy guns were duly dispatched by sea from Berwick and six batteries were set up outside the castle. Within 10 days of the massive bombardment opening up on 16 May, much of the east side of the castle had been reduced to rubble, including most of David's Tower, the Constable's Tower and the stretch of wall in between. The east elevation of the palace, where King James VI had been born just seven years earlier, was badly damaged and its three fine oriel windows largely destroyed. With the main water supply choked by the collapse of David's Tower, Kirkcaldy of Grange had no option but to surrender. He was hanged for treason afterwards.

In 1603 Queen Elizabeth of England died unmarried and without children. Her heir was King James VI of Scotland, descended from her grandfather. The new monarch headed south for London, returning only once, in 1617. In advance of this royal 'hamecoming', the castle was again refurbished, the showpiece being the east front, facing the Old Town. Unlike the other sides, which were of rubble masonry, this side was finely constructed, with parapets, mullioned windows and ornamental panels, including one displaying the 'Honours of Scotland' — of which more later.

With continuing improvements made to the Palace of Holyroodhouse, at the far end of the Royal Mile, Edinburgh Castle was used less and less as a royal residence. But despite the obvious amenities and domestic advantages of Holyrood, the castle remained symbolically the heart of the kingdom. Efforts continued to be made to secure the defences of 'the first and principal strength of the realm' but scant attention was given to the royal accommodation. The last occasion a reigning monarch slept in the castle was when King Charles I, on his only visit, spent the night there before his coronation as King of Scots in 1663. After that, the castle increasingly became the centre of the military arm of government. Almost all the medieval buildings were either converted to military use or demolished, and the old medieval defences were replaced by new artillery fortifications.

King Charles's execution and the unequivocal Scottish support for his rightful successor, King Charles II, brought Oliver Cromwell to Scotland. By Christmas day 1650, the English Roundheads had set up their headquarters in Edinburgh Castle and Cromwell's creation of a permanent standing army was to transform the ancient Royal Castle into a garrison fortress. When King Charles returned to his throne in 1660 he continued the idea of a regular, paid army, and from then until the 20th century a permanent garrison of soldiers was stationed in the castle.

Above: *The Jewels of Scotland in the Old Crown Room of Edinburgh Castle.*

Below Left: *Holyroodhouse got its name when the 11th century queen who was to become St Margaret of Scotland died there leaving her son David a relic of the true cross — a 'holy rood'. Today's palace was started in the early 16th century by James V. After the Restoration Charles II had major works undertaken including the portraits of 89 Scottish monarchs by Dutch artist Jacob de Witt. The oldest rooms are those occupied by Mary Queen of Scots — the James IV tower where her lover Rizzio was murdered.*

Right: *Aerial view of the Palace of Holyroodhouse showing the park beyond. The highest point in the park is Arthur's Seat at 250m (823ft). The buildings at bottom right occupy the area which will be the site of the Scottish Parliament.*

The last time they were called upon to defend their fortress was during the Jacobite risings. In 1715 the Jacobites actually broke through the castle's western perimeter, following which most of the artillery defences now seen protecting the castle on its north and west sides were built. They were soon put to the test during the 1745 rising, but only in a desultory fashion. Bonnie Prince Charlie held court briefly at Holyrood, at the other end of the Royal Mile. His halfhearted effort to take the fortress proved to be the last military action that the castle ever saw.

Yet the ghosts of Edinburgh Castle's violent past remain. In 1689 the Duke of Gordon unsuccessfully held the castle for the exiled King James VII against the forces of William and Mary. The ordinary soldiers who defended the fortress are nowhere recorded. But recently unearthed beside the Old Guardhouse were some bones — the skeletons of 15 well-built men, believed to have been soldiers serving in the garrison at that time. As is so often the case throughout Scottish history, the poor soldiers who fought so defiantly but in vain for their native Scottish soil are remembered only by their bones.

There is one more, very obvious reminder of the military might that was once wielded from within the forbidding stone walls of Edinburgh Castle. From the battlements high above the heads of the citizens of the capital, at precisely one o'clock every afternoon, a signal gun fires a single shot. Visitors jump in fright. Locals simply check their watches . . . as another day passes into the astonishing, tragic, dramatic, glamorous and glorious history of Scotland.

CASTLE ROCK

The Castle Rock and the Royal Mile are perhaps the world's best example of the geological feature known as the 'crag and tail'. Its origin goes back about 340 million years. Hot molten rock rose through the earth's crust and spread ash and lava over the landscape to form a huge cone-shaped volcano. In time the volcano became extinct

Millions of years later great sheets of ice came and eroded the soft sedimentary rocks that had by this time covered the volcano. The last Ice Age, some 10,000 to 20,000 years ago, was so powerful that it removed almost everything but the volcano's solid basalt feeder pipe. The ice, moving from west to east, flowed around the obstacle and gouged out the area to the west. But the hard basalt protected the softer sediments to its east, and by the time the streams of ice merged once more near the site of Holyrood Palace, the 'crag and tail' — the Castle Rock and Edinburgh's Royal Mile — had been created.

HONOURS OF SCOTLAND

The refurbishment of the palace of Edinburgh Castle for the 'hame-coming' of James VI in 1617 included the provision of a strong-groom to house the Scottish crown jewels, known as the 'Honours of Scotland'. The Crown Room still houses these gems, the oldest regalia in the United Kingdom and amongst the oldest surviving in the whole of Christendom.

The Honours of Scotland — the Crown, Sword and Sceptre — were shaped in Italy and Scotland during the reigns of King James IV and King James V and were first used together as coronation regalia at the enthronement of the infant Queen Mary in Stirling Castle in September 1543.

From the time they were taken from Edinburgh Castle in 1650 to be used at the coronation of King Charles II at Scone on New Year's day 1651, they have had an eventful history.

Between 1651 and 1660 they were preserved from capture by Cromwell's army, at first in Dunnottar Castle on the Kincardineshire coast and then, with Dunnottar besieged, smuggled out by the wife of the minister of nearby Kinneff Church, and buried under the church floor.

After the 1707 Treaty of Union between Scotland and England, the Honours were locked away in the Crown Room and the doors walled up. The barricaded room became something of a mystery to the soldiers serving in the garrison.

No less than 111 years later, romantic poet and novelist Sir Walter Scott, with the permission of the Prince Regent (the future King George IV), had the room unblocked and the chest forced open. Scott himself tells the story:

'The chest seemed to return a hollow and empty sound to the strokes of the hammer, and even those whose expectations had been most sanguine felt at the moment the probability of disappointment. The joy was therefore extreme when, he ponderous lid of the chest being forced open, the Regalia were discovered lying at the bottom covered with linen cloths, exactly as they had been left in the year 1707.

'The reliques were passed from hand to hand, and greeted with the affectionate reverence which emblems so venerable, restored to public view after the slumber of more than a hundred years, were so peculiarly calculated to excite.

'The discovery was instantly communicated to the public by the display of the Royal Standard, and was greeted by shouts of the soldiers in the garrison, and a vast multitude assembled on Castle Hill. Indeed the rejoicing was so general and sincere as plainly to show that, however altered in other respects, the people of Scotland had lost nothing of that national enthusiasm which formerly had displayed itself in grief for the loss of these emblematic Honours, and now was expressed in joy for their recovery.'

Except for a period during World War 2, when they were buried once again, this time in David's Tower, the crown, sword and sceptre have remained on display ever since — a proud reminder of Scotland's glittering royal past. Of Scotland's Honour.

Glenfinnan Monument.

PART 2:
THE HISTORY

3 Islands at the End of the World

The Shetland Islands are the most northerly point of Scotland. For thousands of years the Shetlands and their neighbours, the Orkney Islands, have been welcoming friendly visitors and, all too often, repelling the not so friendly. Some came by accident, others on planned expeditions — a mix of the wanderers, fishermen, traders, explorers, smugglers and invaders. All travellers.

In addition to the ships and the visitors who have stopped here to conquer, provision or languish, Shetland has provided a welcome landfall for many species of bird as they migrate between Africa and the Arctic Circle. The seashore, voes (small bays or creeks), moors and marshland have also served as a safe haven and animal habitat, the cliffs and rockscapes as footholds for wild plants and as breeding grounds for thousands of seabirds. They still do.

A full appreciation of the ancient history of the Shetland and Orkney Islands came only in the 19th century — and only then by the rude hand of nature . . .

During the 1890s violent storms broke into the low cliffs at Jarlshof, a small promontory near the southern tip of Shetland. The landowner, a Mr Bruce, dug into the sand and revealed a stunning maze of prehistoric structures.

The discovery at Jarlshof is a spectacular and enduring reminder of Shetland's heritage — and is regarded as one of the most fascinating and complex archaeological sites in all Britain. It was a settlement buried in time until the storm exposed the masonry of an entire village. Walls and hearths, wheel houses (circular homes) and Iron Age towers, all reflected the way of life of a long bygone age.

The first people to reach the Shetlands probably landed not far from Jarlshof some 5,000 to 6,000 years ago. The sea has risen since then, drowning and eroding the land, and the point where they beached their boats now lies probably a few metres below the sea and many metres offshore. Their arrival heralded the beginning of an intensive occupation of the site — from the earliest, primitive hunters to the more skilled agriculturalists, from the metal-working Beaker folk right up until the 17th century AD.

Jarlshof must have been a veritable crossroads of sea lanes. The Norwegian coast was only 48 hours away by sailing boat. From the hills around Jarlshof you can see Fair Isle, still one of the most isolated inhabited islands in Britain. (The intricate, colourfully patterned knitwear, which takes its name from the island, has today made Fair Isle famous worldwide.) And from Fair Isle can be seen the Orkney Islands, which lie between the Shetlands and Caithness, on the north coast of the Scottish mainland.

Jarlshof is an astonishing archaeological treasure chest and provides evidence of the scale of communal development of the ancient islanders, particularly during the comparatively 'recent' Iron Age. But what sort of domestic comforts did the very earliest inhabitants of this and other settlements enjoy?

Above: *The cliffs of the Orkneys are spectacular and none more so than those at Marwich Head which rise to a height of 300ft above the raging Atlantic waves.*

There are few clues to the lifestyles of the earliest islanders, except that we know the climate was kinder and the land therefore more arable in that period.

Before 4000 BC, people had begun to grow wheat and barley in Britain. Farmers had reached Shetland and Orkney before 3500 BC, and over the next thousand years built many tombs and settlements on the islands. They grew wheat and bere, an early form of barley still grown in Orkney today.

Their earliest dwellings were of wood. But when all the larger trees had been cut and used for construction, stone and turf became the standard building materials. In about 3500 BC the Neolithic farmers laid their dead in stone 'cists', one of which has been unearthed at Sumburgh, near Jarlshof. Although the dead were at first buried simply in stone-lined communal graves, soon the construction of more elaborate chambered tombs began. In Shetland these are comparatively small, with modest chambers which would have accommodated only a handful of burials. In Orkney, however, there are more substantial burial chambers.

These relics of the dead do not give many clues to the lifestyles of the living in this harsh, far-flung land. Here we are helped by an event which parallels the discovery at Jarlshof . . .

In the winter of 1850 a wild storm stripped the grass from the high dune known as Skara Brae, in the Bay of Skaill on mainland Orkney. An immense midden (or refuse heap) was uncovered. So too were the ruins of ancient dwellings. What came to light in that storm proved to be the best preserved prehistoric village in Northern Europe. And it remains so today.

The village of Skara Brae was inhabited before the Egyptian pyramids were built and flourished many centuries before construction began at Stonehenge. It is no less than 5000 years old.

But it is not its age alone that makes it so remarkable and so important. It is the degree to which it has been preserved. The structures of this semi-subterranean village survive in impressive condition. And so, amazingly, does the furniture in the village houses. Nowhere else in northern Europe are we able to see such rich evidence of how our remote ancestors actually lived.

They were careful planners and expert builders. The design of the village would have minimised heat loss, so that the houses could have been kept comfortably warm quite efficiently. A central hearth would have heated each house, as well as providing cooking facilities. The houses would have been very dark apart from the light radiating from the fire in the hearth. There are no surviving objects resembling lamps but it is quite likely that some form of lighting could have been employed by burning oil taken from marine mammals or sea birds. There would have been little ventilation, and the air inside the houses would have been very smoky. There would have been one benefit from this, however, in that food would have been smoked in the roof.

There was no knowledge of metal in the New Stone Age. People made their tools from stone — mainly from flint, although in Orkney and Shetland this was in short supply. So, while the tool kit of New Stone Age people elsewhere was largely made from stone, at Skara Brae it was from bone and wood. A great variety of tools not seen outside Orkney has been recovered from the site.

Gradually sand dunes formed around Skara Brae, separating the village from the sea — and eventually filling up and burying the buildings after they had been abandoned.

Jarlshof sounds as if it gets its name from the Norse word Jarl, meaning earl. Certainly the Vikings lived there and they ruled the Northern Isles from the first Jarl of Orkney and Lord of Shetland, Sigurd Eysteinsson in the 10th century, through to the 15th century. However, in reality the name is a modern invention attributed to Sir Walter Scott.

*Before the Vikings came, the Shetlands and Orkneys had thriving Bronze and Iron Age communities as can be seen from the two wonderfully preserved Neolithic sites at Jarlshof (**Above Left**) and Skara Brae (**Above**).*

Another Orkney treasure is Maes Howe, built about 5,000 years ago. A large mound containing an entrance passage and burial chambers, it is the finest chambered tomb in north-west Europe. It is a remarkable mixture of simplicity and sophistication, its survival owed to the fine building stone used for it.

With the rings of standing stones at Brogar and Stenness, it is one of three great monuments at the heart of Orkney, where the power of a rich society was concentrated 5,000 years ago. Within a few miles of Maes Howe and the rings of standing stones were many other Neolithic and early Bronze Age structures, of which the chambered tombs at Knowe of Onstan or Unstan and at Wideford Hill and Cuween have survived to this day.

The Bronze Age (1800 to 600 BC) inhabitants of Orkney and Shetland experienced a steady worsening of climate which lost to arable farming the greater areas of the islands. Communal burials seemed to die out — perhaps the harsher living conditions did not allow enough time or surplus labour for the construction of elaborate cairns, and memorials seemed to take a simpler form.

Standing stones and stone circles are scattered through the northern and western islands of Scotland. Although they must have been associated with long-forgotten Bronze Age rituals, their pre-

cise purpose is unknown. There are splendid examples of these at Brodgar and Stennes, in Orkney, and at Callanish, in Lewis, in the Western Isles. Further afield the most outstanding prehistoric monument in Scotland is probably the so-called Clava Cairns, five miles east of Inverness — circular burial chambers surrounded by standing stones and dating from before 2000 BC.

Eventually, the apparently peaceful lifestyle of the Bronze Age seems to have lapsed, and in the succeeding Iron Age (600 BC to AD 500) the islanders gathered themselves into more defensive communities. From about 500 BC the inhabitants of Shetland and Orkney began to build strong circular houses as the main dwellings of their farms. Gradually these became more sophisticated in design and formed the centres of small agricultural villages, frequently enclosed by outer defences in the form of ditches, banks or walls. There were also undefended settlements at this time, but these are less well studied. They are harder to locate than the massive structures known as brochs, for which the Northern Isles are famed.

Brochs are large stone-built towers. These imposing dry-stone structures, standing from 5m to 13m (16-42ft) high, were erected for defence by the Iron Age tribes of northern Britain. They are among the most ingenious and impressive military works of prehistoric man in western Europe and are unique to Scotland. Until the 19th century, practically nothing was known about them. They were referred to as 'broughs' (defended places), 'Pict's castles' or 'Pict's hooses' by the local inhabitants and were so entered on the earliest Ordnance Survey maps until the end of the last century.

Above and Right: *The Orkneys — no trees, just peat bogs, sea and a lot of wind. Indeed, you're never far from the sea or the wind in the Northern Isles: the highest gust of breeze ever in Britain was recorded in 1962 on the Shetland island of Unst — 177mph!*

Essentially, a broch was a lofty, dry-stone tower, circular in plan with an immensely thick ring base enclosing a central courtyard. This was entered by a single passage originally provided with a wooden door halfway or so along its length.

From the central courtyard, openings gave access to chambers or 'cells' in or against the wall, and a doorway led to a stone staircase rising upwards within the wall thickness. This led upwards through a series of superimposed galleries, the ceiling of each forming the floor of the one above, emerging at the wall head, which commanded a view of the village, the outer defences and the countryside beyond.

Excavation evidence suggests that each broch may have had an inner structure of stone and wood. The surviving stone tower is to some extent merely a shell within which once sat the real dwelling place, possibly with one or more raised floors and covered by a thatched timber roof.

Because of collapse, the majority of the towers are reduced to mounds of grass-grown rubble covering the circular bases and wall stumps. The finest example of these unique structures is the Broch of Mousa in Shetland, which still survives to its original height of 13m (42m). At Mousa the visitor can see all the basic features which make up broch architecture. It stands on a natural rock bastion dramatically overlooking the sea. At nearby Clickhimin can be found the most extensively excavated example of brochs.

The nature of brochs was neatly summed up by the anonymous author of *Orkneyinga Saga*, written in the 12th or 13th century but telling tales of a far-distant past. Writing of the Broch of Mousa, which had been briefly reoccupied more than a thousand years after its construction, he wrote: 'It was an unhandy place to get at.'

When surrounded by outer ramparts and ditches, the brochs were manifestly unwelcoming to any predatory tribe. But impressive as they were, they were often merely the central points of more complex settlements. The broch was the residence of the principal family of the community, and probably also served as a gathering place for communal activities ranging from meeting for war to entertainment on winter evenings. It also provided the last defensive resort of the community.

As brochs became widespread, they probably became indicators of the importance of the leading families of each community, so that no group was felt to be of significance in society unless it had a broch at the heart of its lands. More than 500 broch sites are known or suspected. They are concentrated in Orkney, Shetland, the north mainland counties of Caithness and Sutherland, and in the Western Isles, with a few in southwest and southeast Scotland. By around 100 BC there were more than 120 brochs on Orkney alone.

The people who built the brochs were farmers, successors to those who, many centuries before, had built the great chambered tombs of Orkney. Although they were in regular communication with other parts of Scotland, and perhaps ventured farther afield, there is no good evidence to suggest, as archaeologists once believed, that there was an invasion of 'broch builders' from outside the region.

The Iron Age farmers of Shetland, Orkney and the north Scottish coastline were, by the standards of northern Britain, prosperous and secure, with their mixed farming economy bolstered by the produce of the sea. They were probably well-connected, and trade or marriage would have brought fresh contacts, new ideas and innovative minds into the community. Orkney in the Iron Age was probably remarkably cosmopolitan.

Although considerable quantities of grain, mainly barley, were grown, farming was centred around the rearing of cattle, which provided meat, milk and leather. They may also have served as draught animals for ploughing. But more important, they represented wealth, and possession of cattle was probably the main index of social status, at least during the earlier Iron Age. There is some evidence that, as time went on, more 'modern' indicators of wealth also became current — like exotic jewellery.

Life would have been busy and work hard, but starvation can seldom have been a likely spectre for the Iron Age farmer. Long dark hours during the winter would have afforded time indoors to plan for the following season, weave and spin, tell tales and repair tools, fishing gear and boats. During the summer months much time was spent out of doors, with the late evenings perhaps enlivened by otter trappings along the shores or, for the more lawless spirits, forays to seek out and claim 'strayed' cattle.

So where did the broch builders, or rather their descendants, go? Probably not very far. The pattern seems to be one of slow drift away from the broch villages back to living in scattered farmsteads, once threat of attack was perceived to have disappeared. There is also evidence of a general reduction in population in the Shetland and Orkney Islands between the broch period and the arrival of Norse settlers around 800 AD.

Jarlshof — at the southernmost tip of the Shetlands' Mainland Island — is one of the most important archaeological sites in Britain, showing the development of civilisation from earliest times through to medieval days. It gives us an insight into how early settlements developed from the late Neolithic village through to the Bronze Age oval houses, Broch, Viking settlement and, finally, medieval farmhouse.

It must have been hard life: while the Shetlands' average temperature rarely drops below 39°F, wind and proximity to the sea means that there haven't been trees on the islands for some time. Remains of tree stumps in the peat bogs show that once the climate was different but weather has got colder and wetter and the winds have got stronger.

The pottery and metal artefacts were found during the extensive excavation.

Previous Page: *The Ring of Brogar is one of the great monuments to the rich society which lived on the Orkneys 5,000 years ago.*

Above Left: *An aerial view of Jarlshof showing its proximity to the sea and the extent of the excavations.*

Skara Brae

The wonderfully preserved Neolithic village of Skara Brae, on the west coast of Mainland Island, Orkneys, was excavated in 1928-30 by Australian archaeologist Vere Gordon Childe, professor successively at Edinburgh and London, then the expert on the Neolithic period and one of the leading archaeologists of the time. He found a complete stone-built settlement which, one theory suggests, was abandoned after a Pompeii style inundation — but for Vesuvius's volcanic ash and lava read the invasive fine sand that can be seen on the beach of the Bay of Skaill.

As on the Shetlands, proximity to the sea and substantial winds mean that the Orkneys have no wood for building or burning. Peat bogs solve the heating problems, but the lack of wood on the island meant that Skara Brae — like the comparable Neolithic site of Jarlshof on the Shetlands — was completely made of stone. The six or seven houses and a workshop hut were clustered together and linked by alleyways which would have been roofed over with stone.

*The craftsmanship of the stonework shows the sophistication of the building techniques (**Far Left**) as do the interior furnishings and shelves (**Above**).*

The main livelihood for the people of Skara Brae would have been the sea — their main source of food, although sheep and cattle were kept. That being said, there are distinctions apparently between Shetlanders and Orcadians: the former are fishermen with crofts and the latter crofters with boats.

Brochs

While the usual theory of the purpose for the brochs is defensive — at a sign of danger the lookout on the top would sound the alarm and all the settlement's people and livestock would make for the security of the stone walls — there have been other theories. Many experts feel the size of the brochs precludes their use as a place of protection — they are just not big enough. One idea, proposed by the Orkneys' best-known writer, Eric Linklater, is that they were the structures upon which primitive catapults could have been placed to stop any invading foe before he reached the shore by sinking his boats.

They are unique to Scotland and of the c. 500 brochs discovered so far, the best preserved are in the Northern Isles. Here (**Left, Below and Bottom**) Clickhimin Broch, Shetland, the best excavated of the brochs. The Broch of Mousa on Mousa Island to the east of Mainland is worth visiting too: its 40ft tower is almost intact. There are about 100 brochs in the Orkneys: they aren't as well preserved as those in the Shetlands except Midhowe and Gurness (**Right**).

4 The Western Isles

The story of ancient Shetland and Orkney is paralleled by that of the Western Isles. This unique archipelago, otherwise known as the Outer Hebrides, is a beautiful, remote area — a chain of islands lying close to the northwest of Scotland, on the very edge of Europe and bordering the wide Atlantic Ocean. The combinations of land, sea and inland waters have produced landscapes of international importance.

The Western Isles stretch about 200km (130 miles) north-south from the Butt of Lewis to Barra Head, with the St Kilda group 22km (35 miles) to the west and lonely, uninhabitable Rockall a further 320km (200 miles) out into the North Atlantic.

The St Kilda archipelago is noteworthy in its own right. Remote and spectacular, it lies 176km (110 miles) from the Scottish mainland. A self-sufficient community lived there throughout ancient history. Fowling among the great colonies of sea birds (puffins for feathers and meat, young fulmars for oil and young gannets for meat) was the main employment, augmented by sheep herding, crofting and fishing. Its main island of Hirta maintained its population until 1930, when the islanders were evacuated at their own request.

By contrast, the islands of Lewis and Harris are combined like Siamese twins at the northern end of the Western Isles. They have been inhabited for more than 6,000 years but today only 30,000 people live on the 12 populated islands (Lewis and Harris, Bernera, Scalpay, Berneray, North Uist, Baleshare, Grimsay, Benbecula, South Uist, Eriskay, Barra and Vatersay). The people of the Western Isles are Gaels, bilingual Gaelic and English speakers.

The islands are formed from some of the oldest rocks in the British Isles. But despite this primeval ancestry, traces of the earliest inhabitants who set foot upon them are more elusive than in Shetland and Orkney. For much of the landscape of the Western Isles is relatively recent and is still changing.The reason is that the isles are generally low-lying and prone to blanketing by wind-blown sand. Remains of settlements from the Neolithic, Bronze and Iron Ages were generally sandwiched between sand dunes and the hinterland's more fertile uplands. Over the centuries, the drifting sands have alternately buried them and re-exposed them. For a brief while they may have stood crumbling by the shore — only to be finally swept away by the waves for ever.

These predations of the sea continue to the present day, with the comparatively recent settlement of Old Arnol, on Lewis, succumbing to the Atlantic breakers. While today only 12 islands support human habitation, yet the remains of post settlements, tombs and places of work and worship have been found on more than 50, many of them no more than dots on the map.

The principal monuments of the early Neolithic period, when farming first became established, are communal burial mounds, known as chambered cairns, and the great stone alignments and circles. Although excavations at the cairns of Uneval and Clettraval, on North Uist, have established that these great mounds of stone served as burial places, many questions remain. Were they reposi-

The Western Isles have standing stones aplenty: these two are on Arran in the Firth of Clyde.

Above: *Machrie Morr; there are Bronze Age burial chambers inside a stone circle on the moor.*

Right: *Standing stone outside Brodick — the main village on the island where the ferry arrives.*

tories of the remains only of the tribal leaders? Since we know that the cairns were used over several centuries, how often were they cleared out and refurbished? And why are the cairns so concentrated in certain areas, particularly North Uist?

Then there are the standing stones and circles. Like the great chambered tombs, which generally predate them, they represent considerable feats of communal effort by a society where everyday life was a harsh battle with nature carried out around the humblest of stone homes of the most modest construction.

The group of about 20 intervisible standing stone sites around *Calanais* (in English Callanish), on the west coast of Lewis, represent the most varied collection in the whole of Britain — second only to Stonehenge in the United Kingdom for their grandeur.

The principal circle stands on a low ridge, visible for many miles. The plan is unique: a circle of 13 gneiss stones, up to 3.5m (11ft 6in) high, has a central stone 4.7m (15ft 5in) high. The circle is the terminus for a double row of stones leading north. Further single rows lead off the circle towards east, south and west. Apart from the circle and avenues of the main complex, the area boasts simple circles or near circles, arcs, alignments and single stones.

What was their significance? Although no one knows for certain, there is no doubt that some of the circles contain alignments with the heavenly bodies at specific times of the year. The rising and setting of the sun was obviously marked. And at Callanish the equinoxes and the winter and summer solstices seem to have been particularly significant events.

The Uists, Benbecula and Barra are rich with archaeological sites. North Uist contains some two-thirds of the chambered cairns found in the isles, with Barpa Langass, 8km (5 miles) from Lochmaddy, of particular importance. Settlement sites dating from the Neolithic and Bronze Ages have also been excavated at Northton on Harris, Loch Olabhat on North Uist, and Allt Chrisal on Barra. At these sites, small, oval, stone houses were surrounded by abundant broken pottery and midden material (domestic refuse that was allowed accumulate and rot before being spread on the fields). But apart from burial cairns and standing stones, very few sites or monuments dating before the Iron Age give us any insights into the domestic life of those who created them.

The social history of the Western Isles at the end of the Bronze Age and the beginning of the Iron Age (around 500 BC) is representative of the major changes wrought through the whole of Scotland. As we have seen in Shetland and Orkney, the new forms of settlement were designed for defence. Nowhere is this change more obvious than in the Western Isles where the archaeological record, almost empty for the Bronze Age, is represented in the Iron Age by more than a hundred fortified sites.

Clifftop promontories and islands in the middle of lochs were the natural choices. They would have been easy to fortify with a simple wall, and not too inconvenient for working the nearby fields or tending cattle. Perhaps these duns, as they are now called (from the Gaelic word for a fort), were temporary refuges. In time, however, they became permanent, with stouter walls and stone building. Access, originally by boat, was often provided by boulder causeways lying just below the surface and following a winding course to impede unwelcome visitors.

Eventually the fortifications were widened and heightened until they emerged as the classic Iron Age monument of the Scottish north and west: the broch. There is a theory that the brochs were designed by specialist builders who travelled around Scotland's Atlantic coast, contracting their skills to local communities. Just a

few miles away from Callanish on Lewis stands one of these circular dry-stone fortified towers: the 2,000-year old Carloway Broch or Dun which is one of the best preserved examples of the few surviving brochs in the Western Isles.

By the time history came to be recorded, other structures appeared in the landscape: castles and religious buildings. Outstanding is Kisimul Castle on Barra, with its main tower dating from 1120. Other castles, now ruined, include Borve in Benbecula and Ormacleit in South Uist. Teampull na Trionad (Trinity Temple), near Callanish in North Uist, dates back to the early 13th century, and the sites at Teampull Chalum Cille in Benbecula, and at Tobha Mor (Howmore), in South Uist, reflect these very early times. The chapels at Cille Barra are well preserved.

But despite these later, perhaps more sophisticated structures, it remains a credit to those early dry-stone builders that the ancient duns and brochs of the Scottish northern coast and its islands continued to be occupied right up until the Middle Ages.

Above, Below and Right: *On the west coast of the Isle of Lewis, at Callanish at the head of East Loch Roag, stands the awesome collection of stone circles and avenues of standing stones called the 'Hebrides' Stonehenge'. Why early man spent so much of his time 4,000 years ago building these impressive monuments no one knows for sure — although astronomical religious reasons seem the most likely. The more romantic legend says that the stones are actually giants whom St Kieran turned to stone for refusing to be baptised.*

Left: *The Isle of Lewis is the most populated of the Outer Hebrides and the largest, boasting the only Outer Hebridean town, Stornoway. On the west coast of Lewis is Arnol Black House Museum. With a thatched roof tied on with ropes, six-foot thick walls, no chimney and a central peat fire the Black House gives an excellent impression of life on the island in times gone by.*

Above: *Dun Carloway is on the west coast of the Isle of Lewis overlooking East Loch Roag. It is a substantial and well presented broch with nearly 22ft of walls in places and a substantial diameter of 47ft.*

Right: *Inscriptions or ornamentation from Carn Ban, a 100ft long chambered cairn dating from the neolithic period.*

5 Outpost of the Empire

The Iron Age in Scotland lasted until relatively recent times; it is generally regarded as stretching from 500 BC to AD 560. It is a period that saw the incursion of the Roman Empire through mainland Britain and, of course, the advent of Christianity. Yet in material terms, the northern and western islands have little to show for these global changes. Forts, duns, brochs and wheel houses continued to be adapted and occupied. Archaeologists have discerned only minor changes in the pottery of the northern inhabitants of Scotland — and the few exotic items that might have assisted them in dating sites have been imported from other regions.

The influence of the Roman Empire fell far short of these northern realms, although legend has it that they explored the seas as far as the Shetland Islands. They certainly knew of a cluster of 100 islands at the confluence of the North Sea and the North Atlantic. They called them 'Ultima Thule'.

But to see the effect of this new civilisation transplanted from the Mediterranean to the chill climes of Scotland, we must move south from the mysterious Celtic seascapes of the broch builders to the Lowland moors and plains. For its was here in the 1st century AD that the Roman legions — which had landed in southeast Britain, conquered and subdued the whole of England — marched into Scotland. Incidentally, it is only from this period that we come across the first written records of Scottish history.

In AD 81 Gnaeus Julius Agricola, governor of the Roman province of Britain, invaded southern Scotland with Legio IX Hispana and advanced to a front-line position betwixt the estuaries of the Rivers Clyde and Forth — a line that today would link the cities of Edinburgh and Glasgow. In Lothian stands a 2.7m (9ft) tall sandstone monolith, known variously as the Caiy Stone, Kel Stone and General Kay's Monument, which traditionally marks the site of a battle between the Picts and the Romans.

Agricola built a chain of forts across the land and threw forward one major bastion at Stirling, which he made his headquarters. Sustained by the Roman fleet, which matched his progress along the sinuous eastern coastline, in AD83 Agricola vanquished the local Caledonians in the battle of Mons Graupius, believed to be the Hill of Moncrieffe.

We know of these events from the writings of the Roman historian Tacitus, who happened to be Agricola's son-in-law. Tacitus wrote proudly of his relation's victories, principally against the Caledonian chieftain Calgacus, but criticised subsequent Roman strategy. For in AD84, only months after Agricola had subdued the Lowland tribes, the general received sudden orders from Rome to withdraw. As Tacitus wrote: '*Perdomita Britannia et statim omissa*' (Britain is conquered then is at once thrown away).

Imperial strategy became defensive rather than offensive. The Emperor Hadrian himself visited Britain in AD121 and ordered the building of the famous Hadrian's Wall as a deterrent to the raiding parties of the factionalised northern tribes. Bits of it still stand today between the estuaries of the Solway and the Tyne — a line back into England and far south of Agricola's earlier frontier.

Above: *Rough Castle is one of 13 forts built by the Romans and so far found along the Antonine Wall. At less than an acre in size, it would not have housed a major unit.*

Right: *The Caiy Stone in Lothian traditionally marks the site of a battle between the Roman legions and the Picts.*

Less than 20 years later, however, new Emperor Antoninus Pius ordered the restoration of Roman rule over the defiant northerners. Within months of succeeding Hadrian in AD 138, the tough new emperor decided to abandon Hadrian's Wall, which was still being modified, and move the frontier north some 160km (100 miles) and to reoccupy Lowland Scotland. The then governor of Britain, Lollius Urbicus, was given the task of pushing the frontier of Rome back to Agricola's advanced positions.

The Antonine Wall was constructed during the years following AD 142. The new wall was built across the narrow waist of Scotland formed by the Rivers Forth and Clyde and their tributaries the Carron and the Kelvin. It ran for exactly 40 old Roman miles (about 37 modern miles or 60km) from present Bo'ness on the Forth to old Kilpatrick on the Clyde, following for most of its length the southern slopes of the central valley of Scotland.

The Antonine Wall was a less permanent structure than Hadrian's earlier wall, perhaps reflecting the Roman Imperial Army's manpower shortages. It had a stone and turf rampart base 4.3m (14ft) wide and almost as high, topped by timber. In front of the rampart was a deep ditch, the earth from which was tipped onto the north side to form a further mound. At intervals of about 3.5km (2 miles) along the wall were forts, some housing small detachments but others designed for major forces, linked by a military road and beacon-platforms. And between the forts (Rough Castle, some 5km (3 miles) west of Falkirk, is a well-preserved example) lay still more outposts, each garrisoned by up to 30 men.

These soldiers, all highly trained, were charged with the task of defending the province of Britain. Most of the summer they would have spent north of the wall patrolling the central Lowlands, chasing off raiders and supervising the local tribes. Recruits for the maintenance of the Antonine Wall would have been mainly local in origin. For like the Britons in the south, the Pictish-Scottish inhabitants of the agricultural Lowlands were now beginning to learn the long, slow lesson of living as neighbours with the Romans. The best preserved remains of a Roman fort, at Bearsden, reveal the domestic, as well as military, lifestyle of an army whose area of operations extended from the Clyde to the Euphrates.

It was under the Emperor Severus and his son Caracalla that the Roman Empire arranged a peace on its northernmost boundary which would last in the main for 200 years. During the war Severus had fought to win the his position, the Roman armies had been pulled away from frontier duties in Britain and the northern tribes had overrun the weakened defences. Severus had to conduct the campaigns of reconquest himself, invading Scotland in AD 208.

He died at his headquarters in Eboracum (York) and was succeeded by Caracalla who brought the war to a conclusion. The peace centred on the Wall of Hadrian with strong outposts as far north as Carpow on the Tay from which a large garrison of Legio VI and II Augusta patrolled the area.

As the history of the Roman Empire became one of civil war and wars of succession, the British legions played their part, leaving the province to fight on the Continent but each time they returned to reconquer lands taken in their absence by the Pictish tribes. By the end of the 4th century, Hadrian's Wall had become the frontier again and the farther outposts in Scotland abandoned. As troubles closer to home caused the empire to contract, one by one the legions were recalled from Britain to defend Italy and Rome herself from the Goths. By AD 430 not only Scotland but the whole of Britain had been abandoned for the final time.

The departure of the Roman legions did not bring peace to Scotland. The reverse occurred. At first the Caledonian tribes, growing ever bolder, pushed further and further south — but they soon encountered a mass movement of humanity that was exploding upon the British Isles in the vacuum left by the retreating Romans. Teutonic invaders, the Angles and the Saxons, held back for so long by the Roman east coast forts, swarmed across the North Sea and drove the native Britons westwards and northwards into southern Scotland. The native Scots also had to watch their back, because Saxon raiders were establishing a hold on the east coast. The history of Scotland was about to take yet another, dramatic turn.

Above Left: *Aerial view of Rough Castle.*

Below Left: *A depression in the ground, a piece of wall, a section of ditch: not much remains of the northern boundary of the Roman Empire.*

Below: *Defensive positions around Roman encampments used what were called 'lilies' — pits dug to a depth of about three feet with sides which tapered slightly towards the bottom where fire-hardened, sharpened stakes were projecting from the bottom. The pits were then covered with brushwood to hide the trap.*

Left: *Croy Hill Fort is to the west of Rough Castle separated along the Antonine Wall by forts at Westwood and Seabegs. The ditch in front of the wall was about 12m (40ft) wide and 3.75m (12ft) deep although at Croy Hill there is a patch of rock which defeated even the patient professionalism of the legions.*

Right and Below: *The wall started at Old Kilpatrick on the Clyde and there was a fort — Duntocher — between the start and Bearsden. These two photographs show the Bearsden bath house — always an important part of any Roman establishment. Every permanent fort had its bath house which consisted of a series of rooms of varying temperatures and humidity*

6 Invasion of the Norsemen

It is worth here pausing to re-examine the racial mix that was Scotland in the first half of the first millennium. The ancient inhabitants of Scotland were Celts, who had sailed across the seas and settled in these northern lands in a series of minor migrations stretching back to 1000 BC and beyond. By Roman times, Scotland was divided between four main races — the Picts, Britons, Teutonic Anglo-Saxons and the Scots.

The most powerful of these were the Picts who reigned supreme from Caithness in the north to the Forth in the south. Of Celtic stock, some historians say they originally arrived from the continent of Europe as part of the Celtic migration to the British Isles during the first millennium before Christ. Others say they were of Scythian origin.

The neighbouring Britons of the Strathclyde region were another Celtic race, speaking a kindred tongue and controlling the area stretching from the Clyde to the Solway and beyond into Cumbria.

The Teutonic Anglo-Saxons, who hailed from lands lying between the mouth of the Rhine and the Baltic, occupied the country south of the Forth and controlled an area stretching southwards into Northumbria.

Finally, to the west, embracing what is now Argyll, Kintyre and the neighbouring islands, lay the Scots. This warlike Celtic race from Dalriada in northern Ireland had arrived in force in the 3rd century AD and began colonising a sister kingdom of Dalriada in an area roughly coincident with the old counties of Argyll and Bute.

The Scots found themselves at first overshadowed by the Picts. But as Roman influence waned in the north of Britain — at this time known as Alba or Alban — the Celtic newcomers pressed their advantage and filled the vacuum. Although Picts and Scots occasionally joined forces to harass the Romans, the Scots' first loyalties were to their fellow men across the sea in Irish Dalriada. Their conflict with the Picts was to take several hundreds years and the spilling of much blood before it was resolved.

When they sailed across the sea from Ireland, they brought their culture to lands less remote than those we have so far visited — to the hospitable peninsulas and shore hugging isles of the central west coast, like Arran and Iona. They first brought with them the Gaelic language and in due course gave Scotland its present name. They also heralded an extraordinary new cultural 'invasion' — Christianity.

Of its effects on Scotland, and the gloriously rich architectural heritage it has left, we shall learn in a later chapter. Meanwhile, however, we must examine an invasion that was less welcome, less gentle — but which eventually embraced Christianity and helped spread it not only around Scotland but the known world.

In the 9th century AD, the whole western world was rocked by the movement of Norsemen away from their own countries, their longships leaving the fjords for new lands across the sea. Their adventuring and colonisation in time took them south to the Holy Land and west to Greenland and almost certainly North America.

The Scandinavians arrived in Britain in force shortly before AD 800. Not only the Northern and Western Isles and Caithness, but also the Isle of Man and much of Ireland and eventually England, succumbed to these forays, and the predominantly Pictish inhabitants were forced to give way to this powerful force. To pick up the earliest threads of the story of the feared and fearless men from Scandinavia, we must return to the far north of Scotland. Back to now-familiar Jarlshof, in Shetland, that extraordinary time capsule which, as we have learned, is a mere two days' sail by Viking longboat from the coast of Norway.

In the 9th century the Shetlands became an important link in the raiding and migration routes 'west over sea' to Britain, Ireland, Iceland and Greenland. Between AD 830 and 860 Kenneth MacAlpin united the Picts and Scots and it was probably after Pictland became Scotland that the Norsemen first settled at Jarlshof. The earliest known Scandinavian burials in the Scottish islands date to the latter half of the 9th century.

It has been suggested that the first Norse settlers in Scotland came from the More-Trondelag district of Norway, and that later settlers came from the districts of East and West Agder. It does appear that the people who came to Shetland and Orkney hailed from at least some part of southern Norway.

From 872 AD, a Viking earldom was established in Orkney. Not only warriors but farmers and their families came and stayed, bringing with them a new and enduring culture. Wherever the Vikings went, they took their law and their language. In the Western Islands of the Outer Hebrides, the place names are almost all of Norse origin. The Vikings invaded and settled the islands from the 9th century onwards and it was not until 1280 that Norway handed the Western Isles over to the kingdom of Scotland under the Treaty of Perth.

Equally, of Shetland's 50,000 place names, the vast majority are 'Norn'. The local parliament was held at Lawting Holm, an islet in Tingwall Loch. Enduring folklore and sagas are associated with many other legendary sites, such as the Broch of Mousa, the Loch

of Girlsta, Haroldswick on Unst, the 'Bears Bait' on Fetlar, and the beach at Gulberwick. The latter is the site of the wrecking of two longships of Norse ruler Earl Rognvald Kali as they were on their way to the Crusades in the 12th century.

For it is a myth that the Norsemen were Vikings intent on only 'rape and pillage'. The Christian ethos was strong in the islands. The *Orkneyinga Saga* tells us that Earl Rognvald Kali gathered crusaders together in Orkney in 1150. After wintering on the islands — not without squabbles over money and love affairs — they sailed for Jerusalem. While the earl was away rivals struggled for mastery over the islands. One of the claimants, Harold Maddadarson, son of the Earl of Atholl, tried a surprise attack on Orkney. On 6 January 1153 he landed at Stromness and marched eastward; caught by a storm he and his men took shelter for three days in Maes Howe. Two of his men went mad there. But they were not the only Vikings to enter the tomb. The proof is in the runes Earl Rognvald's men and women carved when they returned from the crusade later in 1153.

The 'City and Royal Burgh of Kirkwall', capital and administrative centre of the Orkney Islands, is one of the best preserved examples of an ancient Norse settlement, being mentioned in the *Orkneyinga Saga*. Founded around 1035 by Earl Rognvald Bruason, Kirkwall's name comes from the old Norse 'Kirkjuvagr' meaning 'church-bay'. This is a reference to a church much older than the present cathedral that dominates the town.

St Magnus's Cathedral was founded in 1137 by Earl Rognvald Kolson to the memory of his uncle, St Magnus. Built of local red and yellow sandstone more than 850 years ago, it was at the time

Far Left: *Viking graffiti from Maes Howe. It's evident from what's written on the walls of the tomb that Vikings ransacked it: 'Haakon alone bore the treasure out of this tomb', says one. 'Thorny was bedded. Heigi says so,' says another. It seems that the urge to deface is not confined to modern aerosol wielding youth!*

Above Left: *Illustrations from Jarlshof on stone and slate of Viking longboats. It may seem hard to believe that Norsemen went to the Holy Land on crusade but they actually went even farther than that. The Varangian Guard of the tsars of Kieven Russia were Vikings who probably reached Kiev via the Black Sea.*

Above: *Inside the chambered cairn of Maes Howe on Orkney.*

Below: *Steatite (soapstone) lamp from Jarlshof.*

one of Europe's great architectural achievements. Today, weathered but untouched by pollution, it is still bright and clean.

Viewed today, Kirkwall's main street is little changed in centuries: a narrow, winding thoroughfare that echoes the shape of the shoreline. Viking influence is still prevalent in the northern islands. Even though Orkney was sold to Scotland in 1468, there are still lingering loyalties, and Kirkwall's stone houses annually echo to such celebrations as Norwegian Constitution Day!

Equally, Scandinavian rule in Shetland was to last for more than 600 years until the mid-15th century, when the islands were finally given as a dowry to Scotland. As a reminder of this heritage, the Shetland capital of Lerwick annually holds a midwinter festival known as 'Up Helly Aa'. This spectacular celebration features a procession of 1,000 torch-carrying revellers, a squad of Vikings in horned helmets and full regalia, and a longship dragged through the streets of Lerwick before its ceremonial burning.

Above and Top Right: *Jarlshof, showing the size of the site and the remarkable state of preservation of the buildings.*

Right and Far Right: *The Brough of Birsay is a small island off the northwest of Mainland Island, in the Orkneys. From it, Norse jarls ran an empire which, at its peak under Earl Thorfinn the Mighty in c1100, controlled the Northern Isles, the Western Isles, a large part of northern Scotland and much of Ireland. On the Brough remains can be seen of a palace, cathedral, houses (as illustrated* **Far Right***) and other things like this cross-inscribed grave slab (***Right***). Thorfinn's grandson, Magnus Erlendsson, was canonised following miracles at the site of his murder and his body, with an axe wound in the skull, has rested ever since in St Magnus' Cathedral in Kirkwall, which was founded in his memory.*

Above and Right: *The Broch of Mousa is the best preserved of all the brochs and shows to great effect how imposing and substantial these buildings were. It is on a small island to the east of Sandwich on the southern peninsula of Mainland in the Shetlands. The aerial view shows clearly the double skin which allows for rooms and an inner courtyard. As a defensive establishment the broch would certainly have been difficult to penetrate and Mousa is mentioned in Norse sagas as being strong enough to withstand Viking raids. Mousa Broch is still 12m (40ft) tall and before gunpowder it would certainly have been a difficult nut to crack.*

Left: *Pottery from Jarlshof. The Norse occupation of Jarlshof saw major building work. At first a 21m (70ft) rectangular stone farmhouse was erected and later extended; a long house was added subsequently as was a third farmhouse.*

LANGUAGE

In 10th century Scotland, the principal language was Gaelic. In the last thousand years, its use has contracted first becoming the language of the Highlands, then in recent times losing even more ground to English as the Highlands emptied of its native population.

Today Gaelic has its stronghold in the Western Isles, where it remains a vigorous force in written and spoken prose and poetry. However, it is in place names all over Scotland that it will be most apparent to the visitor — each craggy outcrop or lowering loch has its usually descriptive Gaelic name.

Gaelic	English
aber, abhair	river mouth or confluence
achadh	field
ard, aird	high point
allt	burn, river
ban	white
beag	small
bealach	pass
bodach	old man
buidhe	yellow
cam	bend, bay
caol, caolas	strait (cf kyle)
chailleach	old woman
coille	wood
coire	cauldron, or corrie
dearg	red
dubh	black
drochaid	bridge
drum, druim	ridge
garbh	rough
gobhar	goats
gorm	blue
kin, ken (ceann)	head
liath	grey
lomond	beacon
meall	round hill
mor	big
ros, ross	promontory or moorland
stob	top, peak
tigh	house
uig	bay
uisage	water

Scotland's other language is Scots, a form of 'English' which has grown from a Northumbrian dialect of Anglo-Saxon. Scots has absorbed French, Germanic and Norse influences and was the standard speech of court until James VI of Scotland inherited the English crown in 1603 and moved to England.

From then on, it also lost ground — never, for example, gaining a standard mode of spelling. This process was accelerated by the King James Bible being printed in English but not Scots. Finally with the Union of Parliaments in 1707, English became the official language of administration.

Right: *Viking writing — runes on the wall at Maes Howe.*

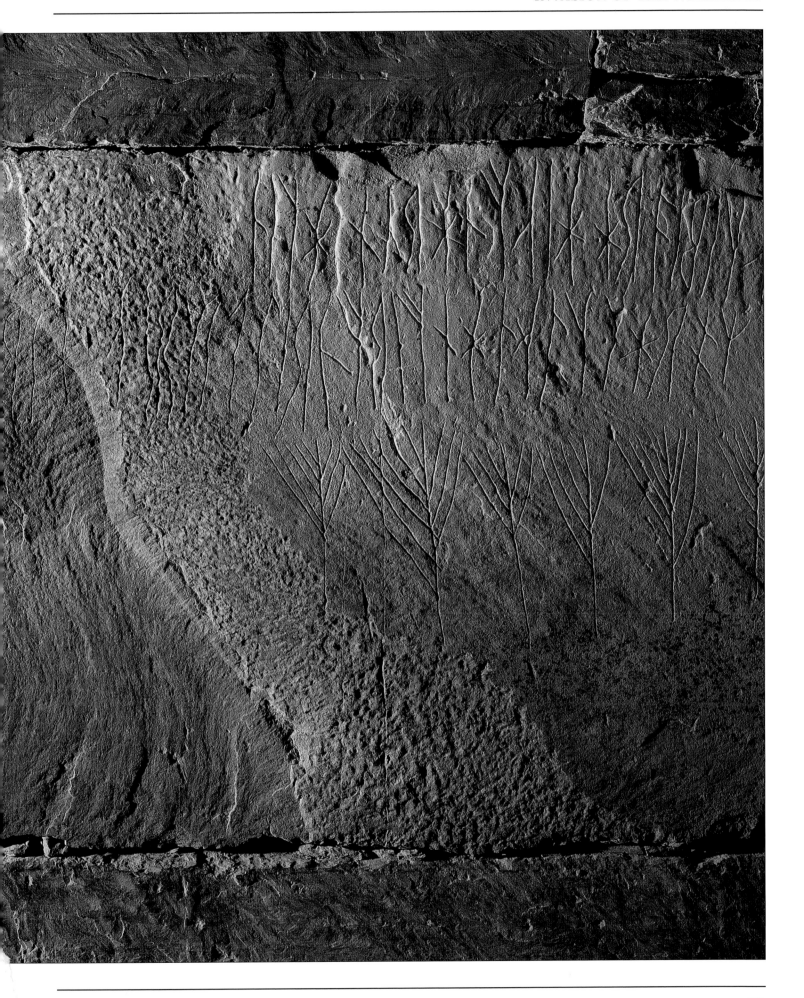

7 The Norman Conquest

Much had occurred in England in the early days of the second millennium. In 1066 King Harold resoundingly crushed a renewed Viking offensive in north-eastern England, then marched his exhausted troops south to the Sussex coast where yet another invasion force was challenging his supremacy. The resultant Battle of Hastings — between King Harold's Anglo-Saxons and the northern French invaders of King William of Normandy — was the single most important turning point in the 'recent' history of the British Isles. For when, after a closely fought conflict, Harold was carried dead from the field of battle, the spoils of war fell to a French-speaking hierarchy who changed the old British lifestyle, language and culture for ever.

A chain of vast fortifications was thrown up across the land to maintain the Norman overlords' stranglehold on the recalcitrant islanders. It took many decades before the Normans could finally claim to have subdued their newly conquered lands.

When the Normans ventured to the north of the British Isles, they found a people who were, for the first time in its history, coming together almost as one nation. It was under the rule of Duncan, King of Strathclyde (1034-40), that we can first speak of the kingdom of Scotland. Indeed, it had virtually the same borders as it does today. Duncan was killed by Macbeth, who successfully ruled Scotland for 17 prosperous years, to be succeeded in 1057 by one of Scotland's most significant early monarchs, Malcolm III.

There was some uneasy unity when Malcolm took the throne. Most commonly known as Canmore, a Gaelic name literally translated as 'big-head', Malcolm married Margaret of the royal house of Wessex, giving him some interest in the English throne. But when William the Conqueror finally invaded Scotland in 1071, he forced Malcolm to pay homage to him at Abernethy. In the intervals between the fighting, amicable relations were maintained between England and Scotland, for Malcolm remained a popular figure at the English court. But his death in 1093, while raiding Alnwick, in Northumberland, plummeted Scotland into 30 years of turmoil, ruled over by a succession of weak, insecure kings.

The first of these was Malcolm's 60-year old brother Donald Ban. Donald clashed with William Rufus, the new king on the English throne, who made several attempts to usurp him. Donald's half-brother Edgar became king in 1097, followed by his brother Alexander in 1107. Alexander married King Henry I's daughter and his sister Maud became the wife of the king himself. Ties with England grew closer and the Norman influence even greater.

When Alexander died in 1124, he was succeeded by his brother David, the ninth son of Malcolm and already the ruler of most of southern Scotland. He was to reign for 30 years. Like his brothers, David had been brought up in England where he had had a Norman education and made many Norman friends. In addition to being King of Scotland, he was also Prince of Cumbria. Further, by his marriage to a rich Norman heiress, he held the title Earl of Northampton and Huntington. Because of this he was one of the most powerful barons in England as well as being the English

king's brother-in-law. He was also to prove one of the most innovative of Scotland's early kings.

On returning to Scotland, David began distributing large estates amongst his Anglo-Norman friends and associates who then became landowners on both sides of the border. At the same time, David introduced something akin to a feudal system of ownership to the Lowlands of Scotland. In the Highlands, however, the king's ideals counted for little while the Northern and Western Islands and some coastal regions gave a loose allegiance to Norway.

David did his best to establish a national system of justice and administration with a specially selected governing body to advise him. He appointed sheriffs to administer justice. He also encouraged trade with foreign countries and established two royal mints and a standard system of weights and measures. David granted the status of burgh to a number of towns, together with a freedom from tolls and the right to hold markets and fairs. He was a devout man and established more parishes, built more churches and endowed monasteries. He died in 1153, ending a rule which had brought with it dramatic change.

The focus of this short narrative of Scotland's ancient history now turns to its central heartlands — to Stirling, the 'crossroads' of the nation. Set at the highest navigable point of the Forth, and on the line of the main pass through the northern hills, Stirling guarded both the principal north-south and east-west routes across Scotland. The coincidence of strategic significance and a naturally strong site meant that the great rock upon which old Stirling stands was a prehistoric fortress and the likely site of the city of Iudeu, which figures in accounts of British kings in the 7th century.

However, Stirling Castle does not begin to appear in recorded history until the early 12th century, by which time it is already a residence of Malcolm's Canmore dynasty. Alexander I had founded a chapel here, and probably died within the walls of the castle in 1124. The castle next comes on record exactly 50 years later, when it was handed over to Henry II of England, along with five other castles, to pay for Scottish King William the Lion's release after his capture at the battle of Alnwick. Scottish control of Stirling was regained in 1189, and 25 years later King William died within it.

In all this time, we have no idea of Stirling Castle's physical appearance, although most of the buildings would have been of timber. The castle probably began to assume more permanent masonry from the late 13th century — something the turmoil of the succeeding century was to obliterate.

Right: *Old Scone Palace was the spot to which Kenneth MacAlpin is said to have brought the Stone of Destiny. Generations of Scottish monarchs were crowned on it until it was taken to London by Edward I: it resided in the coronation chair at Westminister until returned north of the border during John Major premiership. Scone Palace today is a castellated mansion enlarged in 1802-13 around 16th century and earlier buildings. It is the home of the Earls of Mansfield whose family has owned the property since it was given to Sir David Murray by James VI after 1600.*

Edward I of England was the scourge of the Scots. Nicknamed 'Longshanks', he had long coveted the Scottish kingdom. As one of the most important castles in the kingdom, Stirling naturally played a major part in the Scottish struggle for independence of English overlordship. In 1291 Edward I took custody of all Scottish royal castles while he adjudicated on who was the rightful king of Scotland, and the castle's history over the next 50 years is mainly that of a struggle for its occupation by the forces fighting on behalf of the rival claimants. During the course of this struggle, Stirling was the scene of several of the finest triumphs of the Scottish patriots — although the benefits derived from these triumphs were short-lived.

In 1297 an army led by that great Scottish hero William Wallace overthrew the English in a famous victory at Stirling Bridge, and thus secured the castle for a time. Wallace was forced to defend his victor's crown the following year at Falkirk, and this time Edward I wrought his revenge. The English and Welsh archers shot down the Scottish foot and so enabled a charge by Edward's heavy cavalry to prove decisive.

By 1304 Stirling was the only castle left to the patriots. In that year Edward I instigated a successful siege, using fire-throwing equipment and a siege machine known ominously as the 'War Wolf'. The castle was again in English hands. The country seemed to lie at his mercy. And when the Scots' champion Wallace was captured and put to death at the king's orders in London in 1305, hope ran out and final surrender seemed inevitable.

Scotland was occupied from end to end and a foreign garrison lay in every town from Annan to Dingwall. Yet some did not despair and, in 1306, Robert the Bruce was crowned King of Scots at Scone, with a mission to recover his kingdom and regain freedom for his subjects. For the victories won by the first Edward were not followed up by his son. In the years which followed the tide slowly turned, almost imperceptibly at first and then with gathering impetus, to the chagrin of Longshanks's successor, Edward II. One by one the towns and fortresses were retaken until by the spring of 1314, of only three castles which were still in English hands, Stirling remained the most important.

In that year, Stirling Castle was under siege by a Scottish force commanded by King Robert's brother, Sir Edward Bruce. Extraordinarily, under the laws of chivalry of the day, an agreement had been made between Edward Bruce and the English governor of Stirling castle, Sir Philip Moubray, whereby it was to be surrendered if not relieved before Midsummer Day (24 June 1314).

Edward II of England, realising the blow that failure would mean to his prestige, determined to relieve the castle in time. In doing so, he believed that he could draw the main Scots army out to oppose him, rather than allow them to conduct the campaign by their previous, highly successful guerrilla tactics. With one mighty stroke, Edward felt that he could recover all the ground lost since his father's death. Robert the Bruce was made aware of the English king's intentions by March 1314 — and determined to accept the challenge.

Above: *William Wallace's statue at the entrance to Edinburgh Castle.*

Left: *Strategically placed on the main communication and trade route south, Stirling Castle was the most important piece of real estate in Scotland in medieval times. It had to withstand sieges by both Scots and English as it changed hands in the 13th and 14th centuries. In more peaceful times the castle changed from fortress to royal residence and from the late 15th, through the 16th centuries it was used heavily by the Stuart kings. Illustrated is the Renaissance south facade of King James V's Palace which can be seen behind the crenellated curtain-wall built by James IV, his father. The end result of these building works was an important early classical exterior outside and sophisticated royal apartments inside.*

Right: *The Wallace Monument — the arousal of interest in Wallace caused by the film* Braveheart *is not the first time he has been hero-worshiped from beyond the grave. The Victorians went to town over this romantic hero and the epitome of this can be seen in the 67m (220ft) stone structure perched atop a rocky outcrop near Stirling. It was completed in 1870.*

8 One People, One Nation

The dramatic set-piece battle which followed was probably the greatest which ever took place on Scottish soil. It is known to all Scots as the Battle of Bannockburn and to the English of earlier days as the Battle of the Pools, or sometimes as the battle near the Bannock Burn, near Stirling. In Gaelic the battle is known as *Blar Allt a Bhain-chnuic* or 'the Battle at the Burn of Bannock'. By this clash of armies, Scotland was to win its independence from England — at least temporarily — on 23 and 24 June 1314.

Edward had already sent out summonses to the English counties, to Wales and Ireland, for levies and he ordered the army to concentrate at Wark on the Tweed, near Berwick, by 10 June. The army, led by Edward himself, consisted of 2,000 heavy cavalry, and upwards of 17,000 archers and foot.

The cavalry was furnished by the nobles, knights, squires and landowners, all with their own paid men-at-arms. The horsemen wore chain-mail and armour, bore a 3.6m (12ft) lance and had a mace or battleaxe as a close combat weapon. The horses, some with light armour, were gorgeously equipped with flowing blankets, known as 'trappers', their function being to trap or entangle swords and spear thrusts. Edward was relying for victory on the charge of this mass of heavy cavalry which was accustomed to strike terror into the hearts of any but the most highly trained and disciplined body of foot.

The archers carried a long bow, a quiver with 24 arrows and in addition they had a short sword or dagger as a personal weapon. The foot soldiers were spearmen, each carrying a 3.6m (12ft) spear, a shield and a sword or dagger.

By contrast, Robert the Bruce is believed to have had only about 5,500 trained men to meet the English army of nearly 20,000. The Scottish soldier bore a 3.6m (12ft) spear, a sword, axe or dirk as a personal weapon, and carried a targe or shield. Bruce's few archers provided a longbow and 24 arrows. His horsemen were organised into a small body of some 500 light cavalry, under Sir Robert Keith.

As a kind of reserve, a goodly number of the 'small folk', often erroneously called gillies or even camp followers. These 'small folk' were minor tenant farmers, townspeople, labourers and craftsmen who had joined to strike their blow for Scotland , but whom Bruce wisely kept out of his divisions because of their lack of equipment, training and discipline. They were even expected to supply their own arms. Despite this, the numbers of these 'small folk' gradually increased to some 2,000 as small parties of clansmen joined from remote areas.

The fact that nobles, knights, landowners and tenant farmers fought together, with their men on foot, made for a high standard of leadership, cohesion, training and discipline. In the English army, by contrast, most of the natural leaders were serving together in the cavalry and the infantry felt the loss.

On 23 June, Bruce, unarmoured, and mounted on a sturdy Scottish pony, was riding round his forward troops encouraging them when the leading English mounted patrols were seen just after

Above: *Could there be anything more fearsome than a charge of heavily armoured knights? At Bannockburn the charge was halted and the Bruce won the day.*

Right: *King Robert I and his second wife. His daughter Marjory married Walter Steward of Scotland and their son became Robert II, the first Stewart king.*

crossing the Bannock Burn. Recognising the Scottish king by the gold coronet he was wearing, one of the English knights, Sir Henry de Bohun, set his lance and charged. But Bruce skilfully avoided the deadly point and, rising in his stirrups, cleft de Bohun's helmet and skull with his battleaxe. On being reproached by his generals for the risk he had taken, it is said that he merely remarked: 'Alas I have broken my good battleaxe.'

King Edward was relying on the pomp and chivalry of his large host over-awing the Scots whom at last he had drawn into a set-piece confrontation. But the Scotsmen stood calmly and firmly as the mass of galloping horses bore down on them. The horses pulled up and shied off in front of the serried ranks of spears. The Scots counter-attacked, driving the English from the field — at the cost of only one Scotsman killed.

With English morale low, Edward decided to end the fighting for the day and move his army to new and stronger positions nearer Stirling. Bruce and his commanders watched this vast English army moving away in the distance and crossing the Bannockburn. The disparity in numbers was so great that Bruce was advised to withdraw westwards to carry on guerrilla warfare. Then Sir Alexander Seton, who had been leading a Scots contingent in the English army, defected to Bruce's headquarters and described the miserable plight of the English in the Carse and their low morale. 'Now's the time and now's the hour,' he cried, 'and Scotland shall be free!'

Bruce knew he now had his enemy where he had always wanted him — where he could not manoeuvre or use his cavalry effectively. He would attack after first light on the following day.

The 24th June broke fine and sunny, and the Scots, after an early meal, moved down to the plain. Mass had been celebrated, for it was St John's Day, and when they came to within some hundreds of yards of the English, they again knelt for a few moments in prayer. Edward, seeing the Scots kneel, is reported to have called out: 'Ha! They kneel for mercy!'

'Yea, sire,' said one of his staff, 'they kneel for mercy, but not from you. These men mean to attack.'

At that moment the English trumpets sounded the alarm and the cavalry rushed to saddle up, don their armour and surcoats and make ready. The Earl of Gloucester, who led the English main body, at once ordered it to charge. He had not time to don his surcoat, with his glittering crests, and, unrecognised, fell dead on the Scottish spears and the charge was halted much as Clifford's had been by Moray the day before. Both sides now became locked together so that archer support was impossible. The English vanguard broke — and its wounded and riderless horses, careering back upon the main body, threw it into confusion.

The English archers tried to reform but the inferior Scottish cavalry rode them down. Jubilant Bruce now saw brought his own strong reserve division into the fight. Turning to his commander Angus Og, he exclaimed: 'My hope is constant in thee' — and the Islesmen rushed upon their foes. The English line began to give.

Edward II, sensing the day was lost, was at last persuaded by his own commanders to retreat to Stirling Castle. Having seen his king safely on the way, Sir Giles d'Argentine is reported as saying: 'Sire, your reign was committed to me; you are now in safety. There is your castle, where your person can be in safety. I have not been accustomed to flee, and I will continue no further — I bid you adieu.' With that, he returned to the battle and charged straight into the Scots. So perished Sir Giles, famed at the time as the bravest knight in all Christendom.

When the royal standard was seen leaving the field, the whole army began to waver. At this juncture, whether on Bruce's orders or from sheer exuberance, the 'small folk' abandoned their reserve position and came rushing down the escarpment on to the plain to join the battle. At the sight of what they took to be further Scottish reserves, the whole English army disintegrated and fled, pursued in every direction. A party of Scots horsemen followed King Edward towards the castle, one man reportedly seized the royal rein. But the stout escort of knights beat him off and the King escaped capture.

The centre of the English army fled to the Forth and to destruction, while the luckless left flank were forced back into the muddy gorge of the Bannockburn at high tide, where the most of them perished. In the words of contemporary chroniclers: 'Bannockburn betwixt the braes was so charged with horses and men that men might pass dry over it upon drowned horses and men.'

The guards left with the English supply train were massacred after the battle and the spoils captured were enormous. The English casualties were very heavy, nearly all the foot and archers being killed or captured, while contemporary records give 700 of the cavalry as dead, including many nobles and knights. Many other nobles were taken prisoner and were later held to ransom. The Scottish casualties are not known, but must have been considerable.

Bruce himself seems to have rated the charge of Angus Og's clansmen as of the highest importance in the battle, for the MacDonalds claimed the honour of always being the 'Right of Line' in royal armies and he gave into Angus's domain many valuable lands and islands in the west. The king's exclamation to him at the crisis of the battle is preserved today in the Clan Ranald motto.

And what of Edward II? Sir Philip Moubray rightly refused the king entry to Stirling Castle as this would have meant his certain capture. With a small but devoted escort and pursued all the way, Edward escaped to Dunbar where he secured a small rowing boat which took him to Berwick. It was an ignominious end to his campaign to conquer Scotland, which had begun with his boastful resolution to wipe out 'Robert de Brus who calls himself King of Scotland'.

King Robert the Bruce proved himself at Bannockburn to be not only a superb leader of men but also a very great general. His place as a great national hero is assured for all time. By the Battle of Bannockburn, Scotland became again a free and independent country. It was the greatest victory that the Scots ever gained, although it took some years before the English, in the Declaration of Arbroath (1320) and then the Treaty of Northampton (1328), gave formal recognition of the results achieved — by acknowledging Bruce as an independent monarch and formally renouncing English overlordship of Scotland. Bannockburn had certainly made Scotsmen feel, more than ever they had done before and possibly since, that they were one people and one nation.

As so often in Scottish history, the benefits of a great achievement or a mighty victory were soon dissipated. Bruce died in June 1329, aged 53. In 1331 his son David, aged just six years old, was crowned king. Bruce's nephew Thomas Randolph became regent before dying a year later. But trouble was brewing. In 1332, urged on by Edward III of England, a number of Scottish nobles, who had been deprived of their lands for siding with the English against Bruce, landed in Fife. Edward took Berwick in 1333. Seeing the way things were going, large numbers of Scottish nobles and clergy changed sides, with the result that the Lowlands of Scotland were easily overrun and garrisoned by the English who filled them with their own merchants, clergy and settlers.

In this turbulent period, the 10-year old king David and his child wife were sent to France for safety. The regency was entrusted to Bruce's 17-year old grandson Robert Stewart who put up a valiant fight. He drove the English garrison out of Bute and in 1339, with the help of a French expeditionary force, captured Perth. In 1340, he had cleared Scotland north of the Forth. Finally, in 1341, he was able to bring his young uncle David back from France and hand over to him the government of the country.

The English were by now fully engaged in France with the Hundred Years War. This gave the Scots a badly needed respite. Stirling and Edinburgh were recaptured, but in 1346 David was taken prisoner by the English after rallying to help out the French army. There followed 12 years in England — which David found an easier life than the burdens of kingship in Scotland. Robert Stewart once more became regent, and following David's death in 1371 took the throne as Robert II, the first Stewart king. He died in 1390 after an unremarkable reign and was succeeded by his son Robert III, who in turn quickly abdicated when he learned he was expected to fight off invaders!

Right: *1929-vintage statue of Robert the Bruce alongside the entrance to Edinburgh Castle.*

This then was the pattern of Scotland's misrule — as all the benefits of Robert the Bruce's victories were wasted. The reasons were clear, however. Of the eight kings who followed the Bruce, only the two Roberts had been adults. David II was five, James I was twelve, James II was six, James III was ten, James IV was fifteen, and James V was just over one year of age — so that for decades Scotland was ruled by regents. Among these royal novices, it was the young James IV who was to be immortalised — following the infamous Battle of Flodden.

Relations between England and Scotland had already rapidly deteriorated following Henry VIII's succession to the English throne. And so James was only too willing to answer the French queen's plea for support against the English following Henry's attack on France in 1512. James sent word that if Henry did not withdraw from France then he, himself, must invade England. His message was ignored.

Thus, with perhaps the biggest Scottish army ever assembled, James crossed the border, captured key English strongholds and awaited the oncoming English army. As the armies came into sight of each other on 9 September 1513, James committed the deadly error of allowing his enemy to place themselves between the Scots and their road back to Scotland. His final error was to order his men to leave their position upon Flodden Hill and toil over marshland to attack the English.

The English foot soldiers were better armed, their 'bills' (short spears with axe heads on their shafts) outmatching the Scottish spears. The English were able to close in upon the tight Scottish ranks. The Scots, as ever, defiantly held their ground and were killed where they stood. In the end, the battle became a massacre.

King James IV was himself killed by an arrow in his throat and an axe wound to his head. With him died, too, the flower of Scottish chivalry. Nine earls and 14 lords, the chiefs of many of the great Highland clans, James's natural son Alexander, Archbishop of St Andrews, the Bishop of Caithness, the Bishop of the Isles, the Dean of Glasgow and the Provost of Edinburgh, together with as many as 10,000 of some of Scotland's finest young men, perished that day. Never had their been such a disaster. Hardly a family in Scotland was not mourning the loss of a son or brother or father. Their untimely end is commemorated in the most moving of laments: *The Flowers of the Forest are a' Wede Away*.

The new king, James V, was aged 18 months. Edinburgh's city leaders hastily built the Flodden Wall, expecting further English attack. But the English had suffered heavy losses too, perhaps as many as 6,000 dead, and hadn't the stomach to renew the fight.

By 1541, however, the English were becoming aggressive yet again. Having himself broken with Rome in 1534, their King Henry VIII was set on making Scotland Protestant and so turning her against France. James resisted this. Then, in 1542, James was offered the Crown of Ireland. This gave Henry the pretext he was looking for. Sending his troops across the border, he proclaimed himself Lord-Superior of Scotland. James, already ill and at odds with his nobles, replied by invading England. But his nobles refused to march. On 24 November 1542, James's little army was defeated at Solway Moss. Sick at heart, the Scottish king rode to Falkland. He died shortly after hearing that his wife had given birth to a baby girl. The child was christened Mary and was proclaimed Queen.

SCOTTISH DECLARATION OF INDEPENDENCE

At Bannockburn, the so-called 'small folk' — the ordinary people of Scotland — were determined, as patriots, under Robert the Bruce's great leadership, to defend the independence of their land with their lives. Their spirit was reaffirmed a few years later in 1320, in the immortal words of the Declaration of Arbroath:

'As long as a hundred of us remain alive we will never be subject to English dominion, because it is not for glory or riches or honours that we fight, but for freedom alone, which no worthy man loses except with his life.'

After nearly 30 years of struggle, there is good reason for this great document often being referred to as the Scottish Declaration of Independence.

Above and Right: *This statue of Robert the Bruce at Bannockburn, just south of Stirling, was unveiled in 1964. His grave in Dunfermline Abbey is marked by a plaque of 1818. His heart is said to be at Melrose Abbey — the story goes that he asked Sir James Douglas to take his heart to Jerusalem. Sir James was killed en route and the heart was returned to be interred in Scotland. Robert I was an enlightened ruler and his reign saw frequent parliaments including the first — in 1326 — to include representatives of both the Scottish nobility and burghs.*

9 Fortress Scotland

Scotland is dotted with castles — ruined or renovated, rugged or just rural retreats for the rich — but Stirling and Edinburgh are the two which are most closely identified with the nation's history. Each castle occupies a secure volcanic outcrop, which has been made even more easily defensible by the scraping of glaciers in the Ice Ages. This same action has in each case left a gentle tail-like ridge at one end of the outcrop, along which a town developed. Both castles were favoured residences of successive Scottish kings, who progressively rebuilt them to become the magnificent structures they are today. Of Edinburgh and its castle we will learn more later. Stirling's importance we know from the previous chapter.

For much of the Middle Ages, the effective capital of the kingdom was wherever the king happened to be in residence. As a result, the town of Stirling, like Edinburgh, shows many of the characteristics of a medieval capital. Both were provided with fine parish churches, which eventually achieved collegiate status. Both also had a magnificent royal abbey of Augustinian canons.

Following his victory at Bannockburn, Robert I (the Bruce) ordered that Stirling Castle should be rendered indefensible, so that it could not be held against him again. However, in the disturbances which followed his death it was once again repaired and occupied by English forces until they were constrained to surrender to Robert the Steward (later to be Robert II) in 1342.

From the later 14th century onwards, there was a great deal of building, and the North Gate of 1381 may be the earliest identifiable building in the castle still to survive. In the course of the 14th and 15th centuries, Stirling provided a prominent backdrop to the continuous turbulence of medieval Scotland. Amongst the best-remembered of such events was the murder by James II within the castle of William, the 8th Earl of Douglas, in 1452, followed by the ejection of his mutilated corpse from a window.

The esteem in which the castle was held as a royal residence continued to increase throughout the 15th century, and probably reached its climax in the first half of the 16th century during the reigns of James IV and V, both of whom were prodigious builders.

Above: *Scalloway Castle is situated on the southwest coast of the Shetlands' largest island, Mainland. It was built at the end of the 16th century by Patrick Stewart, Earl of Orkney — the Royal Bastard. A cruel despot he ruled the islands with terror and used forced labour to build his castle.*

Left and Above Right: *The House of the Binns, West Lothian. Begun in the 15th century, the house saw remodelling in the 17th and 19th century.*

Right: *Dirleton started its life as a Norman earth and timber castle built by the de Vaux family. Extensive 13th century stone building on this site produced a formidable cluster of towers which were added to in succeeding centuries. Besieged and taken by Edward I's troops in 1298 it was retaken by Robert the Bruce. Subsequently it was taken by General Lambton for the Parliamentary forces in 1650 and is today a ruin.*

Further events which have earned the castle a place in Scottish folk memory took place in the reign of Mary Queen of Scots — including her coronation within the chapel in 1543, her escape from death by fire in 1561 and the baptism of her son, the future James VI, in 1566.

James VI, who as a baby had been crowned in the parish church at Stirling, had a close connection with the castle throughout his precarious reign, it being the centre of the struggles between rival factions trying to dominate the youthful king.

In 1594 his first son, Prince Henry, was born here, and grandiose schemes for reconstruction were drawn up. Most were abandoned, however, when in 1603 James moved south to accept the English Crown. Despite a promise of regular 'homecomings', the castle entered a twilight phase of royal occupation.

However, Stirling is just one of a chain of romantic castles, most sited in the most gloriously dramatic settings. The builders of these castles had good natural resources, like stone and timber, readily available to them. In an age of seaborne transport and communication, the waters around the islands and sea lochs of Scotland were aids, not barriers, to the establishment and maintenance of maritime lordships and castles.

Proof of the soundness of these building methods is Castle Sween, the oldest standing castle in Scotland, dating from the late 12th century. Situated on a low rocky ridge on the picturesque eastern shore of Loch Sween, Kintyre, both castle and loch take their name form Suibne, progenitor of the MacSween family, rich and powerful Lords of Knapdale and important landowners in Ireland.

Sween Castle is just one of the famed castles of Argyll, which stand like sentries on its deeply indented coastline and are subject to the assaults of the weather of the western seaboard. They conform to the romantic notion that castles are best fitted to a wild, landscape. In fact, inland there is much fertile land which was settled in the Middle Ages, and therefore needed defending. In the Middle Ages, Argyll became a frontier zone between Norwegian dominion over the islands of the west coast, the 'Innse Gall', and the growing power of the kingdom of the Scots on the mainland. But the undisputed sovereignty of the Kings of Scotland over the whole of the western mainland and islands was not finally recognised until the Treaty of Perth (1266), following the Battle of Largs (1263).

Royal works at Tarbert, Skipness and elsewhere show that long after the removal of the Norwegians, the authority of the kings of the Scots still remained precarious, due to the threats of the MacDonald Lords of the Isles. James IV found that declaring the chief of Clan Donald forfeit and getting the other West Highland chiefs to submit to him at Dunstaffnage Castle in 1493 was simply not enough. In the second of two expeditions in the following year he strengthened Tarbert Castle and took control of Dunaverty.

Multi-storey tower houses, lofty, versatile and defensible, became, from the 1400s, the favoured homes for all ranks of landholders for more than three centuries. The west coast towers at Kilchurn, Skipness and Tarbert belong to this classic age of the tower; others of note include Dunollie, Moy, Breachacha and Saddell. Later structures of this style include the rock-island tower of Castle Stalker, a remarkable offshore mid-16th century house of the Stewarts of Appin. But the largest and most distinguished would undoubtedly have been the first Campbell edifice built at Inveraray about 1450 and removed in the 18th century.

The great square tower of Drum Castle, at Drumoak near Banchory, is one of the three oldest tower houses in Scotland. It was the work of Richard Cementarius, first Provost of Aberdeen and King's master mason, in the late 13th century. In 1323 Robert the Bruce gave the charter of the Royal Forest of Drum to his faithful armour-bearer, William de Irwyn.

Gradually, castles became less fortifications, more homes — sometimes palaces — for the landed gentry of Scotland. The following few are but examples to whet the appetite of any visitor.

The five towers of Fyvie Castle, north-west of Aberdeen, enshrine five centuries of Scottish history, each being named after one of the five families who owned the castle. The oldest part dates from the 13th century and is now probably the grandest example of Scottish baronial architecture.

Set in Morayshire parkland, Brodie Castle is a magnificent edifice. It is old but the family association with the area is even older. The Brodies were endowed with their lands by Malcolm IV in 1160, and a Thane of Brodie is recorded in Alexander III's reign.

House of the Binns, at Linlithgow, West Lothian, is the historic home of the Dalyells, among them General Tam Dalyell who raised the Royal Scots Greys there in 1681. It reflects the early 17th century transition in Scottish architecture from fortified stronghold to more spacious mansion.

The royal palace of Falkland, in Fife, was the country residence of the Stewart kings and queens when they hunted deer and wild boar in the Fife forest. Mary Queen of Scots spent some of the happiest days of her tragic life 'playing the country girl in the woods and parks'. The palace was built between 1501 and 1541 by James IV and James V, replacing the earlier castle and palace dating from the 12th century. The roofed south range contains the Chapel Royal, and the east range the King's bedchamber and the Queens Room (both now restored by the National Trust for Scotland).

Not all castles have survived so perfectly. Dirleton Castle, in East Lothian, is now a cluster of beautiful ruins dating back to 1225, with additions in the 14th and 16th centuries. The castle has had an eventful history, from its first siege by Edward I in 1298 until its destruction in 1650. But despite its ruination, the romantic setting reveals a flavour of a bygone age . . . its garden still encloses a 16th century bowling green surrounded by yew trees.

These are but a few of the castellated treasures Scotland boasts. A more comprehensive list is given at the back of this volume.

Top Right: *Skipness Chapel was re-sited in the castle grounds in the 13th century.*

Right: *An atmospheric detail of Dirleton Castle.*

Far Right: *Skipness Castle is an enclosure castle which was started by Dugald MacSween in the 13th century and was considerably modified over the years. Located on the strategically important northest coast of Kintyre, it controlled the confluence of Loch Fyne, Kilbrannan Sound and the Sound of Bute.*

Left and Right: *Drum Castle — a 13th century great tower — was given to Robert the Bruce's armour bearer, William Irvine, in the 1310s.*

Bottom and Below Right: *Situated on the shores of Loch Awe, Kilchurn Castle is a beautiful ruin. Built in the 15th century by Colin Campbell, it was remodelled by another Campbell — John — in the 1690s to accommodate a private army; it was abandoned in the mid-18th century.*

Below: *Smailholm Tower, near Kelso.*

Previous Page: *Edinburgh Castle, pride of Scotland.*

Above and Left: *Castle Sween stands on the coast of Knapdale on what used to be called Loch Sween. The massive, uncomplicated early design (it was started in the late 11th/early 12th century) has been masked by later medieval additions but its state of preservation is perhaps unsurprising when you consider how thick — over 2m (6.5ft) — the original walls were. It is now a romantic ruin having been slighted during the Civil War.*

Above Right and Below Right: *Falkland Palace, Fife, was built by James IV to the south of an older, 13th century castle, built by James II. James V made major additions and alterations 1537-42, through the services of his architect Sir James Hamilton. The latter had spent some years at the French court, the workmen were all French and the result was a splendid Renaissance facade to delight James's French wife Madelaine, daughter of the powerful French monarch François I.*

Above Left: *Brodie Castle is owned by the family of the same name and stands on land which had been the family's for over 800 years. The castle we see today was built in the 16th and 17th centuries and rebuilt after a fire in 1645. It contains a good art collection.*

Left: *Another view of Kilchurn Castle brooding in early morning mists.*

Above: *Fyvie Castle is a spectacular fortified palace. The earliest part dates back to the 14th century — when the Preston Tower was erected. The other tower — the Meldrum — went up in 15th or 16th century and the imposing gatehouse is also late 16th century.*

10 From Dawn of a Christian Age

Just as the castles of Scotland tell a story of its violent history, forever threatened by attackers and invaders, so the churches and abbeys of Scotland tell of a different type of cultural 'invasion' — Christianity. In this section, we will look at just a few of the great and beautiful buildings that reflect this civilising influence.

When the Romans left this land, they left behind them not only forts, villas and straight roads, they also left Christianity. The new religion was brought to Scotland by the imperial soldiers and administrators, and for the last hundred years of Roman rule, that empire was officially Christian.

Yet it was a Scotsman, born in the Solway area but educated in Rome, who must be given the credit for introducing Christianity to his homeland. This little-known 4th century missionary, St Ninian, preceded the more celebrated St Columba and St Augustine by almost 200 years. The gospel was first been introduced by St Ninian in AD 397 at Whithorn, where he established his stone church 'Candida Casa'. From there his followers spread the Word through the country.

The island of Iona, however, is more usually credited with being the launch point of Christianity in Scotland. The tiny 1,800-acre west coast isle has a special significance for all Christians because that is where, in AD 563, Columba and his followers arrived from Ireland to extend the religion in Scotland and the north of England. An abbey, other sacred buildings and historic sites are visited by pilgrims from all over the world.

In this section, we will look at only a smattering of religious sites (a fuller list can be found at the back of the book) in a journey from Columba's west to the gentler Borders of Scotland. Columba and his followers took the same journey in their mission to spread their Gospel. Indeed, as we shall learn from the accompanying panel about beautiful Loch Ness, his journey was not without drama.

It is, however, to the south that we now journey — to see a very different Scotland, one which most graphically shows how both the warlike and peaceloving aspects of this country's history have left their marks side by side. For in the beautiful Scottish Borders, alongside the ruins of battered castles and forts, stand examples of Christian architecture at its most perfect.

Hidden in this forgotten country nestling in Scotland's southeastern corner, between England and Edinburgh, is a land of great contrasts and surprises. Contrasts between soft fields and rugged shoreline, and between splendour and ruin. High hills and moors bound the region on three sides, the North Sea on the other. Through its lush river valleys the great waters of the Tweed, Teviot, Yarrow and Ettrick flow. Almost half the region's 1,800 square miles are more than 305m (1,000ft) high.

The Scottish Borders greatly prizes its peaceful way of life. It was, after all, hard won. As history records, before the area could

Below: *King David I (1124-53) founded Melrose Abbey, now ruined but hauntingly beautiful.*

Above Right: *Detail of the ceiling of Iona Abbey.*

Below Right: *Dryburgh Abbey burial place of Sir Walter Scott.*

establish its own identity and way of life, it had to fight off the advances of first the Romans and then the English. In between, there were numerous internal scores to settle. It was a struggle that was to continue unbroken for almost seven centuries, through the wars of independence and the time of the Border Reivers. While much of the Borders was inevitably destroyed in the course of these tumultuous times, happily much remains today to tell the tale.

Traces of camps and hill forts survive from the days when Celt, Pict, Scot and Saxon did battle with one another. Tower houses — like 16th century Aikwood Tower in the Ettrick Valley — that held out the English border raiders stand proudly and defiantly on commanding hilltop sites.

Less blemished by time and conflict is Traquair, said to be the oldest inhabited house in Scotland. It has colourful historical associations with Mary Queen of Scots and the Jacobite risings.

Four of Scotland's greatest historical prizes lie in these lands, together representing the greatest concentration of medieval religious houses in Scotland. With a medieval majesty that still manages to shine through the spoiling and the dereliction they have suffered, the great Border abbeys of Jedburgh, Kelso, Melrose and Dryburgh stand testament to the past. Their story is perhaps best told through the ruins of the proud Abbey of Melrose . . .

A little to the east of the town, beside the winding River Tweed, is a secluded spot called Old Melrose. It is here that Melrose's story begins with the arrival of Celtic monks deep in the Dark Ages, shortly before the year 650. It was at this time that St Aidan of Lindisfarne established a monastery, 'Mailros', bringing monks from the Columban monastery on Iona. Mailros then lay within the Anglian kingdom of Northumbria, and its first abbot, Eata, was one of 12 Saxon youths taught by Aidan. The first prior, St Boisil, a quiet and unassuming monk, gave his name to the local village of St Boswells.

The abbey's story continues with the advent of the Cistercians in 1136, who through their diligence and hard work created one of the richest and most magnificent buildings in Scotland. The abbey church of Melrose is one of the finest expressions of 'the architecture of solitude' practised by the Cistercians. Much of the rose-coloured ruin visitors see today dates from a rebuilding of the war-damaged monastery in the late 14th and 15th centuries, by which date the austere architecture for which the Cistercians were famed, had given way to a far more ornate style.

Melrose Abbey has close associations with many famous historical figures, among them St Aidan, St Cuthbert and St Waltheof, King David I and King Robert the Bruce of Scotland and King Richard II of England.

The historian the Venerable Bede, in his *Life of Saint Cuthbert*, wrote of the great missionary's visit to the abbey: 'Now he [St Cuthbert] entered first the monastery of Melrose which is enclosed for the most part by a loop of the River Tweed, and which was then ruled by its abbot, Eata, the most meek and simple of all men.'

Within a radius of just a few miles are the splendid ruins of the three other great Border abbeys: Kelso, Jedburgh and Dryburgh.

Kelso Abbey, even in its fragmentary state, is a great piece of architecture. What can still be seen today is the west end of the great abbey church of the Tironseians, brought to Kelso in 1128 by King David I to demonstrate that his control stretched right down to the English border.

Jedburgh Abbey is in a more complete state. Also founded by David I, around 1138, it is memorable chiefly as a dramatically sited ruin viewed soon after a traveller's arrival from England. Its position, however, meant that it was the target of raids by more belligerent visitors from across the border, becoming devastated in the 16th century.

Dryburgh Abbey, remarkably complete, is situated beside a most picturesque stretch of the River Tweed. Here, on a sheltered tongue of lush ground, the White Canons of the Premonstratensian Order established their first home on Scottish soil in 1150. Though the monastery never quite aspired to the heights of wealth and political influence enjoyed by its neighbouring three abbeys, it proved nonetheless their equal as a source of attraction to the many English raiding parties that bedevilled Border life for some three centuries. The monastery never recovered from the ravages of English armies in the 1540s. Today, Dryburgh is perhaps best remembered as the burial place of poet and novelist Sir Walter Scott.

Scott wrote: 'Who knows not Melville's beechy grove and Roslin's rocky glen. Dalkeith, which all the virtues love, and classic Horthenden.'

He was talking about the architectural treasures — like 15th century Rosslyn Chapel, one of Scotland's outstanding works of Gothic architecture — of Midlothian, the region sandwiched between the Borders country and Scotland's capital, Edinburgh.

Midlothian and the Borders, by virtue of their strategic position, have been at the heart of Scottish drama and culture over the centuries, and a sense of history everywhere surrounds one. They boast a rich heritage of prehistoric earth dwellings, ancient monuments, hill forts, picturesque churches, historic houses and dramatic castles like Borthwick and Crichton, famed in literature. But their green and tranquil valleys were once the scenes of clashes of arms between feudal lords and, later, between rival monarchs. And perhaps the most famed of these was the amazing lady who held an entire nation in thrall . . . Mary Queen of Scots. It was due to her disputed claim to the throne of England that so many churches and the four beautiful Borders abbeys were reduced to ruins, as we shall see in the following chapter.

Below and Right: *Urquhart Castle stands on the shores of Loch Ness. While today's ruins date back to the 12th century we know that the site has been in continuous occupation for 2,000 years and was visited by St Columba in AD 465.*

NESSIE

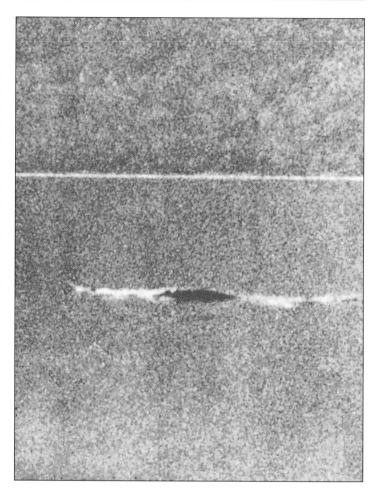

More than 200 million years ago, a great movement of the Earth's crust created the Great Glen, a 96km (60 miles) long cleft cutting diagonally across the heart of Scotland. 20,000 years ago glaciers scoured and smoothed the glen, creating four great lochs along its length: Linnhe, Lochy, Oich, and Ness. Loch Ness is by far the largest — nearly 40km (25 miles) long and only about 3km (2 miles) at its widest point. From the air, Loch Ness looks like a giant 'slash' across the map of Scotland. The loch is more than 300m (1,000ft) deep, with waters blackened by the peat-stained rivers that flow into it.

In recent years, new roads were built along the bank of Loch Ness, opening up the Great Glen, and visitors to the magnificent area 'discovered' the now-famous Loch Ness Monster. But how could a supposedly prehistoric beast, whose ancestors must have lived in the loch for thousands of years, have remained hidden for so long? The truth, of course, is that the existence of this creature from the deep had been recognised by the local Scots for centuries.

The first recorded sighting of Nessie, as it has become affectionately known, was as far back as the birth of Christianity in these northern reaches. It was made by no less than a personage than Saint Columba himself.

The saint travelled from his home in Celtic Dalriada, west Scotland, to the Great Glen in AD465 converting the heathen Picts to Christianity. During the course of this trip, Columba called at the home in Glen Urquhart of a noble named Emchath and converted him and his household. The discovery of a fragment of a brooch recently revealed that this Pictish home was probably a location that has since enthralled visitors as being one of the most dramatic vistas in Scotland: the site of Urquhart Castle, which sits on a rocky promontory jutting into Loch Ness. Although the earliest record of the castle is from the 13th century, it is now clear that the site has been occupied for 2,000 years.

During his mission to Loch Ness, Columba found the locals recovering the body of a neighbour who had been attacked by a beast of the depths while out swimming. One of the saint's followers swam out into the loch to retrieve a boat when he, too, was confronted by the creature.

According to St. Columba's biographer Adomnan, abbot of Iona: 'A strange beast rose from the water something like a frog, except that it was not a frog.' Columba ordered the monster: 'Go no further, nor touch that man.' At which the wild predator sank meekly back into the deep.

That was the beginning of the legend of the Loch Ness monster. It is a legend that has been kept alive over the centuries through Scottish folklore, which tells of kelpies (malignant water sprites) disguising themselves as horses to lure and kill human victims. Locals have always referred to their mysterious neighbour as a 'water horse' rather than a monster. Children were warned not to swim in Loch Ness because of the giant kelpie. In Gaelic, the creature was known as *Niseag*.

It was only in the 1930s, when a new road was being cut into the rocky north shore of the loch, that outsiders began to take notice of Nessie. Now monster hunting has become a minor industry, with underwater cameras, echo sounders and even miniature submarines plumbing the depths — but nevertheless failing to find conclusive proof of Nessie's existence. The loch presents investigators with problems. It can play tricks on the eyes. Its high shorelines cast deep shadows and reflections. It is sometimes completely calm in a way that the sea rarely is, and ripples in the water can appear exaggerated. Sceptics have attempted to explain away many mysterious sightings of unidentified creatures as being the result of boats' wakes or wind changes or simply logs in the water.

However, one of the world's most respected naturalists, the late Sir Peter Scott, who helped launch the Loch Ness Phenomena Investigation Bureau, was sufficiently impressed with research to announce: 'I believe there are between 20 and 50 creatures down there — and I believe they are related to the plesiosaurs.'

Since the plesiosaur is long extinct, Scott's theory means that the creatures in Loch Ness must have been cut off from the sea at the end of the last Ice Age. That makes Nessie and her ancestors up to 70 million years old!

If Nessie exists, why have no bodies or bones ever been found on the shoreline? Scientists say that water pressure in the great depths slows down decomposition and allows time for eels to dispose of the remains of any defunct monsters. And so cold is it that bodies of drowned men — never mind monsters — seldom return to the surface.

Above: *It's hard to believe that Nessie exists but when such experts as Sir Peter Scott don't rule it out . . . you begin to wonder.*

Right: *Moody Urquhart Castle has a long history changing hands many times. It stands on a promontory jutting into the peat-blackened waters of Loch Ness. It was here, perhaps, that St. Columba met Emchath*

Above: *Another abbey founded by David I, Kelso was one of the most spectacular Romanesque abbeys in Britain. Particularly wealthy, by 1300 it controlled the revenues from some 40 churches.*

Right: *The ruins of Melrose Abbey in the lush hills of the Borders east of Galashiels. Probably founded by St Aidan in the 7th century, David I invited the Cistercians to establish the medieval abbey we see today.*

Left and Below: *Kelso Abbey.*

Previous Page, Right and Below Right: *Melrose Abbey.*

What caused the deterioration and decay of such wealthy foundations? War certainly played its part: the Borders' abbeys resounded to the brute noise of war regularly, but neglect was probably the main culprit. Following the Reformation when the fixtures and fitting were removed, along with the windows and roof lead, stone robbing — a time-honoured practice the world over — took hold. Many a local farm or country house would have accepted gleefully the cheap, fine quality stone available for reuse! The most vandalised Scottish abbey of them all was that of Scone which was so destroyed by a mob, following John Knox's tirade against idolatry in 1559, that it is not even listed as an ancient monument because too little remains.

Today, as with the great English medieval foundations at Jervaulx, Rievaulx and Fountains, all that remains are beautiful skeletons which still seem to retain a fragmentary feeling of quiet, reflective solitude.

Above and Left: *Melrose Abbey. The beautiful detail of the window exemplifies the style of Gothic architecture called 'Decorated' which can be described as 'more tracery than glass'.*

Right: *Dryburgh Abbey ceiling detail.*

Left, Below Left and Right: *Dominating the Jed Water, Jedburgh Abbey was founded in 1138 as a priory of Augustinian canons.*

Below: *The Cross of St John outside Iona Abbey.*

Below Right: *It was to Iona that St Columba came by coracle from Ireland in AD563 to spread the Word. The island is just off the west coast of Mull, separated by the Sound of Iona, which is just over 1km (0.75 miles) wide. The island has a long religious history: used by the druids before the birth of Christ, under St Columba it became the centre of European learning. The Book of Kells may have been started here (it is preserved today in Dublin); written in Irish with magnificent illustrations it is a manuscript of the four gospels.*

Left: *Iona Abbey and the replica of St John's Cross. St Columba died in AD597 and Iona settled down to a long period of peace which was shattered by roving Norsemen in 795, 801, 806 — when 68 monks were massacred at Martyrs' Bay — 825 and finally 986 when the abbot and 15 monks were killed. The monastery was rebuilt in 1074 and in 1430 the Bishopric of the Isles was formed. Iona became a cathedral in 1500, but the Reformation was just around the corner and all the religious buildings were broken up and most of the crosses on the island defaced. It would not be until 1910 that the abbey was restored.*

Bottom: *The burial ground on Iona — it was recorded in 1549 that 60 kings of Scotland and Norway were buried here.*

Right: *Iona Beach.*

Below: *Iona Abbey detail.*

11 Mary, Queen of Scots

Few other figures in Scottish history are as well known as Mary Queen of Scots, who lived from 1542 to 1587. Her reign in Scotland lasted only seven years, yet she played her part in a drama which still fascinates historians and visitors alike. She had in full measure the strange charm of the Stewart (the spelling was later changed to Stuart) dynasty which so often added turbulence and uncertainty to Scotland's story. But this queen's life was part of a larger drama, played out in the royal houses of Scotland, France and England.

Mary was born at a troubled time for Scotland, which was experiencing the first upheavals of the Reformation. The Protestant reformers favoured an alliance with England, as King Henry VIII of England was a vigorous opponent of Catholicism. Meanwhile the supporters of Catholicism looked towards France.

Mary's grandmother was Henry's sister, Margaret Tudor. But Mary's mother, Mary of Guise, was of the French royal house. Her husband, King James V, died at Falkland Palace only a week after Mary was born at Linlithgow Palace. With the religious struggle intensifying between France and England, France expected Scotland (with its Catholic monarchy) to side with it against the English King Henry. Thus Scotland was drawn into an English-French quarrel — a dangerously unstable political situation for the young queen.

Just before her birth, a half-hearted attempt by Scotland to aid France had ended in defeat by England at Solway Moss. Soon King Henry VIII was well aware that several Scottish lords were unhappy with the established church and demanded that the infant Mary should marry his own son Edward, thus creating a Protestant dynasty on both sides of the border. Before Mary was three years old, Henry had sent an army to back his claim in an episode known as the 'rough wooing'.

The English armies destroyed the Border abbeys, and burned the palace of Holyroodhouse in Edinburgh and many other parts of southern Scotland. By the time Mary was five years old, even though King Henry VIII had died, English forces under Edward VI defeated the Scots at the Battle of Pinkie, near Musselburgh, in September 1547 and occupied their country.

Many Scots did not know which way to turn. Though the tide of anti-Catholicism was gradually rising, the English invaders, representing the new Protestantism, were unpopular. In the absence of a strong monarch, the nation was indecisive — then finally appealed to France to rid the country of the English invaders. Already a pawn in a political game, the price for this was the removal of the future queen to France. At the age of only six, amid much conflict and bloodshed, Mary sailed from Dumbarton Castle in 1548.

She returned to Scotland at the age of 18, already widowed following the death of the king of France. Contemporary accounts speak of her beauty: she was tall, dark-eyed and graceful.

Although the new Protestant religion had by no means claimed all influential Scots, by the time of Mary's return reformers like

Above: *Wooden ceiling panel in Mary Queen of Scots' outer chamber at the palace of Holyroodhouse. Poor Mary spent much of her life in confinement: from her sojourn aged three on the Isle of Inchmahome to keep away from Henry VIII's 'rough wooing', a year in the castle of Loch Leven where she was forced to abdicate her crown and then 19 years in the hands of English Queen Elizabeth I until the Babington Plot led to her execution at Fotheringay in 1587.*

Right: *Mary's bedroom in Holyroodhouse.*

John Knox were already preaching armed resistance to any attempt by the monarch to interfere with their style of worship. However, Mary had particular support in the Highlands, which were still mainly Catholic.

Mary fell in love with Henry, Lord Darnley, whom she described as 'the lustiest and best-proportioned lang man' that she had ever met (he was over six feet tall). They were married in 1564 in the Chapel Royal at Holyrood. He soon proved to be arrogant, impetuous, fond of taverns and thoroughly unreliable. Mary thereafter excluded him from court business. He also became jealous of her secretary and close friend, Italian musician David Rizzio. As part of a wider power-plot, Rizzio was murdered by Darnley and his supporting conspirators before the queen's eyes in the Palace of Hollyroodhouse.

Shortly after, Mary gave birth to a son, destined to be James VI of Scotland — later James I of England, after the childless English Queen Elizabeth. Factions and plots among Scotland's noble families were rife at this time, in a complex political situation involv-

ing the church and state. It was rumoured that Mary was to be removed from the throne and Darnley set up as regent over her child.

By 1567, the year after the birth of her child, Mary had pardoned the murderers of Rizzio, failed in her attempt to reconcile Darnley and had become attracted to one of her staunch supporters, the Earl of Bothwell. Then Darnley was found murdered after a mysterious explosion at the Kirk o' Field, Edinburgh. Bothwell was implicated but soon had himself acquitted of the accusations.

The Earl of Bothwell abducted Mary and took her, perhaps willingly, to Dunbar Castle. Scotland was shocked and rebellion loomed when it became known that they had married. Besieged on their honeymoon in Borthwick Castle, Midlothian, both Bothwell and Mary escaped and raised an army. Their forces assembled at the Palace of Seaton, in East Lothian. They were challenged by an army of confederate lords at Carberry Hill, southeast of Edinburgh, where they were defeated on 15 June 1567. Bothwell slipped away (he eventually ended his days in prison in Denmark) while Mary was taken captive. After being led in an unseemly short red petticoat through the jeering crowds of Edinburgh, the deposed queen, still only 24, was imprisoned in Loch Leven Castle.

Loch Leven Castle will forever be associated in the memory of Mary Queen of Scots. She had been a frequent visitor during her short, tragic reign, perhaps because it was a marvellous place from where she could enjoy her favourite sport of hawking. She probably visited first within months of her return from France in 1561. Two years later she debated long and hard with John Knox in the castle's great hall as to whether Roman Catholics should be persecuted or tolerated. In 1565 Mary, with her second husband Lord Darnley, dined at Loch Leven.

But within two days of her defeat at the battle of Carberry Hill she was a prisoner at the island castle which had given her so much pleasure. Her jailer was Sir William Douglas, Laird of Loch Leven and a die-hard rebel. 'Guard was continually kept at the castle day and night, except during supper, at which time the gate was locked with a key,' wrote Giovanni Correr, Venetian Ambassador to France, reporting in May 1568 on Mary's imprisonment.

Loch Leven Castle, whose surviving buildings are outstanding, is among the most important medieval monuments in Scotland. Indeed, the lofty tower house on the island which was Mary's prison for much of her stay has a claim to be among the oldest in the country, and parts of the courtyard may well perpetuate defences erected as early as 1300.

Above: *Dumbarton Castle, nestling below Dumbarton rock, volcanic basalt, jutting into the Clyde.*

Below Left and Right: *Loch Leven Castle will always be remembered for its associations with Mary Queen of Scots who spent nearly a year in unhappy captivity within its cramped confines. For the castle is a small structure with spartan facilities — very different from her usual quarters in Holyroodhouse. The keep was started in the 14th century; the walls and drum tower were 16th century additions. Entrance was by means of ladder to the second floor of the five-storey keep. As can be seen from the photograph (**Right**) the stonework is immaculate, although the interior of the keep is gutted.*

Mary, who miscarried twins within a month of her arrival, was housed in the third floor of the tower house. Because of her state of health, she was allowed a doctor, in addition to two ladies-in-waiting and a cook. She occupied her time during captivity in needlework and walking in the castle grounds.

The most momentous event during her imprisonment occurred in June 1567 when she was forced to abdicate in favour of her infant son, christened Charles James. He succeeded to the throne as James VI and was crowned at Stirling five days later. The Laird of Loch Leven had the castle's guns fired and bonfires lit in the courtyard to celebrate the event. The recently deposed Queen was not amused.

The castle walls held Mary for less than a year. In May 1568, with the help of boatman Willie Douglas, she escaped across the loch. She fled to the west, rallying supporters as she went. Yet within a matter of days of her escape her army was decisively defeated by Protestant forces (often known as the Lords of the Congregation) at Langside, near Glasgow. She fled southwards and her last night in Scotland was spent at Dundrennan Abbey, in Galloway.

Mary, former Queen of Scots, went into England, and in May 1568 threw herself on the mercies of the Queen of England, her cousin Elizabeth. Not forgetting Mary's long-standing claim to the English, as well as Scottish, throne, Elizabeth promptly imprisoned her once more. Without ever seeing Scotland again, Mary remained in captivity south of the border, a pawn in the political game played around her, for 19 long years.

Despite many calls for her execution as a traitor, Elizabeth refused to send her to the block, until a plot — the so-called Babington Plot — was uncovered to assassinate the English queen and replace her with Mary who would bring back Catholicism to England. Mary was found guilty of complicity and, four months later, was led to the block at Fotheringay Castle, Northamptonshire. Before some 300 spectators, she calmly walked to her death dressed in black on 8 February 1587. Her outer clothes were removed, revealing a dark red petticoat and bodice, the colour of blood and the Catholic church's colour of martyrdom. Before the axe fell, Scotland's most romantic queen forgave her executioners, saying: 'I hope you shall make an end of all my troubles.'

Below and Right: *Dumbarton Castle was the capital of the ancient Kingdom of the Britons of Strathclyde until it merged again into the Kingdom of Scotland in about 1018. It was also used by the Hanoverian kings as one of the garrison points to control Scotland. Without doubt it can lay claim to being the strongpoint with the longest history in Scotland.*

12 Clans, Witches, and Giants

In Gaelic, the word 'clann' means family or children. The peculiarly Scottish social system of clans was a distinctly Gaelic tribal culture — but one which eventually encompassed many peoples of different ancient origins, whether Celtic, Norse or Norman-French. By the 13th century, the clan system was well-established in the Highlands of Scotland. And in its 15th century heyday, it even threatened the authority of the monarchy.

The geography of the Highlands and Islands may, in the distant past, have played a part in the formation of the clans as social groups, each on its own territory, divorced from its neighbours. And the clans were completely separated by language, custom and geography from the southern 'Sassunachs' (nowadays spelled 'Sassenachs' — meaning of Saxon origin, a word applicable both to the English and to Lowland Scots).

Though increasingly brought into contact with the rest of Scotland, the clan system survived intact until, as we shall see, it was partly dismantled following the Jacobite uprising which ended at Culloden in 1746. Nevertheless, the tribal pride in belonging to a clan lives on to this day and is still a vital part of the richness of cultural life in Scotland. Indeed, with the migrations of Scots in recent centuries, the clans have spread their individual identities throughout the world.

The clan was basically a tribe. At its head was the chief, who was also the owner of its lands. A large clan might have branches or septs, headed by chieftains who originally would be related to, or appointed by, the chief. Not all members of a clan were related, for outsiders could be accepted. When the clan system was at its height, when it had least contact with 'Lowland ways', it was common practice for the sons of the clan chief to be 'boarded out' to other families living nearby.

Growing up with other members of this extended family helped to bond the clan unit together and to foster allegiance. Thus the chief was a kind of tribal father to whom both lesser chieftains and ordinary clansmen gave their loyalty. Such incomers might adopt the name of the chief, but surnames are an unreliable guide to kinship as they were not in general use until relatively late in history. What mattered was loyalty to chief and clan.

The clans lived off the land more-or-less self-sufficiently, with cattle as their main wealth. Stealing cattle (sometimes in order to survive) was widespread, as were territorial disputes between clans. The clansmen did not own land, only the chief, sometimes directly from the crown, sometimes from other superior clan chiefs.

Between the chief and the clansmen were the tacksmen, often related to the chief, by whom they were appointed. They rented from him large tracts of land which they sub-let at rents which allowed them a profit. They were responsible for rent collecting and also for calling out the men of the clan when the chief wanted to go to war. Neither of these duties was particularly popular, and the latter could sometimes involve force if a clansman was unwilling to obey the summons to battle. The system, however, meant

Above: *Dunstaffange Castle sits at the mouth of Loch Etive where it meets the Firth of Lorn.*

Right: *Ossian's Cave. Ossian was the mythical son of Fingal — builder of the Giant's Causeway. The cave is on the northern side of Aonach Dubh, the last of the 'Three Sisters', on the left as you travel down Glen Coe from Rannoch Moor.*

that the chief was not personally involved in these operations, and his position as 'father of his people' was unimpaired.

The clan would normally fight with its chief at its head, the immediate members of his family leading its companies, and each man in the position dictated by his social standing within the clan. The priorities were clear; when one chief, a MacDonell of Keppoch, was asked how much his rents brought him, he replied: 'Five hundred fighting men'.

Not all of a clan chieftain's preoccupations were warlike, however. The most powerful chiefs in some places kept expensive courts and retainers for prestige and had autonomy over matters of law and order within their territory. An important member of the chief's retinue was the bard, who could both compose an epic poem, perhaps recalling a feat of heroism in battle, and recite lineage, which was part of his role as the recorder of the clan's story. The clan piper was another hereditary post.

It is romantic to think of the clan tradition as being mystically Celtic. But it is much more broadly based than that. Some clans have Norman roots and married into Celtic society: Cummings (Comyns), Hays (de la Haye), Frasers (La Frezeliere, ultimately linked to the French 'la fraise', referring to the strawberry shaped device on the family crest), Sinclair (St Clair) and Bruce (Brix, a Normandy place name). Following early Viking raids on Scotland, others have Norse connections: the Macleods of Skye are said to descend from Liot, son of a Norse king; the MacDougalls of Lorne come from the Dougall (Gaelic, 'dark foreigner'), grandson of Norse King Olaf, the Black.

Some clans are linked with ancient monastic houses: the Macnabs ('son of the abbot'); Buchanan ('of the canon's house'); MacTaggart ('son of a priest') and MacPherson ('son of a parson').

Clans with uncertain origins include the MacKenzies who appeared in Ross and Cromarty, claiming descent from their 12th-century kinsman Gilleoin, as do the Mathesons, with lands close to Kyleakin in Wester Ross. The Gunns in Sutherland claim a most unusual descent: they may have been an ancient surviving Pictish tribe, forced into the far north of Scotland.

Clan Donald, the Lords of the Isles, was for generations the most powerful clan in Scotland, especially on the lands by the western seaboard. Great seafarers, the clan controlled the sea lanes with its oared galleys (Gaelic: *birlinn*). Living in semi-royal style, the clan's power brought it into conflict with the crown and the power of Clan Donald was broken before the end of the 15th century.

Mention of the Clan Donald brings us to the best-known, or perhaps most infamous, historical event in clan history. The massacre of Glencoe (the village which sits on Loch Leven at the end of Glen Coe)is a bloody example of the perpetual schisms between individual clans, between the clans and the Lowlanders, between the Catholics and the Protestants, and between Scots and English.

But the history of Glen Coe is much more than the story of a massacre. That event occupied a mere two or three hours in a struggle that went on for at least a thousand years. The whole episode can be seen only in the context of the long and often bitter family rivalries of the Western Highlands. It also gives us an opportunity to gaze upon the grandeur of an area that is one of the world's most celebrated landscapes.

Over the years, hundreds of writers have waxed eloquent in their descriptions of the glen. Perhaps none more than Dorothy Wordsworth when she wrote in her Journal in September 1803: 'The impression was, as we advanced up to the head of the first reach, as if the glen was nothing. Its loneliness and retirement made up no part of my feeling: the mountains were all in all.'

One of the first people to report the wonders of Glen Coe was St Mundus, an Irish disciple of St Columba, who came across from Iona round about the year 600 and settled briefly on a small island in Loch Leven, opposite the mouth of the glen. For centuries this island, Eilaen Munde, the isle of Mundus, was to be the religious centre of the region. But it is not surprising that in a realm as melodramatic, magical and mist-shrouded as this, religion should mix easily with myth and legend.

Glen Coe has produced more than its fair share of giants, monsters and witches. The most famous of the witches was the wicked

Corrage who, at her death, was surprisingly offered Christian burial on Eilean Munde. But the waters of Loch Leven erupted in anger and prevented her crossing, so she was buried on the mainland. She returned subsequently to use her storm-raising powers to sink one of the stray ships of the Spanish Armada which was trying to win home by this route. Another well-known witch was Bean Nighe who was occasionally to be seen washing her clothes in the River Coe. Anyone who saw her was doomed to die soon after . . . and it is not surprising to learn that she made an appearance the night before the famous massacre. Amongst the monsters, the most famous was '*Tarb Uisge*', the water bull of Loch Achtriochtan, named after Ossian, who seems to have been one of Scotland's more amiable monsters and did harm to no one.

When it comes to giants, Glen Coe, as befitted its grandeur and the size of its mountains, was the legendary home of one of the greatest Celtic heroes, Fingal. Fingal, or Fionn McCumhail, was the leader of the Feinn tribe and father of the totally mythical Ossian.

Fingal, if he was a historical figure at all, is credited with a defeat of the Vikings in Glen Coe. The first part of this battle took place at Laroch, by Ballachulish, when the Vikings, led by King Erragon of Sora, came up Loch Leven to Inverscaddle Bay with 40 of their ships full of warriors. Most of Fingal's men, the Feinn, were away hunting deer and the crafty Fingal kept the enemy talking until their return. King Erragon suggested that each side should provide their best 140 warriors who would fight it out formally on the field of Achnacon. This suggestion was accepted and the Scots won — but the whole exercise had to be repeated six times, with great bloodshed, until the Vikings at last retreated. King Erragon was killed with many of his followers in the shallows of Loch Leven, and grave slabs known as the Ringed Garden, at West Laroch, are popularly thought of as Viking tombs.

About the 11th century, Glen Coe passed into the hands of the powerful MacDougall clan, a family of Viking descent, who built up a small empire based at Dunstaffnage Castle, near Oban. In 1308, however, the MacDougall power was shattered when the clan sided with the English against Robert the Bruce. The rival MacDonalds and Campbells fought side by side for Bruce to destroy the MacDougalls at the Battle of the Pass of Brander, 20 miles south of Glencoe. As part of his reward, Angus Og, chief of the MacDonalds, was given the area by the Bruce — for the next 500 years it was MacDonald.

THE KILT

The traditional attire of the clansmen was the kilt of tartan. But neither the garments nor the patterns we know today would have been familiar in the ancient Highlands.

The traditional dress was the belted plaid (*plaide* is Gaelic for blanket). This was a rectangle of cloth about 6ft wide, and was held in place by a belt round the waist. The upper part could be arranged in a variety of ways and, the belt having been loosened, it could serve to wrap the wearer in at night.

The modern kilt is simply the lower half of this garment with its pleats stitched.

Credit for its invention is often given to an Englishman, Thomas Rawlinson, who ran an ironworks in Glengarry and Lochaber about 1725. This is not acceptable to all Scots however, and Sir Thomas Innes of Learney, a former Lord Lyon, in his *Tartans of the Clans and Families of Scotland* calls it 'a wretched story' and claims a much longer history.

Right: *Dunstaffange Castle featured importantly in Scottish history from the days when Alexander II and III used it on their campaigns against the Vikings in the Western Isles; Edward I took it — the Bruce took it back; it was held by the Earls of Argyll and was abandoned in 1810. In legend the Stone of Destiny resided here in an ancient building of the Kings of Dalriada until it was removed to Scone by MacAlpin.*

13 The Massacre of Glencoe

The fist hint of trouble in Glencoe came in the 16th century, when the difference in wealth between the subsistence clans of the remoter Highlands and the more industrious fertile Lowlands began to become more pronounced. In 1501 the Glencoe MacDonalds, with others, captured the Campbell's island fortress of Innis Chonnell, on Loch Awe, and briefly rescued from his long imprisonment Donald Dhu, the only surviving grandson of the last Lord of the Isles. This was just one of many clashes which occurred over the next 200 years. Glen Lyon, now Campbell country, became a favourite raiding-ground and the scene of many skirmishes. It was to be the ultimate coincidence that a Glen Lyon Campbell captained the Redcoats sent to conduct the massacre.

Some years later, Scottish clans became entangled in the civil war between the English monarchy and the English parliamentarians — in which the MacDonalds backed the royalist Cavaliers whilst the Campbells were the Scottish equivalent of the parliamentary Roundheads. A large MacDonald contingent, including the Glencoe men under their 11th Chief, fought for the brilliant Marquis of Montrose in his spectacular campaign to save Charles I. It was the Glencoe men who helped Montrose to find the famous short-cut over the mountains at the Devil's Staircase, east of Glencoe, which enabled Montrose to attack a much larger Campbell army from the rear, near Fort William. More than 2,000 Campbells were killed and the strategically important town of Inveraray was captured by Montrose. After the fall of Montrose, Glencoe MacDonalds still fought vainly for the Royalist cause.

In 1646 came another famous incident when, on one of the Glencoe raids into Glen Lyon, the MacDonalds attacked the Clans Menzies and Campbell after a wedding. They killed 36 of them and returned home with great booty.

Decades of cattle-rustling culminated in the so-called Atholl Raid of 1685. Two successive Earls of Argyll had been executed in Edinburgh, and the Campbells were weakened by defeats. The Glencoe men took advantage of the situation to pillage huge tracts of Campbell territory. The rights and the wrongs of the massacre of Glencoe, therefore, were less clear cut than folklore and clan rivalry would have us believe.

The massacre was carried out on a branch of the Clan Donald by a regular regiment of the British army, raised from the Clan Campbell. The latter had a long history of anti-Jacobitism and support for the Hanoverian (or otherwise Lowland) government. The Campbell regiment acted under orders from King William III in London who wanted the MacDonalds punished ('extirpated') as part of a government policy designed to bring rebel clans to heel.

The story of the massacre has been told many times. On 27 August 1691 King William offered a pardon to all Highland clans who had fought against him or raided their neighbours, on condition that they took the oath of allegiance before a magistrate by the close of the year. It was a fair enough offer. Old Alastair MacDonald had four months to pluck up courage to make the dread journey to Inverary to obtain pardon for himself and his followers.

Above: *Looking toward Stob Corrie nan Lochan which can just be seen over the top of the Aonach Dubh.*

Right: *The slopes of the Aonach Eagach are reflected in the still waters of Loch Achtriochtan.*

Previous Page: *Dunstaffanage Castle from the shore of Loch Etive.*

The alternative was death. Perhaps not taking the threat seriously, Alastair MacDonald left this act of subservience to the last minute, not taking the oath until five days past the deadline. Nevertheless, MacDonald believed that he was safe.

However, a punitive force had already been built up at Fort William and it appeared that the MacDonalds had made enough enemies — King William himself, Secretary of State Sir John Dalrymple of Stair and John Campbell Earl of Breadalbane — to make them seek excuse to regard the oath as invalid. On 1 February 1692 two advance companies were sent to Glencoe under the command of another man who had a grudge against the MacDonalds: Captain Robert Campbell of Glen Lyon a 60-year old alcoholic and a gambler who had by this time lost anything that the MacDonalds had left of his estates.

Robert Campbell had not received specific orders to attack the MacDonalds when he set out for Glencoe. So, since his niece was married to the Glencoe chief's younger son, he asked for quarters for his two companies. All were entertained in the homes of the Glencoe MacDonalds most hospitably for 10 days.

On 12 February, Campbell received written orders from Duncanson to kill all MacDonalds under 70 years of age at five o'clock the following morning. It was the way in which Campbell of Glen Lyon turned on his hosts, on his own niece and her husband, in breach of the ultimate ethic of Highland hospitality, which later gave special notoriety to the massacre.

It was mere coincidence that, while he was there as a commissioned officer of King William and acting under direct orders from his superiors, he happened to belong to one of the Campbell families who had suffered most at the hands of the Glencoe MacDonalds. He was bankrupt and now totally dependent on his army pay. He had very little pride or principle left and was not the sort of person to stand up to his superiors. The other macabre feature of his plight was that, with a force of around 120 men, he was ordered to destroy, in darkness and very poor weather, several hundred people spread over a distance of at least 10 square miles. They expected substantial reinforcements but they were late, perhaps deliberately, leaving all the dirty work to Captain Campbell.

Of the 130-odd officers and men, no more than a dozen bore the surname Campbell. They may have harboured a personal bitterness, but it was not ruthless efficiency which marked the massacre but general incompetence. The force killed only about 10 percent of the numbers they had been ordered to destroy.

The massacre was merciless enough. At Inverrigan, where Captain Campbell had his quarters, eight or nine MacDonalds were tied up and shot. At Invercoe, one man was shot crossing the river. At Carnoch, where the chief had his house, the old man was shot as he got out of his bed and his wife had her clothes and rings stripped from her. At Achnacon several more were killed, including an old man of 80 and a child. At Achtriochtan, the community where the clan bards used to live, a further group was killed.

In all, about 38 were killed but at least 300 escaped into the hills. By the time reinforcements arrived, there was only one old man left alive in the villages and he was promptly killed. Of those who escaped, many are believed to have died of cold and starvation. Most, survived, including the old chief's two sons — despite specific orders 'to root out the old fox and his cubs.' On the army side, three soldiers were believed killed when they pursued MacDonalds up into the hills. And there was a rumour that two officers had resigned their commissions rather than take part in the massacre.

About two weeks later, news of the massacre began to filter through to London. But it was a piece of investigative journalism by an Irishman, Charles Leslie, which turned Glencoe into a political scandal. His pamphlet, arguing a high-level cover-up and breach of trust, excited sympathy for many who were not wholly enamoured with Dalrymple as secretary of state, or William of Orange as king. But there were to be no official reprimands for a full three years. Of those responsible for the massacre, Dalrymple had to resign but soon made a political comeback, and Captain Campbell died a pauper in Bruges, Belgium.

The clan system was now slowly heading for collapse — not just in Glencoe and the western Highlands but throughout the land.

Some chiefs were becoming more interested in money than in men, espousing agriculture and forestry, and dispensing with the tacksmen as costly intermediaries. By the 18th century, with agricultural improvements spreading from the Lowlands and with some road-building taking place which made communications easier, clans and their chiefs were brought more and more into contact with 'southern' ways, which subtly eroded their independence and values. The old clan system was gradually being absorbed into a modern economic society

This process of change was noted by Sir Walter Scott in his novel *Rob Roy* where Rob can be seen as a symbol of the old, self-sufficient ways, which contrasted with his distant cousin, Bailie Nicol Jarvie, a Glasgow merchant preoccupied with progress and business. Even so, Rob also acts as a Jacobite agent and sympathiser (as did the real life Rob Roy), demonstrating that, inevitably, the clan system was a part of Scottish politics.

Ultimately, Lowland authority moved against the clans simply because the chiefs could call on loyal fighting men in time of war or rebellion. These 'private armies' were perceived as hotbeds of Jacobitism or at the very least liable to undermine authority.

Of the two MacDonald brothers who escaped the massacre of Glencoe, John, the 13th Chief of Glencoe, was formally allowed the king's pardon and rebuilt the family home at Carnoch. His brother Alastair rose for the Jacobite cause in 1715 — and fought alongside John Campbell, son of the captain who had led the massacre. Both men forfeited their estates when their cause was lost.

Thirty years later, Alastair, the 14th Chief of Glencoe, who had escaped as a baby from the massacre, turned out with his men to fight for Bonnie Prince Charlie and was made a member of the prince's council. The Glencoe men fought at Culloden . . . and that was truly their last stand. In the miserable period that followed the defeat, their homes were burned once more, their cattle driven away, their clan headquarters at Carnoch destroyed and the chief imprisoned. The chieftainship of the MacDonalds of Glencoe lost all its meaning. (The title was eventually sold to Lord Strathcona, of the Hudson's Bay Company, Canada.) That year of 1746 also saw the chase in Glencoe which Robert Louis Stevenson included in his novel *Kidnapped*.

To what would have been a gradual social change by the clans of Scotland, the Battle of Culloden was to give a brutal and bloody impetus.

Right: *Artist's impression of the MacDonalds fleeing for their lives into the snow, chased by English soldiers. Surprisingly few died in battle — 38 out of 300 — but many died from the cold in the aftermath.*

Above: *The Lost Valley runs between Beinn Fhada and Geàrr Aonach — two of the three sisters of Glencoe. The arrête at the head of the valley leads to Bidean nam Bean, at 1,150m (3,770ft) the highest mountain in Argyll.*

Left: *Glencoe during the warmer months.*

Above Right: *The northern side of Glencoe is dominated by the Aonach Eagach, a long knife-edged ridgewalk, which can be dangerous in extreme conditions. At the Rannoch Moor end of the glen, at the start of the ridge, sits Am Bodach from where this photograph was taken.*

Below Right: *The weather can change very quickly in winter, a cloudless sky can quickly grey over. But the mountains do look spectacular in the snow.*

14 The Jacobite Cause

The 17th century was a troubled time both in Scotland and England. James II of England and VII of Scotland was a Roman Catholic, but many whom he ruled were not. His brief reign (1685-88) was marked by unrest and open rebellion in both kingdoms.

By the end of 1688 King James had made himself so unpopular by his despotic methods of government and his attempts to ensure freedom of worship for his fellow Catholics that civil war threatened. A group of Protestants invited James's Dutch-born nephew and son-in-law, William of Orange, to invade. William agreed and James was compelled to flee the country. A convention in England in February 1689 offered the crown of that kingdom to William and his British-born wife Mary Stuart as joint sovereigns. James meanwhile skulked in France where he was welcomed by Louis XIV. A chateau was placed at his disposal and he was given funds to maintain his court. The French king's motives were simple: to use James's presence to cause trouble for his enemy, William of Orange.

But not everyone back in Britain had disapproved of the exiled king. Those who supported him were known as Jacobites, from Jacobus, Latin for James, and they were to play an important part in British history for the next 60 years. Scotland in particular was divided. The Stuart dynasty had ruled for more than three centuries, and loyalties ran deep, especially in the Highlands. The supporters of James, known as the Jacobites, found a leader in John Graham of Claverhouse, Viscount Dundee (the 'Bonnie Dundee' since commemorated in song). Opposing him was General Hugh MacKay, a veteran soldier who was given command of the government troops in Scotland.

The first shots in the Jacobite cause — a conflict that was to tear Scotland asunder — were about to be fired.

In Edinburgh the parliamentary Convention was engaged in proceedings which were to lead to the Scottish crown being offered to William and Mary. At the same time, Edinburgh Castle was being held for James by the Duke of Gordon. At his home in the city from which he took his title, Viscount Dundee was summoned to the Convention. He refused to attend and rode out of the city with 50 followers — an action which Sir Walter Scott later immortalised in his poem *Bonnie Dundee*.

Dundee set about raising the Highlanders and MacKay, with well-trained cavalry and 3,000 foot soldiers, set out on weeks of

The pass of Killiecrankie: the 'Queen's view' (**Below**)*; the 'Soldier's leap'* (**Right**).

fruitless pursuit. Attention focused on Blair Castle, home of the Marquis of Atholl, which was being held by the Jacobites. The castle was strategically important. Whoever held it could command the pass through the hills and the route to the north. So when the news reached Dundee, in Lochaber, and MacKay, in Perth, both marched towards Blair.

Two armies were now on the road that led up Strathtay to picturesque Pitlochry and onwards to the Pass of Killiecrankie.

On the morning of 27 July 1689, as MacKay's army was making its way through the narrow defile of the pass, Dundee had already reached Blair Castle. Dundee led his troops away from the castle, over the hills behind Blair, and took up position on a south-facing ridge. With only 2,500 men and few horse he needed the advantage of ground. In silver and buff coat, with green scarf, he positioned himself with his small troop of cavalry in the centre of the line. Below, MacKay emerging at the north end of the pass, halted his force on level ground above the River Garry.

For two hours the armies waited. Then, at about seven o'clock on the summer evening, when the sun was no longer in the eyes of his troops, Dundee gave the order to charge. Kilt and plaid in those days were one garment. As was their custom, the men discarded this cumbersome cloak. Clad in their shirts, crouching behind their shields to present the smallest target, they rushed at the enemy.

MacKay's troops were armed with a new weapon, the bayonet. This did not clip on to the muzzle, as it did later, but had to be screwed on. A soldier, having fired his weapon, was expected to perform this awkward operation while his enemy was rapidly approaching wielding a double-edged broadsword. The result was that when the two armies met, all was over in a couple of minutes.

General MacKay wrote of his troops: 'With the exception of Hastings' and Leven's regiments, they behaved like the vilest cowards in nature. In the twinkling of an eye, our men, as well as the enemy, were out of sight, being got down pell-mell to the river.'

With a few scattered remnants, MacKay made his escape. He had lost nearly half his army, 2,000 killed or taken prisoner. The Highland losses were 900 — including, though his men did not at first realise it, Dundee himself. He had been hit in the opening minutes as he turned to urge on the cavalry. Wrapped in two plaids, his body was carried to Blair Castle: he was buried in the old church.

The Highland victory was complete. But for the Jacobites, the battle was an isolated success. The clans regrouped and marched on Dunkeld. But the little town had been occupied by the newly formed Cameronians and, without Dundee to lead them, the victors of Killiecrankie were very soon defeated in a bloody battle on 21 August. The Highlanders' rising against the crown was over — for the time being.

When King James died in 1701, French King Louis sent heralds to the chateau where he had spent his exile to proclaim his 13-year old son King James VIII of Scotland and III of England. The boy was to grow up to become known to history as the 'Old Pretender' (Pretender meaning claimant). And his son, Prince Charles Edward Stuart, was to become known as the 'Young Pretender' — or more popularly 'Bonnie Prince Charlie'.

In 1702 William of Orange also died. His horse stumbled over a molehill and threw him. Jacobites toasted "the little gentleman in black velvet." They also had their own version of the loyal toast, passing their wine glasses over water — a silent token that it was to the king over the sea that they drank. It was never easy to estimate the strength of Jacobite support. William of Orange had been unpopular, and exile inevitably increased the attractions of the Stuart monarchy. There were Jacobites in all parts of Britain and they plotted continuously. But not all those who drank to 'the king over the water' were prepared to fight to restore him.

When it did come to real military effort, it was the Highlands of Scotland which consistently provided the largest part of the Jacobite armies. Although not all Highlanders were Jacobites, there were factors which led them to favour the exiled dynasty more than most. One was simple loyalty to a king of Scottish descent. Another was that, since the clans were run on patriarchal lines with chiefs whose word was law, they found nothing untoward in the idea of a despotic king. And, of course, those who were Catholic or Episcopalian had not been repelled, as Protestant clans had been, by James's attacks on their religion.

In 1708 James II's son, now aged 20, made his first bid for the crown. With 6,000 French troops in 30 vessels, he set out from Dunkirk. The fleet anchored in the Firth of Forth. It was the young man's intention to present himself to the Scots as James III, and ask them to break the Treaty of Union with England, which had been arrived at only the previous year. But a superior naval force under Admiral Byng appeared, and the French fled north, to return in disorder to Dunkirk by way of the north of Scotland and Ireland.

Seven years later, James tried again. At his instigation, and in his absence, the Earl of Mar raised the Stuart standard at Braemar on 6 September 1715, proclaiming James, King of Scotland, England, Ireland and France. With nearly 10,000 men, Mar marched south and met George I's army, under the Duke of Argyll, at Sheriffmuir, near Stirling. The battle was indecisive. Mar withdrew to Perth and all initiative was lost. James arrived in Peterhead in December but by this time his support had melted away and Argyll was at his heels. He sailed for France on 4 February 1716, accompanied by the unhappy Mar, and never saw Scotland again.

In England a simultaneous Jacobite rising had also been defeated. On both sides of the border punishment was severe. There were executions — many by the gruesome ritual of hanging, drawing and quartering — sentences of transportation, and the abolition of titles, including 19 Scottish peerages.

Nevertheless, it was only four years later that the next attempt was made. This time it suited Spain, at war with both Britain and France, to play the Jacobite card. A force of 29 ships with 5,000 soldiers and arms for another 30,000 sailed from Cadiz — and was promptly shattered by a storm. An earlier diversionary force, however, including 307 Spaniards, had already sailed. This reached Scotland and made its headquarters in Eilean Donan Castle on Lochalsh. The castle was bombarded by the Royal Navy and its Spanish garrison surrendered. There was little support from the clans, and on 10 June 1719, in the beautiful setting of Glen Shiel, the Jacobite force was defeated by troops from Inverness garrison.

It was to be another 25 years before the next, and last, attempt to put a Stuart on the throne. Meantime the Highlands were changing. Forts were erected and manned. General George Wade, commander-in-chief in Scotland, built some 260 miles of road and 40 bridges to enable government troops to penetrate the mountains. Companies of Highlanders were recruited to maintain order, and were distinguished by their own dark tartan — the origin of the Black Watch. It was against this historically changing background that the drama of the great 'Forty Five' rebellion was to be played.

Right: *The snowy slopes of Kintail.*

15 Bonnie Prince Charlie

At Glenfinnan, on the famous 'Road to the Isles', Highland beauty and Highland history again come together. Great mountains guard the narrow length of Loch Shiel. Their wooded slopes rise steeply from its edge. The scene changes with every change of light. At the head of the loch, a narrow strip of land makes a natural stage in the amphitheatre of the hills. Here stands the monument, a 20m (65ft) pillar surmounted by the statue of a Highlander and surrounded by a stone stockade.

It was built in 1815 by Alexander MacDonald of Glenaladale 'to commemorate the generous zeal, the undaunted bravery and the inviolable fidelity of his forefathers and the rest of those who fought and bled in that arduous and unfortunate enterprise'.

It commemorates the day — 19 August 1745 — when on this spot Prince Charles Edward Stuart, 'Bonnie Prince Charlie', raised his standard and heard his father proclaimed King James VIII of Scotland and III of England and Ireland. It was the first act of the dramatic adventure known in history as the 'Forty Five', the last endeavour to regain for the Stuart dynasty the throne of Britain.

It was a romantic spectacle . . . the young Prince, tall, slim and handsome, surrounded by his army of fierce-looking Highlanders. But it was also an act of war against the ruling British monarch in London. It set in motion a train of events which led, eight months later, to the last battle fought on British soil. To Culloden.

It is tempting to view the Forty-Five as a struggle between Scots and English or between Highlanders and non-Highlanders. The reality was different. Religious and political beliefs dictated diverse loyalties, often within clans and even within families. So, as in all civil wars, there was for many combatants that special agony when facing the enemy, of seeing a brother or a son on the other side.

Prince Charles Edward Stuart's army was predominantly Highland, but by no means exclusively so. Not all the clans rallied to his standard. Had they done so, he might well have marched on London at the head of 30,000 men and the course of history would have been changed. The prince's support came mainly from the Roman Catholic and Episcopalian clans. The Campbells, staunchly Presbyterian, fought for the English — but not all, for those from Glen Lyon served in the prince's Atholl Brigade. Cumberland's forces included three Scottish Lowland regiments. There were clansmen who fought only because their homes and families would have suffered had they not answered their chief's call. There were others, Grants and Macleods among them, who rallied to the cause despite their chief's disapproval.

Perhaps the deciding factor in the Forty-Five, however, was the great majority who did not rise — the Highlanders and Lowlanders, Scots and English, who stayed at home and awaited the outcome.

Had all gone as planned, however, the Forty-Five would have been the Forty-Four, and a much more serious threat to George II. In February of that year, Louis XV planned a massive invasion of Britain. His objective was to place on the throne in London a

The Prince Charles Edward Stuart — Bonnie Prince Charlie — arrived on mainland Scotland at Loch nan Uamh near Arisaig on 25 July 1745. He raised his standard at Glenfinnan on Loch Shiel on 19 August and set off to reconquer his kingdom. Unlike all good fairy stories, this tale did not have a happy ending and the Forty Five — as the rebellion became known — was to lead the Prince to a life in drunken exile and his Highlanders to death.

Above and Right: *Re-enactment of the arrival of Bonnie Prince Charlie at Glenfinnan and the raising of his standard. His father was declared king, and the rebellion had began.*

monarch who would be ultimately dependent upon France. Ten thousand regular French troops were assembled at Dunkirk ready to sail to Essex and march on London. But again weather intervened; a storm wrecked the invasion fleet and the expedition was abandoned. The young Prince Charles Edward Stuart, who was to have sailed with the fleet as the Prince of Wales and representative of his father, found that once his potential usefulness to Louis was gone he was virtually ignored.

The prince was not so easily put off. On 16 July 1745 he set out on his own expedition with only two ships, seven supporters and a small store of arms and ammunition. Off the west coast of Ireland, the expedition encountered a British man-o'-war which saw off one of the ships (containing the bulk of military stores) while the prince's ship slipped away to the Hebridean island of Eriskay.

The Prince's first contact on Scottish soil was not encouraging. On Eriskay, Alexander MacDonald of Boisdale advised him to go home. 'I am come home, sir,' replied the prince.

On 25 July the prince's ship reached the Scottish mainland at Loch nam Uamh, near Arisaig, from where he sent out letters to Highland chiefs seeking support. At Glenfinnan on 19 August, the standard was raised, his father proclaimed James VIII and III, and the prince himself as regent. The Forty-Five had begun.

It was a small force at first, only about 1,200 men. More than half of them were Camerons, under the chief's son, known to his-

tory as 'Gentle Lochiel', the chief, his father being in exile. Most of the remainder were MacDonalds of Keppoch. They gathered strength as they moved eastwards, avoiding the government garrisons at Fort William and Fort Augustus, and crossing by the Corrieyairack Pass into Badenoch, ironically by one of the roads built by General Wade to discourage Highland insurgency. A government army under Lt-Gen Sir John Cope was hurried north but chose not to meet Charles, instead marching to Inverness, so leaving the route south to Edinburgh open to the Jacobites. At Perth, the Prince was joined by Lord George Murray (brother of the Duke of Atholl) who was to prove his outstanding field commander.

Edinburgh was entered virtually unopposed on 17 September, though the castle remained in government hands. The prince occupied the Palace of Holyroodhouse, home of his ancestors. Cope, meanwhile, had marched to Aberdeen and taken ship to Dunbar. He moved towards Edinburgh but on 21 September, in less than 10 minutes, his army was routed at the Battle of Prestonpans.

Charles, magnanimous and humane in victory, was master of Scotland. But it was not enough. On 1 November, in one of the most ambitious military campaigns of history, Prince Charles Edward Stuart turned his army south and began a march on the English capital, London.

Carlisle surrendered on 16 November, 12 days later the army reached Manchester, and on the evening of 4 December, Derby. London was now only 127 miles away and the city was in a state of panic. Catholic support, which had thus far been disappointing, was at last growing throughout England and Wales. Ten thousand French troops were said to be embarking at Dunkirk. A rapier-like thrust at the capital was in prospect.

Such a move could conceivably have succeeded. Charles was all for continuing his march south. But all was not well. The Prince's army had lacked English support, and about a thousand of his Highlanders had quietly left to return to their native glens. Three government armies were threatening to converge on the the Jacobite force. And Charles and Lord George Murray had quarrelled. Cause of the upset was the influence wielded by one of the prince's original seven supporters who had been a thorn in Lord George's side during the entire campaign, and was responsible for much of its failure. He was Irishman John William O'Sullivan, the army's adjutant and quartermaster-general, a great favourite of the prince, and — in Lord George's opinion — an idiot.

On 6 December — 'Black Friday' — the prince took the decision to retreat. It may have been a wrong one. Dispirited, his troops faced the long road back to Scotland.

Glasgow was reached on Christmas Day, but the city was ill-disposed. Only Lochiel's intervention saved it from being sacked, a circumstance which in later years, tradition says, led to the bells being rung whenever the chief of Clan Cameron entered the city.

Stirling town surrendered but not the castle. Reinforcements arrived, including 400 from Clan Mackintosh raised by Lady Macintosh (the redoubtable 'Colonel Anne') whose husband, head of the clan, was on the government side. Men, stores and ammunition arrived from France. From Edinburgh, Lt-Gen Hawley marched to relieve Stirling. The battle of Falkirk, on 17 January, was a victory for the prince's army, but in the confusion of a winter dusk the advantage was neither realised nor exploited. Hawley retired to Edinburgh, there to hang his deserters on gallows erected for Jacobites, while the Prince's army trudged north to Inverness.

Above and Right: *Loch Shiel and the Glenfinnan Monument to the Forty Five. Built in 1815, it stands at the head of the loch, a few miles from Fort Willliam — one of the obvious signs of Hanoverian oppression of the Highlands. Fort William was not to fall to the rebels, but all the other strongholds did — severely unsettling the English who had thought them impregnable after the 1715 rebellion. In fact much vaunted Fort Augustus fell after a two-day siege and the Highlanders made much better use than the English of Wade's roads which were supposed to assist King George's army. At Prestonpans, just outside Edinburgh, Prince Charles won a victory which gave heart and credibility to the revolt. But for all the derogatory comments made about George II (1727-60) he was brave: he was the last British monarch to lead his troops into battle — at Dettingen in 1743 — and would not give up the Scottish crown lightly.*

There were sporadic actions. The Jacobites took Fort Augustus, at the foot of Loch Ness, and near Dornoch defeated government troops under Lord Loudon, who had retreated from Inverness. One of the prisoners taken was the Mackintosh chief, whom Prince Charles gallantly returned to his home, Moy Hall — and to 'Colonel Anne', his wife. It is said that when the chief arrived home, his wife greeted him with: 'At your service Captain.' To which he replied: 'No, at your service, Colonel.'

There was a major setback for the Jacobites, however, when a captured government sloop, dispatched to France to seek support was taken by the English navy off the Kyle of Tongue. Her vital hoard of much needed gold and stores never reached the prince.

Meanwhile, the Duke of Cumberland, second son of George II and, despite his youth, an experienced commander, had built up a formidable army at Aberdeen, reinforced by 5,000 Germans under Prince Frederick of Hesse. Cumberland left Aberdeen on 8 April and six days later, to the surprise of the Jacobites sheltering in Inverness, he had arrived in the neighbouring town of Nairn.

On 14 April the drums beat and the pipes sounded to assemble the Jacobite army for battle. Messengers were sent out to recall the many who were on forays elsewhere. Next day, on the moor which was then called Drumossie but is now Culloden, the army was drawn up in the order in which it was to fight the coming battle.

"Perhaps drinking King George's health in that Glenfinnan pub was a mistake!"

Above, Left and Right: *Until the accession of Edward VII to the British throne in 1901, fingerbowls were never placed on royal dinner tables so as not to allow the secret Jacobite supporters to drink to the 'king over the water'. There were other symbols of support for the Stuart dynasty but when push came to shove most of the Lowlanders and English supporters of the rising sat on the fence to see who was going to win rather than get their fingers burnt.*

Apart from the obvious suitability of location it is therefore apposite that the monument to the rebellion allows Prince Charles to gaze over the Highlands whose sons were ever his support in battle and who felt the backlash of the English establishment in the years to come.

16 Culloden

No place name in Scottish history stirs the emotions more than Culloden. Fought on 16 April 1746, it has all the elements of romantic fiction, all the appeal of a lost cause. It has a hero: young dashing, handsome Prince Charles Edward Stuart, the 'Bonnie Prince Charlie' of song and story. And it has a villain: the brutal Duke of Cumberland, of whom no one now sings.

On the eve of that battle, however, some were indeed singing the praises of Cumberland — but only in drunken revelry. On Tuesday 15 April, the duke was celebrating his 25th birthday, and his men, in camp around Nairn, were drinking his health in brandy.

By a strange irony, these jollifications had some bearing on the battle the following day. As the Prince's army waited at Culloden, his commander Lord George Murray proposed a night attack on the English camp. The celebrating soldiers would be 'drunk as beggars,' he said. The Prince agreed and sent out two columns to catch Cumberland unawares. But their progress across the wastes of Culloden — then known as Drumossie Moor — took so long that dawn was breaking before they could mount their attack. They discovered that Cumberland had broken camp at 5am and, the nocturnal expedition aborted, the clansmen returned to the royal lines with the English army hot on their heels.

Cold, hungry and dispirited, the apprehensive Scots now peered out across the boggy, featureless field of battle to face the hung-over but buoyant English. Lord George Murray was to write later: 'There could never be a more improper ground for Highlanders'. It was not he who had chosen it but the Prince's favourite, John William O'Sullivan, against the urgings of Lord George.

The prince ordered his men to be drawn up, as on the previous day, those on foot in two lines, his weak cavalry in the rear, and his meagre artillery — 13 assorted guns — in three batteries on the right, left and in the centre of the front line. His force was small, under 5,000 men. Detachments on tasks elsewhere had been recalled but not all arrived in time. Among them were the MacPhersons who had only reached Moy Hall at the time of the battle. Many men had gone off in search of food; others, exhausted, were asleep.

Cumberland had nearly 9,000 men — 6,500 foot, including 15 regular regiments, and 2,400 horse, including 800 mounted dragoons. His artillery consisted of 10 three-pounder guns and six mortars. The army force-marched from Nairn to Culloden in three columns, with the cavalry on its left and a screen of Campbell scouts in front.

At 11am the two armies came in sight of each other. Cumberland's three columns wheeled around as if they were on a parade ground, not a boggy moor, and within 10 minutes were facing the Jacobites.

Charles looked every inch the prince as he rode on his fine, grey gelding, in his tartan coat and cockaded bonnet, carrying a light broadsword, and encouraging his men. His front line consisted almost entirely of clansmen, standing from three to six deep. The Jacobite second line was perhaps 100 yards behind, and was much

Above and Right: *Re-enactment of the battle of Culloden.*

Opposing Bonnie Prince Charlie was, perhaps had he known it, a reason for hope — his adversary William Augustus Duke of Cumberland (1721-65). The second surviving son of George Augustus, Prince of Wales who would become George II in 1727 on the death of his father, Cumberland was made major-general in 1742 at the age of 21. A brave man — he fought with distinction at Dettingen in 1741 — he was promoted captain-general of all British land forces in 1745 and was fighting on the continent when the rebellion began.

Unfortunately while he may have been brave, he was also unimaginative, unlucky and some would say incompetent as a general. Apart from victory over the Highlanders at Culloden, he lost with regularity to the French at Fontenoy in 1745, Lauffeld in 1747 and Hastenbeck in 1757 and finally retired in disgrace.

shorter. The contrast between the smart, well-fed English army and the plaid-clad, ill-provisioned Scots must have been stark.

The Highlanders were outnumbered, 5,000 against Cumberland's 9,000, and were destined to die in disproportionate numbers, more than 1,000 against Cumberland's 364. They were ill equipped, their artillery poor, their cavalry few. They were exhausted, having marched all night on an abortive foray. They were hungry, because poor staff work had left their food supplies in Inverness. They were badly led, being required to fight over ground which suited Cumberland's cannon and cavalry and handicapped their main tactic — the charge. Yet they went into battle with a courage which has passed into legend, and which today Scots the world over still salute.

The first shots fired came from a Jacobite gun, and it is said one of them narrowly missed the duke. There was to be no artillery duel however. The English guns returned fire with devastating effect. The round shot cut swathes in the Highland ranks. The Jacobite guns answered ineffectually. With wind, sleet and the enemy gun-smoke blowing in their faces, the long tartan-clad line could do nothing but stand and suffer the slaughter. The ranks were often six deep, and a cannonball could mangle several men. This was not the kind of warfare to which the Highlanders were accustomed.

Some fire was directed over their heads at the prince and his command group; his servant was killed, and his horse shot from under him. The prince was too far in the rear to see what was happening and, despite the murderous barrage, still the order to charge — the word 'Claymore' — was not given. And when the charge did come, it was not what it should have been: a wild, terrifying rush by the whole Highland line.

Yelling their war cries, the clansmen came on; broadswords, axes, scythe blades waving. The carnage was appalling. Only on the right did the charge go home, and there the clansmen had to climb over their dead and wounded to get at the enemy. Elsewhere, the rush did not reach the enemy ranks. Grape-shot and musketry halted the tide. Lord George Murray fought his way to the rear of the duke's army, his wig and his hat blown from his head. He saw what was happening, fought his way back, intending to bring up the Highland second line. But by this time it was over. Defiant, but defeated, the clansmen were moving back. The moor over which they had fought was covered with dead and wounded. The rout was complete.

The prince, bewildered and distressed, some say in tears, was led on horseback from the field. The conflict had lasted less than an hour. But more than a battle had been lost that day. The Jacobite cause was irretrievably in ruins. And its aftermath was to effect the whole future of the Highlands.

What little remained intact of the prince's army withdrew in good order under Lord George Murray, towards Ruthven, in Badenoch. There, the next day, cold comfort awaited them: a message from Charles that each man should save himself.

Worse remained for those who had not managed to flee Culloden. For on the battlefield and beyond, there was being enacted a systematic process of murder and mutilation which an English historian was to describe as 'such as never perhaps before or since disgraced a British army'. On the moor with its dead and wounded, and on the road to Inverness packed with fugitives, Cumberland's dragoons slaughtered indiscriminately — and not only the fleeing clansmen. Innocent bystanders, including women and children, were sabred, and there were casual murders, as of a man who was ploughing and his nine-year old son.

On the battlefield, surgeons cared for the government wounded — while redcoats, watched by their officers, bayonetted or clubbed to death the wounded of the prince's army, often obscenely mutilating their bodies.

There were still men who resisted and whose bravery has passed into Highland legend. Gillies MacBean of Clan Chattan, badly wounded but with his back to a wall and broadsword in his hand, is said to have killed 13 of the enemy before the horses of the dragoons trampled him underfoot. Even then he did not die, but crawled to a barn at Balvraid where he lived until evening.

The Cameron standard-bearer, MacLachlan of Coruanan, wrapped the flag of his clan round his body as he withdrew. This is believed to be the old stained flag which still hangs in Achnacarry, seat of Lochiel, Chief of the Clan. The courage of the men of Clan Cameron, who carried their wounded chief from the field, was matched by that of Iain Garbh Cameron who bore the wounded Grant of Corriemony on his back all the way to Glenurquart, on faraway Loch Ness.

The stories of heroism and of brutality are legion. One of the best known is told of Cumberland himself. He asked a badly wounded man to which side he belonged, and being told 'to the prince', turned to one of his aides, a Major Wolfe, and ordered him to kill 'the insolent rebel'. Wolfe refused, saying he would rather resign his commission. A private soldier was found who obeyed the order. The murdered man was Charles Fraser, of Inverallochy, commander of the Fraser contingent, and it is said that General Wolfe's popularity in Canada among the Highlanders of his army, and in particular the Fraser regiment, stemmed from this incident.

Through acts such as these, Cumberland won the nickname the 'Butcher' — and it did not entirely come from his victims. One of his own officers wrote in a letter that the men engaged in the slaughter on the Moor 'looked like so many butchers rather than Christian soldiers'.

Cumberland issued an order to seek out surviving rebels, stating ominously: 'The officers and men will take notice that the public orders of the rebels yesterday was to give no quarter.' It was a lie. Lord George Murray's orders for the battle contained no such instruction — a copy of those orders having been captured and the 'no quarter' phrase added as a clumsy forgery.

But it served its purpose. The killing continued for days as the search parties discovered survivors, mostly wounded, in their hiding places. They found more than 30 officers and men in a barn on Old Leanach farm, barricaded it and set it alight. A woman who had given shelter to another 12 watched as they were led away by redcoats who had promised them medical attention. They were shot within yards of her house. A widow returning from burying her husband in Inverness found 16 dead men at her door . . .

Cumberland returned to London in triumph. The self-styled 'deliverer of this Church and Nation' had the flower 'Sweet William' named after him (the Scots retaliated by christening a weed 'Stinking William'). From the rarefied atmosphere of the English court, he advocated his own 'final solution' to the Highland problem: the transportation of whole clans 'such as the Camerons and almost all the tribes of the MacDonalds (excepting some of those in the Isles) and several other lesser clans'.

On his orders, the process of laying waste the glens began. Garrisons at Inverness, nearby Fort George, at Fort Augustus and at Fort William looted, demolished houses, stole horses, cattle and sheep. The Highlands had never been rich; now many of its people faced starvation.

Prince Charles Edward Stuart was little better off himself. There was a £30,000 price on the head of this fugitive in the heather but it failed to bring forth a single informant. The search for him was unremitting; thousands of troops and a small fleet were engaged.

Above and Above Right: *Re-enactment of the battle.*

Below Right: *Culloden Moor. The last pitched battle on British soil would see 1,000 Highlanders lost for about 50 English casualties. In conditions that did not suit their fighting strengths, harried by accurate and sustained artillery fire, tired after a long night march, the Highlanders succumbed on that bloody April day in 1746 and the hopes of their prince died with them.*

Accompanied by only two or three companions, he hid in Scotland's north-west Highlands and Islands. Flora Macdonald, whose father was with the government forces, gained everlasting fame by conveying him 'over the sea to Skye'. From 'safe houses' in South Uist and the Isle of Skye, he eventually returned to the mainland, hungry, bitten by lice and midges and suffering from dysentery. Yet from those who shared his hardships he won golden opinions for his courage and gaiety. Finally, at Loch nan Uamh, where he had landed 14 months earlier, he boarded *L'Heureux* and sailed for France.

'Bonnie Prince Charlie' was to live for another 42 years and die, drunken and dissolute, in Rome. But in the few brief months when he flashed across the pages of history, he created an enduring legend. Jacobitism was to become a romantic, nostalgic cause, enshrined in a wealth of song and story, as it continues to be today.

The actual story of the Highlanders is less lyrical. In London, the Privy Council decided that prisoners be tried in England, a flagrant breach of the Treaty of Union between Scotland and England. The result was that 120 prisoners were executed; four of them, peers of the realm, being beheaded, as was the privilege of their rank, and the rest suffering the barbaric ritual of hanging, drawing and quartering. Another 936 were transported to the colonies, there to be sold to the highest bidder; 222 were banished, being allowed to chose their country of exile: 1,287 were released, exchanged or pardoned, and there were nearly 700 whose fate is unknown.

But this was far from the end. The spectacle of the Highlander, armed and again in rebellion, haunted the government. It had to be

eradicated and it was. The so-called Disarming Acts demanded that all weapons be surrendered. Bagpipes too, were a weapon of war, a court in York decreed, and had the piper executed. Wearing tartan, a kilt 'or any part whatever of what peculiarly belongs to the Highland garb' was outlawed, the penalty being six months' imprisonment or, for a second offence, transportation for seven years. Most damaging to the Highland way of life, however, was the Heritable Jurisdictions Act of 1747 removing from clan chiefs their hereditary powers and turning them into mere landlords. Their wealth had been reckoned in men, and now, with the dissolution of the clan system, men were no longer important.

Twenty-seven years after the Battle of Culloden, the English diarist Dr Samuel Johnson, himself no lover of the Scots, travelled through much of the country and, in his *Journey to the Western Isles*, wrote: 'It affords a legislator little self applause that where there was formerly an insurrection there is now a wilderness.'

The Highland way of life had for ever been eradicated.

Right: *Aerial view of the battlefield of Culloden.*

Far Right: *One of the immediate consequences of Culloden was the hounding of the clans and the determination of the English that there should be no repetitions of the lack of success enjoyed by the small forts erected after the Old Pretender's rebellion of 1715. Fort George was to be a base for the exercise of Hanoverian might. It's a wonderful study of the art of military fortification of the time — but it was destined to be a waste of money. So cowed were the Highlanders that by the time work finished on it in 1769 it was virtually redundant: by 1795 it was garrisoned by a company of soldiers unfit for active service.*

Below: *Old Leanach cottage, Culloden.*

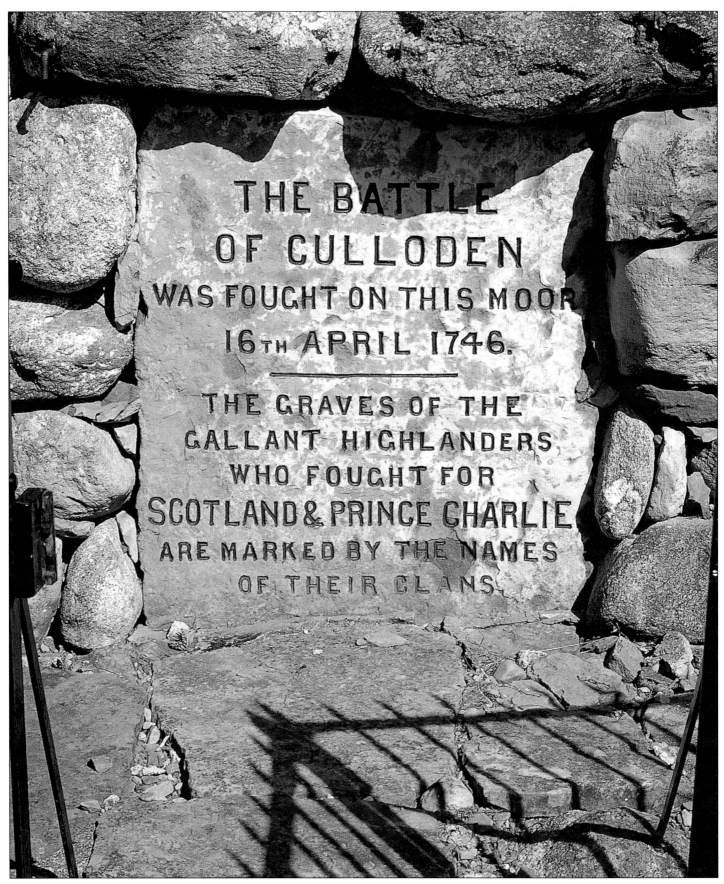

Above and Right: *The Culloden Memorial Cairn. It reads:*
'The Battle of Culloden was fought here on 16 April 1746. The
graves of the gallant Highlanders who fought for Scotland &
Prince Charlie are marked by the names of their clans.'

THE BATTLE
OF CULLODEN
WAS FOUGHT ON THIS MOOR
16TH APRIL 1746.

THE GRAVES OF THE
GALLANT HIGHLANDERS
WHO FOUGHT FOR
SCOTLAND & PRINCE CHARLIE
ARE MARKED BY THE NAMES
OF THEIR CLANS.

Above: *Fort George detail.*

Right: *Fort George is built on a promontory to the Moray Firth near Nairn and opposite Fortrose. Its great bastions epitomised 18th century military architecture and even the great General Wolfe, when still a colonel, was moved to call it 'the most considerable fortress and the best situated in Great Britain'.*

Above and Right: *Bonnie Prince Charlie's immortality was assured before he fled the field at Culloden: but the romance was increased many more times by the story of his escape. Despite a price of £30,000 on his head and an unremitting search, he was hidden in farm houses and made a circuitous route through the Highlands and Western Isles before eventual safety. The line did not die out with him: his claim to the throne passed, on his death, to his brother Henry, a Catholic cardinal who died in 1807; by 1914 the Jacobite claimant to the throne of Britain was the eminently unsuitable Queen of Bavaria.*

Left: *The Clan Cameron memorial on Culloden Moor.*

Below: *The Clan Mackintosh memorial on Culloden Moor.*

Previous Page: *Fort George looking out over the Moray Firth.*

17 Industial Revolution and Highland Clearance

In historical terms, it was not to be so long after the disastrous Forty Five — the last Jacobite uprising — that the Industrial Revolution was to arrive in Scotland. Historians debate the starting date of this new revolution, with some arguingfor a date as early as 1759 when the Carron Iron Works opened at Falkirk. Although Carron was indeed the first of Scotland's great industrial concerns designed on a modern pattern, it was merely a precursor of what was to come: little else during the 1760s showed a major departure from the economic structure of the past. is Probably a better starting point is the end of the American War of Independence in 1783, when the the cotton industry began to blossom thanks to the application in several different parts of Scotland of the new technology of Lancashire.

From the 1780s onwards the industrial sector in the Scottish economy grew at a rapid rate: J. B. Neilson's discovery of the hot-blast smelting process, patented in 1828, enabled the Scots for the first time to utilize their immense resources of black-band iron-stone. Before this manufacturing industry in Scotland had been restricted almost entirely to textiles, but Neilson's process made possible the use of ores which led to the rise of the great heavy industries of Scotland — iron, steel, and shipbuilding, along with a great new expansion in coalmining.

At the start of the 19th century Scotland was still a country dominated by the rural and agricultural character of her economy and institutions, but taking place was an agricultural change which would have dramatic social consequences to the Highlands in the form of the 'Clearances'. In the 1750s cattle — the traditional source of wealth for the Highlander — and sheep populations were about the same, but by 1800 sheep were dominant. During the 18th century sheep husbandry expanded in the Borders and, through the use of sheep enclosures, selective breeding was facilitated. From the Lowlands, southern shepherds moved into the Highlands with their flocks of thousands of Cheviot and Blackface sheep.

After 1815 increases in the price of wool and mutton led to a major influx by Borders farmers wanting to rent sheiling areas from Highland lairds for summer grazing of their sheep. The farmers were also looking for arable stretches of land for wintering at lower levels. This commercial interaction between the Highlands and the Lowlands led to a massive disruption of the traditional forms of Highland life. Highland landlords realised that it would make better business to evict the crofters, who eked out a bare living farming their lands, and replace them with more profitable flocks of sheep. Populations were moved, 'cleared' from the sheltered straths down to windy coasts, inhospitable peat bogs, and moorland edges. Not only were whole families evicted, but Highland soldiers returning from the Napoleonic wars were greeted with the blackened remains of their burnt-out houses.

The outbreak of the Crimean War in 1854 presented the opportunity of work for the men of the glens, as had Britain's imperial wars before. This time, however, the 'thin Red Line' that had fought with courage at Balaclava was raised with difficulty. An elderly tenant explained to the Duke of Sutherland why there were problems mustering soldiers from the Sutherland domain:

'I am sorry for the response your Grace's proposals are meeting here today, so near to the spot where your maternal grandmother by giving some 48 hours' notice marshalled 1,500 men to pick out the 800 she required, but there is cause for it and a genuine cause . . . these lands are now devoted to rear dumb animals, which your parents considered of far more value than men. I do assure your Grace that it is the prevailing opinion of this country that should the Czar of Russia take possession of Dunrobin Castle (family seat of the Sutherlands), we could not expect worse treatment at his hands than we have experienced in the hands of your family for the past 50 years.'

Some Highlanders agreed voluntarily to leave their crofts, accepting that they must make room for the sheep; they went without protest though they must have known that within a short time they would be destitute, as any small compensation they received would not last for long. In some instances they were not even given spiritual support from the kirk. Local ministers berated them, declaring that the evictions were a judgment of God brought upon them for their sins. This broke the spirit of many Highlanders and these economic and social changes shattered and changed their traditional way of life for ever.

The Highland region suffered a massive depopulation and many of the evicted emigrated to the New World. Scottish people have fought against endless hardship, albeit some of it self-inflicted, so much that Scotland's largest export has always been people. Between 1871 and 1901 a quarter of Scotland's total natural increase in population — 483,000 — emigrated away from the Old World to Canada, America, and Australia.

From an economic point of view, the history of Scotland from the middle of the 19th century to the depression of the 1920s can be seen as a successful one. From the textile trade in the first phase of the industrial revolution, through the success of iron and coal in the second, to the triumph, after 1860, of steel, ships, jute, and high farming. The central belt of Scotland became, in the process, one

Right: *Clansmen at the 250th anniversary of the Battle of Culloden scene of the last occasion Highlanders gathered together in battle. Of the 5,000 Highlanders who took the field, an estimated 2,000 men died in just over half an hour, prey to the devastating musket fire of the troops led by the Duke of Cumberland.*

of the most intensively industrialised regions anywhere in the world.

Whisky production also became big business where previously the distillation of the spirit had been a cottage industry. This happened when Robert Stein invented a steam-heated still, which enabled the spirit to be manufactured in one continuous operation. Then Aeneas Coffey invented his 'patent still' which could distil quickly and cheaply and made large-scale production possible. In 1865 William Usher of Edinburgh pioneered whisky blending and was the first to sell the drink under a 'propriety' label which guaranteed its quality. Towards the end of the century the Scottish whisky industry had changed out of all recognition as the grain distillery giants of the Lowlands, (for example Walkers of Kilmarnock and Dewars of Perth) bought out the small Highland malt distilleries and made fortunes out of blending the products of both. By 1898 there were 161 distilleries in Scotland.

Right: *The Linn of Tummel in Perthshire is the meeting point for the River Tummel and Loch Tummel. It lies about 25 miles north-east of the town of Pitlochry and not far from the Pass of Killiecrankie where in 1689 the Highlanders, under the leadership of Claverhouse, defeated the troops of King William III.*

18 Victoria and Balmoral

It was during Victoria's reign that the British monarchy started its love affair with Scotland — although the queen's image of Scotland was a contrived one. She wrote that Scotland was 'the proudest, finest country in the world' and she perceived the Scotsman as a valiant but pacified Celt. Victoria first visited Scotland in 1842 and when she visited the Highlands her heart was captivated. The Queen's Scottish physician, Sir James Clark, recommended Balmoral, on the banks of the River Dee, to Victoria as he thought the climate would be beneficial to both her and her consort Albert's rheumatism. In 1848, she wrote of Balmoral in her diary:

'All seemed to breathe freedom and peace and to make one forget the world and its sad turmoils.'

Prince Albert paid £31,000 for the castle in 1852, and, using grey granite quarried on the Balmoral estate, he had it rebuilt in the grand Scottish Baronial style with distinctive pepperpot turrets. Victoria liked her pleasures simple, and life at the estate was consequently free from protocol and court etiquette. She favoured Deeside for the rides and walks the estate offered, and Albert liked it because it reminded him of his native Germany and because he loved to stalk the local deer.

Victoria would often take her family and guests to the local beauty spot of the Linn of Dee — about 12 miles from the castle. Here the young river races through a narrow gorge and the steep cliffs either side need to be negotiated with great care. John Brown, the queen's faithful ghillie, and the Balmoral footmen must have endured many a nervous moment keeping an eye on the royal offspring as they teetered on the edge of these slippery rocks. Queen Victoria was once told that Ben Macdui 1,309m (4,295ft), in the nearby Cairngorms, was the highest mountain in Britain. She set out from Balmoral and rode a donkey to its summit. When she was later informed that Ben Nevis 1,343m (4,406ft) was higher she was not amused.

When residing at Balmoral, Victoria often donned a tartan plaid or sash and Albert and the royal male offspring would wear the kilt. The Consort designed a special tartan for his family and this is still worn today when the present royal family visit the castle. Victoria also took a lease on Abergeldie Castle, a couple of miles away from Balmoral, where guests could be accommodated. The Queen's mother, the Duchess of Kent, lived there for many years until it eventually became the Scottish home of the Prince of Wales, later King Edward VII. The prince would have been only too pleased to move into Abergeldie as he had been known to describe Balmoral as 'the Highland barn with a thousand draughts.' Close to Abergeldie Castle is the Lochnagar Distillery whose fine whisky has a subtle flavour of sherry absorbed from the casks in which it matures. The distillery was founded in 1829 by a former smuggler, and when Victoria and Albert visited it in 1848, they ordered supplies for Balmoral and thereafter granted permission for the whisky to be described as Royal Lochnagar.

Left: *Prince Albert paid £31,000 for Balmoral in 1852 and had it rebuilt. It would become a favourite location for Queen Victoria, her family and the British royal family in general: over the years since Victoria's reign, each new monarch has spent time in Balmoral.*

Right: *Queen Victoria lived from 1819 to 1901, acceding to the throne in 1837. She married Albert of Saxe-Coburg in 1840 and with him discovered the joys of Scotland. She continued to travel to Balmoral after Albert's death in 1861, although some say that this was more because of her affection for John Brown than her rheumatism.*

Overleaf: *Mar Lodge on the beautiful River Dee.*

19 The Twentieth Century

Scotland's contribution to Britain has been quite out of keeping with its size, with a disproportionate role in creating an empire called British, but in reality, more Scottish than English. The country has also bred people of remarkable talent; the world as a whole has benefited from geniuses like Alexander Graham Bell, James Watt, Alexander Fleming, John Logie Baird, and Thomas Telford and few immigrants influenced the history of modern America more than Andrew Carnegie, born in Dunfermline in 1835. He built a massive business empire and when he sold out in 1901 he gave away $350 million to libraries and universities throughout the world. The archetypal capitalist is best remembered for his philanthropy and his success in the New World has been an inspiration to his countrymen.

When the First World War broke out, Scotland's population was a tenth of England's, yet Scottish regiments made up a seventh of Britain's army. The Lowland regiments, the Royal Scots, the King's Own Scottish Borderers, and the Royal Scots Fusiliers, together with the Scots Guards, fielded over 70,000 men and between them they won 71 battle honours and six Victoria Crosses. The Cameronians raised 27 battalions and fought in France, Flanders, Macedonia, Egypt, and Palestine and the 7th Battalion was the last to leave the shores of Gallipoli.

Of the Highland regiments, 21 battalions of the Gordon Highlanders were raised, winning 65 battle honours and four VCs; 19 battalions of Seaforth Highlanders and 13 battalions of Cameron Highlanders were also recruited. The Argyll and Sutherland Highlanders, the victors of Waterloo and Balaclava, won 79 battle honours and some 30,000 joined the Black Watch. Nearly 8,000 were killed and 20,000 came home wounded or maimed. Glasgow supplied enough able-bodied men to form 26 battalions and enlisted a higher proportion of men than any other British city. Of these battalions of Highland Light Infantry, 11,000 men were killed in action. In silence, the cinemas of Scotland proclaimed to audiences:

Where Scotland's thistle sways on High,
And foemen meet here knee to knee,
Blow up the pipes and then ye'll see,
Her courage wake,
And learn how Scotland's sons can die for
Empire sake.

During the Second World War the River Clyde became Britain's main port and as such received much attention from Hitler's Luftwaffe. In March 1941, in two night raids, 439 planes flew to the limits of their fuel to drop over 500 tons of high explosive and nearly 2,500 incendiary bombs on the city of Glasgow. They were principally aiming for the shipyards of the Clyde, which built the capital ships *Duke of York*, *Howe*, the battleship *Vanguard* and the aircraft carrier *Indefatigable*, and were responsible for the building and repairing of hundreds of smaller craft. In the first year of the war the Clyde also launched the *Queen Elizabeth* which, with her sister ship the *Queen Mary*, were to prove invaluable as troop transports. Clydebank's greatest achievement, perhaps, was not a ship but the Mulberry Harbours. Dozens of firms were involved in constructing and equipping the massive concrete pierheads that would facilitate the Allied invasion of Normandy in June 1944 and the ultimate defeat of Hitler's Third Reich.

Above: *Alexander Graham Bell, 1847-1922, the inventor of the telephone.*

Above Right: *The Forth Bridge was started in 1882 and opened in 1890 at a cost of £2.25 million. It was money well spent! The bridge celebrated its centenary in style and will continue to be used well into the 21st century.*

Below Right: *The tubular Britannia bridge across the Menai Straits is one of Thomas Telford's greatest achievements. It was completed in 1849.*

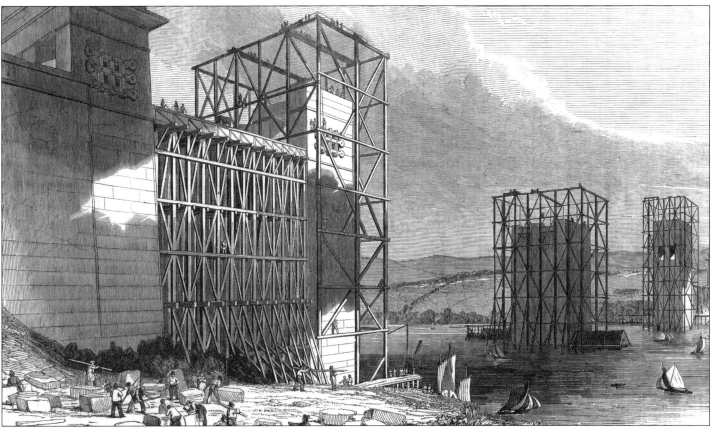

In many respects the whole history of Scotland since the end of the 17th century is overshadowed by one event — the Union of Parliaments — which reduced her to the status of a 'region' in the new hybrid kingdom of Great Britain. 1707 is a watershed that seems to split our view of the past into two distinct halves.

During the 19th and 20th century a wider form of democracy came to Britain in general. The Great Reform Bill of 1832 took the first steps towards giving political representation to the middle classes and led to further Reform Bills, which gave the franchise to a wider and wider spectrum of the Scottish people. By the end of the 19th century, adult male suffrage was almost complete, and after the First World War, adult female suffrage as well.

With the coming of democracy all Scots, for the first time, attained the freedom to decide what form of government they wanted. From the end of the 19th century until well after the middle of the 20th century it never seriously crossed their minds that government from Westminster was not appropriate for Scotland. In the 1979 referendum for a Scottish Assembly less than 33 percent of the Scottish electorate voted 'Yes'; sadly, given the history of the Scottish people after parliamentary union with England in 1707, over 36 percent didn't bother to vote at all. The 1997 referendum held by Prime Minister Blair's New Labour government may yet prove to be another 'watershed'. The overwhelming 'Yes'

Above: *The kilts go to war! The soldiers of Scottish regiments served with distinction and honour all over the world and in two world wars. This picture shows a Scottish regiment moving up to the front during the Great War.*

vote by the Scottish people for devolution may open a new chapter in their history as the founding Scottish Parliament, with its own tax raising powers, opens for business in the new millennium.

Since the Union in 1707 and the disaster of Culloden a severe lack of confidence has undermined the Scottish nation, often been made to feel the underdog by the more powerful and numerous English. The two countries have been rivals for the best part of a millennium with the English still wary of their northern neighbours: the prospect of the 'tartan army,' Scottish soccer fans, invading London for a game against the 'auld enemy' resurrects all the old animosity. To the Scots history remains real and is a story, for the most part bloody, but always lively and never dull.

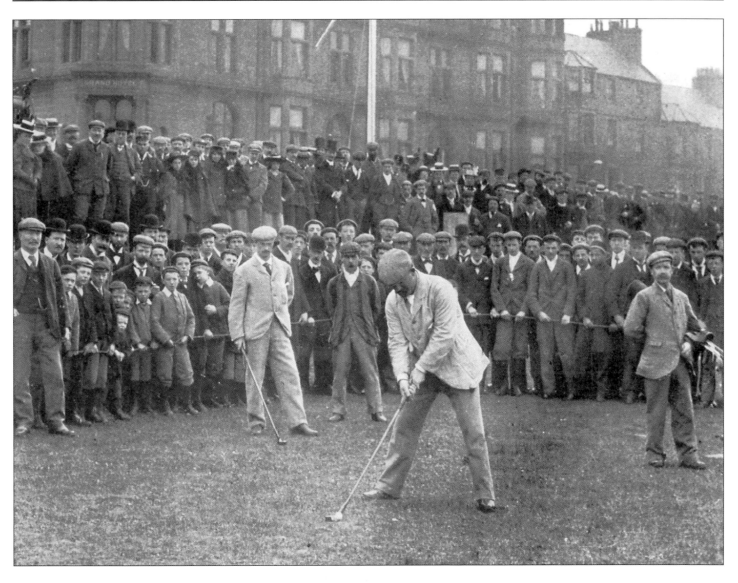

Above: *One of the Scots' greatest gifts to the world — or a good walk spoiled? Golf has become a major part of the sporting world in the 20th century. Here a drive from the home tee at the Royal and Ancient Club, St. Andrews. The Society of St Andrew's golfers was formed on 14 May 1754 by 22 local noblmen; the name was changed to the Royal and Ancient in 1834.*

Left: *Logie Baird made the first television transmission in 1924.*

PART 3:
THE ARTS

Scots dominated their fields: Thomas Telford, the son of an Eskdale shepherd, was the greatest engineer of his generation and of his notable contemporaries John Rennie, John Smeaton, and Robert and Alan Stevenson (of lighthouses fame) were all Scots.

Not all these men did their work in Scotland — James Gibbs, for example, is represented by a single church; Sir William Chambers by only two houses; and there are no works at all by Colin Campbell or James Stewart. The most famous of the Scottish-born did their most spectacular works out of their native country. Although Telford built over a thousand bridges in Scotland, including cast-iron bridges at Craigellachie over the Spey, the Dean Bridge at Edinburgh, and the seven spans over the Tay at Dunkfield, none of these compare to the spectacular and innovative span bridge crossing the Menai Straits to Anglesey.

Although the bridge at Craigellachie was a comparatively minor task compared to the grander engineering feats that Telford is associated with, he set about its construction with great zeal. The fast-flowing river bends sharply here and, while the south bank is low-lying, the north side has steeply rising stone cliffs. Telford decided to blast away (300ft) of solid stone at a height of 21m (70ft) for an approach road, and designed a single iron span of 46m 92m (150ft). He added three stone arches to bring the level of the road down on the south side, reckoning they would add stability in times of flood. His judgement was proved correct when in August 1829, the river running over 15ft above its normal height due to catastrophic flooding, came crashing into the bridge. The stone arches did indeed save the main span but were washed away in the process. The minor splendour of Telford's bridge with its romantic battlements can be seen today as you cross its successor.

Scotland's most famous 'modern' architect was undoubtedly Charles Rennie Mackintosh (1868-1928) who, as a leader of the architectural Art Nouveau movement in Great Britain, made a huge contribution of fundamental importance in reappraising the role of function in building. In 1890 a scholarship enabled him to undertake a study tour in France and Italy, and his first executed work on his return was the corner tower of the Glasgow Herald Building (1894). The style revealed here shows the emancipation of the architect from previous academic traditions. In 1897, at the age of 29, he won the competition for an extension to the Glasgow School of Art, which he had attended as a pupil 12 years earlier. These buildings were erected between 1898 and 1909 and were widely praised by European contemporaries. The library, which Mackintosh built as an addition to the art school (1907-1909), incorporates a style hitherto unknown, raising architecture to the level of poetic abstraction.

Mackintosh also displayed a great interest in the decorative arts; the furniture and pieces he designed are noted for their character, their aesthetic forms often going beyond any functional requirements. In 1897 he was commissioned to design the furniture and decorations for Cranston's chain of tea-rooms in Glasgow. For the one in Sauchiehall Street, he was given his head by Miss Cranston who had the soul of an artist. Sauchiehall means 'alley of willows', so the theme of his architecture and design throughout The Willow Tearoom, from top to bottom, was willows. The ground floor of this building is now a jewellers but upstairs you can still marvel at the bold originality of the deluxe tea-room, now nearly a century old.

Above: *Colonel William Gordon of Fyvie by Pompio Batoni hangs in Fyvie Castle, just one of many fine paintings in a magnificent Scottish Baronial castle. The five-turreted castle lies 25 miles north of Aberdeen in Grampian and its earliest parts date from the 13th century.*

Right: *Charlotte Square, Edinburgh, the fine buildings on the north side of the square are masterpieces of Robert Adam's urban architecture.*

In 1900 Mackintosh married a former student of the Glasgow School of Art, Margaret Macdonald, an interior decorator and talented artist, whose sister Frances had married the architect Herbert McNair. This tight-knit little family group, with similar professional and aesthetic interests, gained international recognition as 'The Four'. As leader of this group, Mackintosh's work was widely praised by European architects but found little favour in his native land outside Glasgow.

Windyhill in Kilmalcolm, Strathclyde, is one of the few private houses that Mackintosh designed in Scotland and, although it shows external stylistic affinities with the Scottish baronial tradition, its internal layout reveals great boldness in the handling of space. It was built in 1900 for William Davidson, a friend and admirer of the architect. Probably the greatest memorials to Charles Rennie Mackintosh in his homeland are the Glasgow School of Art buildings he designed in the first decade of the 20th century: they are still exciting today and were years ahead of their time when they were designed and built.

During the 18th century, at the height of Scottish architectural innovation, visual art was pretty undistinguished — most of the tapestries and paintings which covered the walls of Scottish baronial mansions and town houses were imported. The existence of distinct literary and intellectual traditions in Scotland is generally acknowledged, but a Scottish tradition in the visual arts is less frequently recognised. Like Scottish literature, Scottish painting had a deep-rooted preoccupation with national identity and this played a large part in the development of landscape painting. In the 19th century the distinctive character of Scottish scenery was explored by a generation of painters the best known of whom was Horatio McCulloch.

Not all Scottish painters were concerned solely with Scotland and throughout the 18th and early 19th centuries there was a lively Scottish artistic colony in Rome. This internationalism, building on a strong native tradition, culminated in one of the most exciting episodes in British 19th century painting with the achievements of the Glasgow artists in the last two decades of the century. The Impressionists Sir James Guthrie (1859-1930) and W.Y. MacGregor (1855-1923), along with the Post-Impressionist George Henry (1855-1904), were a formative influence on the 'Scottish Colourists' who continued a close connection with French painting to create a kind of Scottish Fauvism. The 'Scottish Colourists' was the name given to the four Scottish artists J.D. Fergusson (1874-1961), S.J. Peploe (1871-1935), Leslie Hunter (1877-1931) and F.C.B. Cadell, who produced paintings remarkable for their freedom and richness of colour.

Scottish furniture makers also worked with little distinction in the 16th and 17th centuries, so it is quite remarkable that in the single art of making fine silver the Scots excelled to a remarkable degree. In the second half of the 16th century, work by the goldsmiths of Edinburgh attracted the highest admiration of connoisseurs worldwide. In the 17th century, after an Act of 1617 ordering all parish kirks to provide themselves with baptismal basins and communion cups, there was a boom in the production of church plate. Later in the century the silversmiths produced the silver quaich, a two-handled drinking vessel originally made from horn or wood, and now manufactured to beautiful effect in the durable metal. The fine achievements of the Scottish smiths continued in an unbroken tradition well into the 18th century and like their buildings — but not so their literature — it remained unscathed from the effects of Puritanism.

Below and Right: *Standing above the River Clyde in Helensburgh, Hill House was commissioned by the Glasgow publisher Walter Blackie at the turn of the century. He entrusted the work to the innovative Scottish designer and architect, and sometime leader of the British Art Nouveau movement, Charles Rennie Mackintosh.*

Hill House is considered by many connoisseurs to be his finest domestic achievement. In the design of the building he synthesised the Scottish baronial tradition of architecture with a modern vision of the use of space and mass. In this artistic endeavour he was ably assisted by his wife, Margaret MacDonald — a fine artist in her own right — who particularly concentrated on the fabrics for the house.

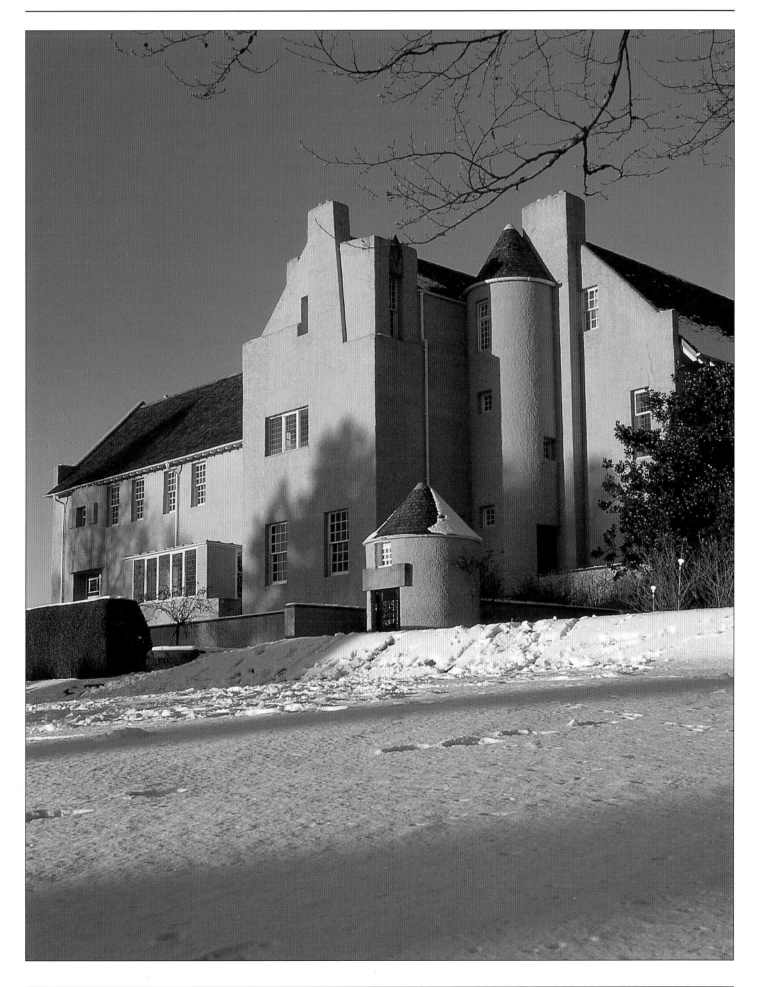

21 Literature

In considering Scottish imaginative literature, we are faced with the curious paradox of why, with the deaths of Robert Burns (1796) and Sir Walter Scott (1832), poetry and prose stopped almost dead in their tracks and ceased with them. They did not cease forever, luckily, but they did lose their continuous tradition. There is no simple answer as to why imaginative literature in the country rose to an apogee in the 18th century and then broke off into virtual silence. It can be argued that the novels of Robert Louis Stevenson, the odd works by George Macdonald and the poetry of Hugh MacDiarmid amount to as fine a body of work as that of the Burns and Scott era, but these are isolated phases in the last century. The tradition of creative Scottish literature has no continuity.

However 200 years earlier the Scottish scholar George Buchanan (1506-1582) achieved much contemporary fame with his varied poems and dramatic tragedies written in Latin. He was considered 'by far the greatest poet of his day' and even Dryden, a century after his death, described him as 'a writer comparable to any of the moderns and excelled by few of the ancients.' Today modern classicists regard his poetry as good of its kind, but still much inferior to that of the Romans. During the 17th century Buchanan had many inferior successors, though the 'Aberdeen doctors' successfully continued a Scottish tradition of supremacy as the finest school of Latin poets in Europe. As Latin declined from a lively literary language to a dead one, Buchanan's reputation faded and the irony is that this poet and dramatist, once more highly regarded than William Shakespeare, is now almost totally forgotten even within his native country.

Scottish poetry entered the 16th centuries with a magnificent double heritage. On the one hand there were the traditional ballads stretching back to medieval times and, on the other, the mellifluous and forceful language of the Renaissance court poets, especially Dunbar, Lindsay, and Douglas. To modern eyes the Scottish tongue of the court poets can make difficult reading but it is worth persevering to find its true riches and surprising scope. In this sonnet Alexander Montgomerie (1545-1610) combined the old Scottish joy in alliteration with Renaissance form:

So sweet a kiss yestreen frae thee I reft,
In bowing doun thy body on the bed,
That even my life within thy lips I left,
Sensyne from thee my spirits wald never shed.
To follow thee it from my body fled
And left my corpse als cold as ony key.
But when the danger of my death I dread,
To seek my spreit I sent by hairt to thee;
But it was so enamoured with thine ee,
With thee it mindit likewise to remain.
So thou has keepit captive all the three,
More glaid to bide than to return again.
Except thy breath their places had suppleit,
Even thine armes, there doutless had I deit.

It has been supposed that the Reformation instantly blighted the writing of poetry in Scotland but performances of plays and music continued for several decades. The kirk did not turn against drama and poetry until after 1574 and, in fact, many of the finest Scottish ballads are dated between 1560 and 1620. The tradition of the 'makaris', the court poets, also thrived into the 17th century. Far from blighting the poetic tradition the Reformation actually added to it with a few fine pieces that were only later left out of the hymn books as 17th century Puritanism took a hold.

The first serious break in the Scottish poetic tradition was not caused by religion but by politics. In 1603 the Union of the Crowns destroyed the court at Holyrood and with it the environment that had created the 'makaris'. The new generation of Scottish poets readily abandoned craftsmanship in their own tongue in favour of the brilliant English verse being written by the likes of Shakespeare, Jonson, and Donne. Unfortunately the idiom was fundamentally alien to them and there is no Scottish poet of the early 17th century comparable to the best English writers.

Scottish Puritanism dealt a second, perhaps greater, blow to poetry; in England, Bunyan and Milton blossomed but Scottish Puritanism was more dogmatic and narrow-minded and suffocated the creative arts for nearly 50 years. The only work of any consequence came from the 'Aberdeen Doctors', who composed in Latin, and the Highland bards who wrote in Gaelic — both well away from the predominantly Lowland Puritans. An aspiring Lowland poet would also have been hampered by finding that the Scottish tongue, in which he thought and spoke, was now considered to be an uncouth dialect of an English language still unfamiliar to him.

By the beginning of the 18th century, Scottish had become the language of the poor, the uncouth, and the humorous. The landed classes and the middle-class intelligentsia wrote English and aspired to speak it without dialect, so as not to betray their provincial origins. Scottish did, however, survive as an acceptable language for poetry, or at least certain types of poetry. This was partly because some poems had remained as part of the national cultural background which even peasants' children heard recited by their elders. Songs in the vernacular, ballads, and lyrical folk songs, were handed down and were acceptable even to the genteel. Despite being constricted, Scottish poetry could draw on the expressive language that was still spoken in the farms, towns, and taverns of 18th century Scotland.

In 1728 Allan Ramsay, a bookseller fascinated by the works of early Scottish poets, attempted to make native literature available in Edinburgh by opening the first circulating library in Scotland. His *Tea Table Miscellany*, published in four volumes between 1724 and 1732, was an anthology of old and new Scottish songs. Later his *Gentle Shepherd*, a pastoral drama set to music, established the ballad-opera tradition in Scotland three years before Gay's *The Beggars Opera* and paved the way for Scotland's better known poets Robert Fergusson and Robert Burns. Born in Edinburgh in

Above: *This modest house is the birthplace of J. M. Barrie (1860-1937) in Kirriemuir in Angus. The author achieved world-wide fame for writing the much-loved children's story* Peter Pan, *although he wrote many other works including* The Admirable Crichton.

1750, Fergusson was the most original voice in the vernacular before the works of Robert Burns. His masterpiece was undoubtedly *Auld Reekie*, a racy survey of 18th century Edinburgh describing a typical day with written portraits of local characters including the working ladies.

Near some lamp-post, wi dowy face,
We' heavy een, and sour grimace,
Stands she that beauty lang had kend
Whoredom her trade, and vice her end.

Fergusson was a dissipated youth and, like many of the 'literati', was a member of one of Edinburgh's numerous clubs who met regularly over noisy suppers of oysters, gin, and ale. In his tragically short life he reawakened the tradition of Scottish poetry but, after a fall that damaged both his mind and body, he died in a madhouse on 17 October at the age of 24. Some critics have dared to suggest that had he lived he would have been the equal of the great Ayrshire poet, if not his superior. There is no doubt Burns himself admired Fergusson and he erected a headstone for him, at his own expense,

in Canongate Churchyard, Edinburgh, where he lies. Burns's own lines are engraved on the headstone:

No sculptured Marble here nor pompous lay
No storied Urn nor animated bust
This simple Stone directs Pale Scotia's way
To pour her Sorrows o'er her Poet's Dust.

Burns was scathing in his attacks on those in Edinburgh who had lavished praise on the boy but done little else and pointed out that the poet's work would stand as his best memorial. There is also a later tribute from Robert Louis Stevenson to Fergusson in the form of a plaque in Canongate Churchyard.

With Robert Burns (1759-1796) Scottish poetry reached its apogee. A great deal of his poetry is concerned with eating, drinking, and wenching but he had the ability, unequalled among either Scottish or English poets, to write marvellous songs — if he had written nothing but his epic ballad, *Tam o' Shanter*, his reputation would have been assured. Amazingly, this epic ballad was written in a single day. It came about because Burns befriended Captain Francis Grose, a famous antiquarian, who was touring Scotland researching material for his latest book. Grose mentioned that he was travelling to Ayrshire and 'Rabbie' asked him if he would make a picture of Alloway Kirk, a place dear to him as his father lay buried there. Burns described the old kirk as a meeting place of demons and witches and related some hair-raising tales of old in an effort to persuade the Captain to visit. Grose agreed to visit the kirk

and provide a picture if 'Rabbie' agreed to write a poem to fit the sketch. According to Jean Armour, Burns's wife, he spent the day in the countryside, strolling the banks of the River Nith (a few miles from Dumfries), sometimes dashing about in the woods gesticulating wildly until he arrived home exhausted — *Tam o'Shanter* had been born, created in a day to live for ever.

Weel mounted on his grey mare, Meg,
(A better never lifted leg,)
Tam skelpit on through dub and mire,
Despising wind, and rain, and fire;
Whiles holding fast his guid blue bonnet;
Whiles crooning o'er some auld Scots sonnet;
Whiles glow'ring round wi' prudent cares,
Lest bogles catch him unawares;
Kirk-Alloway was drawing nigh,
Whare ghaists and houlets nightly cry.
And, wow! Tam saw an unco sight!
Warlocks and witches in a dance;
Nae cotillion brent new frae France,
But hornpipes, jigs, strathspeys, and reels,
Put life and mettle in their heels.
At winnock-bunker in the east,
There sat auld Nick, in the shape o' beast;
A towzie tyke, black, grim, and large,
To gi'e them music was his charge:
He screwed the pipes and gart them skirl,
Till roof and rafters a' did dirl.

In Alloway, near the old Brig o'Doon over which Tam rode his mare Meg with the witches in hot pursuit, there stands a memorial to Rab. On this memorial in the village of his birth a plaque reads:

ONE AUTUMN DAY IN 1790 ROBERT BURNS PACED
UP AND DOWN THIS GRASSY PATH CROONING TO
HIMSELF, IN ONE OF HIS POETICAL MOODS,
THE WORDS WHICH BECAME THE IMMORTAL TALE
OF 'TAM O' SHANTER'
IN THE LAST FIELD ALONG THE PATH THE POET
SAW THE WOUNDED HARE WHICH INSPIRED
'THE ADDRESS TO THE WOUNDED HARE'.

Inhuman man! curse on thy barb'rous art,
And blasted be thy murder-aiming eye:
May never pity soothe thee with a sigh,
Nor ever pleasure glad thy cruel heart!

Go live, poor wanderer of the wood and field,
The bitter little that of life remains:
No more the thickening brakes and verdant plains
To thee shall home, or food, or pastime yield.

Left: *At Ecclefechan in Dumfries and Galloway lies Thomas Carlyle's birthplace. The house was built around 1791 by his father and uncle. From relatively humble peasant origins Carlyle became a prolific writer, political commentator and historian.*

Seek, mangled wretch, some place of wonted rest -
No more of rest, but now dying bed!
The sheltering rushes whistling o'er thy head,
The cold earth with thy bloody bosom prest.

Oft as by winding Nith I, musing, wait
The sober eve, or hail the cheerful dawn,
I'll miss thee sporting o'er the dewy lawn,
And curse the ruffian's aim, and mourn thy hapless fate.

Much has been written about Burns in the two centuries since his death but one fact is obvious: he was undoubtedly 'a lad with eye for the lassies' — and his amorous nature certainly fed his poetry. One of his many passionate love affairs was with a local girl, Mary Campbell, who was probably a dairy maid, and they went through a traditional form of marriage exchanging Bibles over running water. At this time, however, Jean Armour was expecting his child and her father was threatening legal action if he did not marry her. Meanwhile Burns was trying to get a book of his poems ready for a publisher and was planning to flee the country, possibly for Jamaica. When poor Mary died of the fever and Jean bore him twins, he married Jean and forgot all about his planned disappearnce to the Caribbean.

'Rabbie' never forgot Mary Campbell, and the last verse of the poem he wrote in her honor, *Highland Mary*, reveals the continued depth of his feelings:

O, pale, pale now, those rosy lips
I aft hae kiss'd sae fondly;
And clos'd for ay, the sparkling glance
That dwalt on me sae kindly;
And mouldering now in silent dust
That heart that lo'ed me dearly;
But still within my bosom's core
Shall live my Highland Mary.

At Gourock on the Firth of Clyde there is a statue of Highland Mary, which gazes towards Ayrshire. Robert Burns died in 1796 at the tragically young age of 37 from rheumatic fever contracted after falling asleep by the roadside on his way home from a heavy drinking session.

There were numerous poor and unsuccessful imitators of Burns after his death and even though his language was not quite the same Scottish tongue of the 16th century, it was fluent and natural. It was the language of the Ayrshire peasantry he was born into, but even this was rapidly changing. Rich peasants were becoming capitalist farmers, members of a genteel class that spoke English. Everyone was being exposed to the purer English tongue from their employers, the church, and the schools. These were parlous times for Scotland; the clans were broken and scattered, her parliament extinguished and her nationality was being wrenched from her. Englishmen despised Scotsmen and a literary clique ruled in Edinburgh, aping English speech and manners, and totally rejecting any form of 'vulgar' Scottish dialect. The Scottish vernacular became increasingly derivative, forced, and folksy. Most Scots continued to speak with a very different accent to people living in the south of England, but as a distinct, living, and developing language the Scottish tongue had dried up.

Burns himself was at times culpable of going along with the idea that Scottish was an unsuitable language for serious poetry. When he wanted to write especially solemnly he wrote in English but usually with pretty turgid results — he is not best remembered for these efforts! Burn's skills lay in his ability to take a subject as mundane as a mouse, or a louse on a lady's hat, and make it memorable by the use of his language. Compare a verse from *The Cotter's Saturday Night* with the opening verse of *To A Mouse*.

From *The Cotter's Saturday Night*:

Compared with this, how poor Religion's pride,
In all the pomp of method, and of art,
When men display to congregations wide,
Devotion's every grace, except the heart!
The Power, incensed, the pageant will desert,
The pompous strain, the sacerdotal stole;
But haply, in some cottage far apart,
May hear, well pleased, the language of the soul;
And in his book of life the inmates poor enrol.

A farm servant was driving the plough Burns held, when a mouse ran in front of them. The farm hand would have killed the creature, but was restrained by Burns, and this episode led to one of 'Rabbie's' best and best loved poems. *To A Mouse* begins:

Wee, sleekit, cowrin', tim'rous beastie
Oh, what a panic's in thy breastie!
Thou needna start awa' sae hasty,
Wi' bick'ring brattle!
I wad be laith to rin and chase thee,
Wi' murd'ring pattle!

Apart from Burns, the 18th century saw the greatest achievements of Gaelic poetry in the Highlands while the Lowlanders remained oblivious to it. It is difficult for the non-Gaelic speaker to assess the greatness of such works by Alexander Macdonald (c1700-1770), Duncan ban MacIntyre (1724-1808), Rob Donn (1714-1778), and Dugald Buchanan (1716-1768), but those in the know rank them as among the best poets Scotland has produced in any tongue at any time. Macdonald was the poet of love and war. His splendid martial poems, inspired by the landing of Prince Charles, and the 'amorous language' employed in his love poems ensure translation should be approached with some trepidation (see *The Manning of the Birlinn* on page 185). There was great diversity in the subjects these poets covered but they all had the ability to describe in poetic detail their environment and the nature they observed. (See *The Hill-Water — page 198 — and The Hind is in the Forest — page 202 — by Duncan ban MacIntyre*).

Prose did not suffer the same language difficulties as poetry and with Sir Walter Scott (1771-1832) the Scottish novel had a new beginning which extinguished all that went before. Scott's literary debut was, however, with poetry with a collection of ballads he gathered in the Border counties and when he wrote *The Lady of the Lake* it was described by one critic at the time as a 'novel in verse'. In 1814 his novel *Waverley*, based on the Jacobite Rising, was an instant success and over the next dozen or so years he wrote 22 historical novels. Scott's novels generally depicted a deep understanding of the people and period they attempted to portray, although two of his most popular stories, *Ivanhoe* and *Quentin Durward* show little knowledge of England or France or of the Middle Ages in which they were set. In his Scottish novels he treats the history with great care and affection, although his characters appear somewhat unreal, he didn't seem to want to deal with living people in the Scotland of his day, but rather depict a nostalgia for an admirable Scottish past.

Perhaps the Scottish public were addicted to historical novels because it satisfied a need in times of great social change. By the early 19th century the economic revolution was radically altering all the old ways of agriculture and industry after centuries of imperceptible change. People felt they were losing their roots and, although they were better off financially, they had a nostalgia for the past: they had a need for a sense of identity. Economic change brought by the Industrial Revolution affected England and Scotland in much the same way, so it was inevitable that the societies of the two countries would become more alike. There was a certain regret that Scottish national characteristics were being watered down in this way after centuries of proud differentiation. Henry Cockburn (1779-1854), Boswell's only rival in the art of autobiography, sensed this and spoke for many when he wrote in his Journal:

'The prolongation of Scotch peculiarities, especially of our language and habits, I do earnestly desire. An exact knowledge and feeling of what these have been since 1707 till now would be more curious five hundred years hence than a similar knowledge and feeling of the old Greeks. But the features and expression of a people cannot be perpetuated by legislative engraving. Nothing can prevent the gradual disappearance of local manners under the absorption and assimilation of a far larger, richer and more powerful kindred adjoining kingdom. Burns and Scott have done more for the preservation of proper Scotland than could ever be accomplished by law, statesmen or associations.'

Scott deliberately and Burns unwittingly provided the public with the nostalgic stability and sense of nationhood in the past that it sensed it was losing in the present. This did Scottish literature no favors as it progressed into the 19th century, its poetry was always looking back to Burns with his dead language and Scott with his medieval tales entrenched in the past.

At this point it would be churlish not to mention William McGonagall who, in the eyes of one man, was the finest Scottish poet since Burns — unfortunately this critic with the rose-coloured spectacles was none other than himself. McGonegall's hilarious rhymes, with their strange scansion, were written with the utmost sincerity and seriousness. They survive today by reason of their unconscious humour and their some small historical interest.

Beautiful silvery Tay,
With your landscapes so lovely and gay,
Along each side of your waters, to Perth
all the way;
No other river in the world has got
scenery more fine,
Only I am told the beautiful Rhine,
Near to Wormit Bay, it seems very fine,
When the Railway Bridge is towering
above its waters sublime

William McGonagall can be belittled and lampooned but there is absolutely no doubt that he certainly loved his native part of Scotland.

Right: *Robert Louis Stevenson was born in Edinburgh in 1850. He studied law at university but wanted to become a writer. His first books were on his travels around the Mediterranean. In 1883 he wrote the classic* Treasure Island *for his 12-year old American stepson. There followed a number of novels and short stories including* Kidnapped *and* The Strange Case of Dr Jekyll and Mr Hyde. *He died suddenly in 1894 on Samoa at the age of 44.*

Columcille fecit

Delightful would it be to me to be in Uchd Ailiun
    On the pinnacle of a rock,
That I might often see
    The face of the ocean;
That I might see its heaving waves
    Over the wide ocean,
When they chant music to their Father
    Upon the world's course;
That I might see its level sparkling strand,
    It would be no cause of sorrow;
That I might hear the song of the wonderful birds,
    Source of happiness;
That I might hear the thunder of the crowding waves
    Upon the rocks;
That I might hear the roar by the side of the church
    Of the surrounding sea;
That I might see its noble flocks
    Over the watery ocean;
That I might see the sea-monsters,
    The greatest of all wonders;
That I might see its ebb and flood
    In their career;
That my mystical name might be, I say,

    Cul ri Erin; [1]

That contrition might come upon my heart
    Upon looking at her;
That I might bewail my evils all,
    Though it were difficult to compute them;
That I might bless the Lord
    Who conserves all,
Heaven with its countless bright orders,
    Land, strand and flood;
That I might search the books all,
    That would be good for my soul;
At times kneeling to beloved Heaven;
    At times psalm singing;
At times contemplating the King of Heaven,
    Holy the chief;
At times at work without compulsion,
    This would be delightful.
At times plucking duilisc from the rocks;
    At times at fishing;
At times giving food to the poor;

    At times in a carcair; [2]
The best advice in the presence of God
    To me has been vouchsafed.
The King whose servant I am will not let
    Anything deceive me.

St. Columba
6th Century

1 Back turned to Ireland

2 Solitary cell

Stonehaven, Grampian.

Innis Chonnell Castle, Loch Awe.

Such a Parcel of Rogues in a Nation

Fareweel to a' our Scottish fame,
    Fareweel our ancient glory!
Fareweel ev'n to the Scottish name,
    Sae famed in martial story!
Now Sark rins o'er the Solway sands,
    An' Tweed rins to the ocean,
To mark where England's province stands –
    Such a parcel of rogues in a nation!

What force or guile could not subdue
    Thro' many warlike ages
Is wrought now by a coward few
    For hireling traitor's wages.
The English steel we could disdain,
    Secure in valour's station;
But English gold has been our bane –
    Such a parcel of rogues in a nation!

O, would, or I had seen the day
    That Treason thus could sell us,
My auld grey head had lien in clay
    Wi' Bruce and loyal Wallace!
But pith and power, till my last hour
    I'll mak this declaration;-
'We're bought and sold for English gold' –
    Such a parcel of rogues in a nation!

Robert Burns
1759-1796

The Strange Country

Moonrise over the North Sea.

I have come from a mystical Land of Light
    To a Strange Country;
The Land I have left is forgotten quite
    In the Land I see.

The round Earth rolls beneath my feet,
    And the still Stars glow,
The murmuring Waters rise and retreat,
    The Winds come and go.

Sure as a heart-beat all things seem
    In this Strange Country;
So sure, so still, in a dazzle of dream,
    All things flow free.

'Tis life, all life, be it pleasure or pain,
    In the Field and the Flood,
In the beating Heart, in the burning Brain,
    In the Flesh and the Blood.

Deep as Death is the daily strife
    Of this Strange Country:
All things thrill up till they blossom in Life,
    And flutter and flee.

Nothing is stranger than the rest,
    From the pole to the pole,
The weed by the way, the eggs in the nest,
    The Flesh and the Soul.

Look in mine eyes, O Man I meet
    In this Strange Country!
Lie in my arms, O Maiden sweet,
    With thy mouth kiss me!

Go by, O King, with thy crownèd brow
    And thy sceptred hand –
Thou art a straggler too, I vow,
    From the same strange Land.

O wondrous Faces that upstart
    In this Strange Country!
O Souls, O Shades, that become a part
    Of my Soul and me!

What are ye working so fast and fleet,
    O Humankind?
'We are building Cities for those whose feet
    Are coming behind;

'Our stay is short, we must fly again
    From this Strange Country;
But others are growing, women and men,
    Eternally!'

Child, what art thou? and what am I?
    But a breaking wave!
Rising and rolling on, we hie
    To the shore of the grave.

I have come from a mystical Land of Light
    To this Strange Country;
This dawn I came, I shall go to-night,
    Ay me! ay me!

I hold my hand to my head and stand
    'Neath the air's blue arc,
I try to remember the mystical Land,
    But all is dark.

And all around me swim Shapes like mine
    In this Strange Country;-
They break in the glamour of gleams divine,
    And they moan 'Ay me!'

Like waves in the cold Moon's silvern breath
    They gather and roll,
Each crest of white is a birth or a death,
    Each sound is a Soul.

Oh, whose is the Eye that gleams so bright
    O'er this Strange Country?
It draws us along with a chain of light,
    As the Moon the Sea!

Robert Buchanan
Born 1841

The Manning of the Birlinn

The Sailing

The sun had opened golden yellow,
    From his case,
Though still the sky wore dark and drumly
    A scarr'd and frowning face:
Then troubled, tawny, dense, dun-bellied,
    Scowling and sea-blue,
Every dye that's in the tartan
    O'er it grew.
Far away to the wild westward
    Grim it lowered,
Where rain-charged clouds on thick squalls wandering
    Loomed and towered.
Up they raised the speckled sails through
    Cloud-like light,
And stretched them on the mighty halyards,
    Tense and tight.
High on the mast so tall and stately –
    Dark-red in hue –
They set them firmly, set them surely,
    Set them true.
Round the iron pegs the ropes ran,
    Each its right ring through;
Thus having ranged the tackle rarely,
    Well and carefully,
Every man sat waiting bravely,
    Where he ought to be.
For now the airy windows opened,
    And from spots of bluish grey

Let loose the keen and crabbed wild winds –
    A fierce band were they –
'Twas then his dark cloak the ocean
    Round him drew.
Dusky, livid, ruffling, whirling,
    Round at first it flew,
Till up he swell'd to mountains, or to glens,
    Dishevelled, rough, sank down –
While the kicking, tossing waters
    All in hills had grown.
Its blue depth opened in huge maws,
    Wild and devouring,
Down which, clasped in deadly struggles,
    Fierce strong waves were pouring.
It took a man to look the storm-winds
    Right in the face –
As they lit up the sparkling spray on every surge-hill,
    In their fiery race.
The waves before us, shrilly yelling,
    Raised their high heads hoar,
While those behind, with moaning trumpets,
    Gave a bellowing roar.
When we rose up aloft, majestic,
    On the heaving swell,
Need was to pull in our canvas
    Smart and well:
When she sank down with one huge swallow
    In the hollow glen,

Staffa, Inner Hebrides.

Every sail she bore aloft
    Was given to her then.
The drizzling surges high and roaring
    Rush'd on us louting,
Long ere they were near us come,
    We heard their shouting:-
They roll'd sweeping up the little waves
    Scourging them bare,
Till all became one threatening swell,
    Our steersman's care.
When down we fell from off the billows'
    Towering shaggy edge,
Our keel was well-nigh hurled against
    The shells and sedge;
The whole sea was lashing, dashing,
    All through other:
It kept the seals and mightiest monsters
    In a pother!
The fury and the surging of the water,
    And our good ship's swift way
Spatter'd their white brains on each billow,
    Livid and grey.
With piteous wailing and complaining
    All the storm-tossed horde,

Shouted out 'We're now your subjects;
    Drag us on board.'
And the small fish of the ocean
    Turn'd over their white breast –
Dead, innumerable, with the raging
    Of the furious sea's unrest.
The stones and shells of the deep channel
    Were in motion;
Swept from out their lowly bed
    By the tumult of the ocean;
Till the sea, like a great mess of pottage,
    Troubled, muddy grew
With the blood of many mangled creatures,
    Dirty red in hue –
When the horn'd and clawy wild beasts,
    Short-footed, splay,
With great wailing gumless mouths
    Huge and wide open lay.
But the whole deep was full of spectres,
    Loose and sprawling
With the claws and with the tails of monsters,
    Pawing, squalling.
It was frightful even to hear them
    Screech so loudly;

The sound might move full fifty heroes
    Stepping proudly.
Our whole crew grew dull of hearing
    In the tempest's scowl,
So sharp the quavering cries of demons
    And the wild beasts' howl.
With the oaken planks the weltering waves were wrestling
    In their noisy splashing;
While the sharp beak of our swift ship
    On the sea-pigs came dashing.
The wind kept still renewing all its wildness
    In the far West,
Till with every kind of strain and trouble
    We were sore distress'd.
We were blinded with the water
    Showering o'er us ever;
And the awful night like thunder,
    And the lightning ceasing never.
The bright fireballs in our tackling
    Flamed and smoked;
With the smell of burning brimstone
    We were well-nigh choked.
All the elements above, below,
    Against us wrought;
Earth and wind and fire and water,
    With us fought.
But when the evil one defied the sea
    To make us yield,
At last, with one bright smile of pity,
    Peace with us she seal'd:
Yet not before our yards were injured,
    And our sails were rent,
Our poops were strained, our oars were weaken'd,
    All our masts were bent.
Not a stay but we had started,
    Our tackling all was wet and splashy,
Nails and couplings, twisted, broken.
    Feeshie, fashie,
All the thwarts and all the gunwale
    Everywhere confess'd,
And all above and all below,
    How sore they had been press'd.
Not a bracket, not a rib,
    But the storm had loosed;
Fore and aft from stem to stern,
    All had got confused.

Not a tiller but was split,
    And the helm was wounded;
Every board its own complaint
    Sadly sounded.
Every trennel, every fastening
    Had been giving way;
Not a board remain'd as firm
    As at the break of day.
Not a bolt in her but started,
    Not a rope the wind that bore,
Not a part of the whole vessel
    But was weaker than before.
The sea spoke to us its peace prattle
    At the cross of Islay's Kyle,
And the rough wind, bitter boaster!
    Was restrained for one good while.
The tempest rose from off us into places
    Lofty in the upper air,
And after all its noisy barking
    Ruffled round us fair.
Then we gave thanks to the High King,
    Who rein'd the wind's rude breath,
And saved our good Clan Ranald
    From a bad and brutal death.
Then we furl'd up the fine and speckled sails
    Of linen wide,
And we took down the smooth red dainty masts,
    And laid them by the side –
On our long and slender polish'd oars
    Together leaning –
They were all made of the fir cut by Mac Barais
    In Eilean Fionain –
We went with our smooth, dashing rowing,
    And steady shock,
Till we reach'd the good port round the point
    Of Fergus' Rock.
There casting anchor peacefully
    We calmly rode;
We got meat and drink in plenty,
    And there we abode.

Alexander MacDonald
c.1700-1770

Mountain Twilight

The hills slipped over each on each
    Till all their changing shadows died.
Now in the open skyward reach
    The lights grow solemn side by side.
While of these hills the westermost
Rears high his majesty of coast
    In shifting waste of dim-blue brine
    And fading olive hyaline;
Till all the distance overflows,
    The green in watchet and the blue
In purple. Now they fuse and close –
    A darkling violet, fringed anew
With light that on the mountains soar,
A dusky flame on tranquil shores;
    Kindling the summits as they grow
In audience to the skies that call,
Ineffable in rest and all
    The pathos of the afterglow.

William Renton
19th Century

Loch Leven, Western Highlands.

Requiem

Under the wide and starry sky
Dig the grave and let me lie:
Glad did I live and gladly die,
  And I laid me down with a will.

This be the verse you grave for me:
Here he lies where he long'd to be;
Home is the sailor, home from sea,
  And the hunter home from the hill.

Robert Louis Stevenson
1850-1894

Lock the Door, Lariston

'Lock the door, Lariston, lion of Liddesdale;
Lock the door, Lariston, Lowther comes on;
  The Armstrongs are flying,
  The widows are crying'
The Castletown's burning, and Oliver's gone!

'Lock the door, Lariston - high on the weather gleam
See how the Saxon plumes bob on the sky -
  Yeomen and carbineer,
  Billman and halberdier,
Fierce is the foray, and far is the cry!

'Bewcastle brandishes high his broad scimitar;
Ridley is riding his fleet-footed grey;
  Hedley and Howard there,
  Wandale and Windermere;
Lock the door, Lariston; hold them at bay.

'Why dost thou smile, noble Elliot of Lariston?
Why does the joy-candle gleam in thine eye?
  Thou bold Border ranger,
  Beware of thy danger;
Thy foes are relentless, determined, and nigh.'

Jack Elliot raised up his steel bonnet and lookit,
His hand grasp'd the sword with a nervous embrace;
  'Ah, welcome, brave foemen,
  On earth there are no men
More gallant to meet in the foray or chase!

'Little know you of the hearts I have hidden here;
Little know you of our moss-troopers' might -
  Linhope and Sorbie true,
  Sundhope and Milburn too,
Gentle in manner, but lions in fight!

'I have Mangerton, Ogilvie, Raeburn, and Netherbie,
Old Sim of Whitram, and all his array;
  Come all Northumberland,
  Teesdale and Cumberland,
Here at the Breaken tower end shall the fray!'

Scowled the broad sun o'er the links of green Liddesdale,
Red as the beacon-light tipped he the wold;
  Many a bold martial eye
  Mirror'd that morning sky,
Never more oped on his orbit of gold.

Shrill was the bugle's note, dreadful the warrior's shout,
Lances and halberds in splinters were borne;
  Helmet and hauberk then
  Braved the claymore in vain,
Buckler and armlet in shivers were shorn.

See how they wane - the proud files of the Windermere!
Howard! ah, woe to thy hopes of the day!
  Hear the wide welkin rend,
  While the Scots' shouts ascend -
'Elliot of Lariston, Elliot for aye!'

James Hogg
1770-1835

Smailholm Tower, Borders.

Lochinvar

O, young Lochinvar is come out of the west,
Through all the wide Border his steed was the best;
And save his good broadsword he weapons had none,
He rode all unarm'd, and he rode all alone.
So faithful in love, and so dauntless in war,
There never was knight like the young Lochinvar.

He staid not for brake, and he stopp'd not for stone,
He swam the Eske river where ford there was none;
But ere he alighted at Netherby gate,
The bride had consented, the gallant came late:
For a laggard in love, and a dastard in war,
Was to wed the fair Ellen of brave Lochinvar.

So boldly he enter'd the Netherby Hall,
Among bride's-men, and kinsmen, and brothers, and all:
Then spoke the bride's father, his hand on his sword,
(For the poor craven bridegroom said never a word,)
'O come ye in peace here, or come ye in war,
Or to dance at our bridal, young Lord Lochinvar?'

'I long woo'd your daughter, my suit you denied; -
Love swells like the Solway, but ebbs like its tide -
And now am I come, with this lost love of mine,
To lead but one measure, drink one cup of wine.
There are maidens in Scotland more lovely by far,
That would gladly be bride to the young Lochinvar.'

The bride kiss'd the goblet; the knight took it up,
He quaff'd off the wine, and he threw down the cup.
She look'd down to blush, and she look'd up to sigh,
With a smile on her kips, and a tear in her eye.
He took her soft hand, ere her mother could bar, -
'Now tread we a measure!' said young Lochinvar.

So stately his form, and so lovely her face,
That never a hall such a galliard did grace;
While her mother did fret, and her father did fume,
And the bridegroom stood dangling his bonnet and plume;
And the bride-maidens whisper'd, 'Twere better by far,
To have match'd our fair cousin with young Lochinvar.'

Caerlaverock Castle, Dumfries.

One touch to her hand, and one word in her ear,
When they reach'd the hall-door, and the charger stood near;
So light to the croupe the fair lady he swung,
So light to the saddle before her he sprung!
'She is won! we are gone, over bank, bush, and scaur;
They'll have fleet steeds that follow,' quoth young Lochinvar.

There was mounting 'mong Graemes of the Netherby clan;
Forsters, Fenwicks, and Musgraves, they rode and they ran:
There was racing and chasing on Cannobie Lee,
But the lost bride of Netherby ne'er did they see.
So daring in love, and so dauntless in war,
Have ye e'er heard of gallant like young Lochinvar?

Sir Walter Scott
1771-1832

Arran

Arran of the many stags,
the sea reaches to its shoulder;
island where companies are fed,
ridges whereon blue spears are reddened.

Wanton deer upon its peaks,
Mellow blaeberries on its heaths,
cold water in its streams,
mast upon its brown oaks.

Hunting dogs there, and hounds,
blackberries and sloes of the dark blackthorn,
dense thorn-bushes in its woods,
stags astray among its oak-groves.

Gathering of purple lichen on its rocks,
grass without blemish on its slopes;
over its fair shapely crags
gambolling of dappled fawns leaping.

Smooth is its lowland, fat are its swine,
pleasant its fields, a tale to be believed;
its nuts on the boughs of its hazel-wood,
sailing of long galleys past it.

It is delightful when fine weather comes,
trout under the banks of its streams,
seagulls answer each other round its white cliff;
delightful at all times is Arran.

Anon, translated from the Irish by Kenneth Jackson

Isle of Arran.

His Metrical Prayer
(On the Eve of his Own Execution)

Let them bestow on ev'ry Airth[1] a Limb;
Open all my veins, that I may swim
To Thee my Saviour, in that Crimson Lake;
Then place my par-boiled Head upon a Stake;
Scatter my Ashes, throw them in the Air:
Lord (since Thou know'st where all these Atoms are)
I'm hopeful, once Thou'lt recollect my Dust,
And confident Thou'lt raise me with the Just.

James Graham
Marquis of Montrose
1612-1650

[1] north, south, east and west

In Shadowland

Between the moaning of the mountain stream
And the hoarse thunder of the Atlantic deep,
An outcast from the peaceful realms of sleep
I lie, and hear as in a fever-dream
The homeless night-wind in the darkness scream
And wail around the inaccessible steep
Down whose gaunt sides the spectral torrents leap
From crag to crag, - till almost I could deem
The plaided ghosts of buried centuries
Were mustering in the glen with bow and spear
And shadowy hounds to hunt the shadowy deer,
Mix in phantasmal sword-play, or, with eyes
Of wrath and pain immortal, wander o'er
Loved scenes where human footstep comes no more.

Sir Noel Paton
Born 1821

The Reed-Player

By a dim shore where water darkening
    Took the last light of spring,
I went beyond the tumult, harkening
    For some diviner thing.

Where the bats flew from the black elms like
leaves,
    Over the ebon pool
Brooded the bittern's cry, as one that grieves
    Lands ancient, bountiful.

I saw the fire-flies shine below the wood,
    Above the shallows dank,
As Uriel, from some great altitude,
    The planets rank on rank.

And now unseen along the shrouded mead
    One went under the hill;
He blew a cadence on his mellow reed,
    That trembled and was still.

It seemed as if a line of amber fire
    Had shot the gathered dusk,
As if had blown a wind from ancient Tyre
    Laden with myrrh and musk.

He gave his luring note amid the fern;
    Its enigmatic fall
Haunted the hollow dusk with golden turn
    And argent interval.

I could not know the message that he bore,
    The springs of life from me
Hidden; his incommunicable lore
    As much a mystery.

And as I followed far the magic player
    He passed the maple wood;
And, when I passed, the stars had risen there,
    And there was solitude.

Duncan Campbell-Scott
19th Century

Eigg and Rhum from Glenancross, Mallaig.

Venus and Cupid

Frae bank to bank, frae wood to wood I rin
Owrhailit[1] with my feeble fantasie
Like til a leaf that fallis from a tree,
Or til a reed owrblawin with the wind.
Twa gods guides me: the ane of them is blin,
Yea, and a bairn brocht up in vanitie;
The nixt a wife ingenerit[2] of the sea
And lichter nor a dauphin[3] with her fin.

Unhappie is the man for evermair
That tills the sand and sawis in the air;
But twice unhappier is he, I lairn,
That feedis in his hairt a mad desire,
And follows on a woman throu the fire,
Led by a blin, and teachit by a bairn.

Mark Alexander Boyd
1563-1601

1 overwhelmed   2 born of   3 dolphin

To His Mistress

So sweet a kiss yestreen frae thee I reft,
In bowing doun thy body on the bed,
That even my life within thy lips I left.
Sensyne[1] from thee my spirits wald never shed.
To follow thee it from my body fled
And left my corpse als cold as ony key.
But when the danger of my death I dread,
To seek my spreit I sent by hairt to thee;
But it was so enamoured with thine ee,
With thee it mindit likewise to remain.
So thou hes keepit captive all the three,
More glaid to bide than to return again.
        Except thy breath their places had suppleit,
        Even in thine armes, there doutless had I deit.

Alexander Montgomerie
c.1545-c.1610

1 since then

Glencoe, Western Highlands.

The wee, wee German Lairdie

Wha the deil hae we got for a King,
    But a wee, wee German lairdie![1]
An' whan we gaed to bring him hame,
    He was delving in his kail-yardie.[2]
Sheughing[3] kail an' laying leeks,
    But[4] the hose and but the breeks,
Up his beggar duds[5] he cleeks,
    The wee, wee German lairdie.

An' he's clapt down in our gudeman's[6] chair,
    The wee, wee German lairdie;
An' he's brought fouth[7] o' foreign leeks,
    An' dibblet them in his yardie.
He's pu'd the rose o' English louns,[8]
    An' brak the harp o' Irish clowns,
But our thistle will jag his thumbs,
    The wee, wee German lairdie.

Come up amang the Highland hills,
    Thou wee, wee German lairdie;
An' see how Charlie's lang-kail[9] thrive,
    He dibblet in his yardie.
An' if a stock ye daur[10] to pu',
    Or haud[11] the yoking of a pleugh,
We'll break yere sceptre o'er yere mou',
    Thou wee bit German lairdie.

Our hills are steep, our glens are deep,
    Nae fitting for a yardie;
An' our norlan' thistles winna pu'
    Thou wee, wee German lairdie.
An' we've the trenching blades o' weir,[12]
    Wad twine ye o' yere German gear
An' pass ye 'neath the claymore's shear,
    Thou feckless[13] German lairdie.

1 minor squire
2 cabbage patch
3 picking
4 without
5 rags
6 king
7 many
8 fellows
9 swords of Prince Charles Edward's men
10 dare
11 hold
12 war
13 useless

Allan Cunningham
1784-1842

The Hill-Water

From the rim it trickles down
Of the mountains granite crown clear and cool;
Keen and eager though it go
Through your veins with lively flow,
Yet it knoweth not to reign
In the chambers of the brain with misrule;

Where dark watercresses grow
You will trace its quiet flow,
With mossy border yellow,
So mild and soft, and mellow, in its pouring.
With no shiny dregs to trouble
The brightness of its bubble
As it threads its silver way
From the granite shoulders grey of Ben Dorain.

Then down the sloping side
It will leap with glassy slide gently welling
Till it gather strength to leap,
With a light and foamy sweep,
To the corrie broad and deep
Proudly swelling;

Then bends amid the boulders
'Neath the shadow of the shoulders of the Ben,
Through a country rough and shaggy,
So jaggy and so knaggy,
Full of hummocks and of hunches,
Full of stumps and tufts and bunches,
Full of bushes and of rushes, in the glen,

Through rich green solitudes,
And wildly hanging woods
With blossom and with bell,
In rich redundant swell, and the pride
Of the mountain daisy there, and the forest everywhere,
With the dress and with the air of a bride.

Duncan Ban MacIntyre
1724-1808

The Falls of Rogie on the River Blackwater, Strathpeffer.

Loch Moidart, Western Highlands.

McLean's Welcome

Come o'er the stream, Charlie, dear Charlie, brave Charlie;
Come o'er the stream, Charlie, and dine with McLean;
And though you be weary, we'll make you heart cheery,
And welcome our Charlie, and his loyal train.
We'll bring down the track deer, we'll bring down the black steer,
The lamb from the braken, and doe from the glen,
The salt sea we'll harry, and bring to our Charlie
The cream from the bothy and curd from the pen.

Come o'er the stream, Charlie, dear Charlie, brave Charlie;
Come o'er the stream, Charlie, and dine with McLean;
And you shall drink freely the dews of Glen-Sheerly,
That stream in the starlight when kings do not ken,
And deep be your meed of the wine that is red,
To drink to your sire, and his friend the McLean.

Come o'er the stream, Charlie, dear Charlie, brave Charlie;
Come o'er the stream, Charlie, and dine with McLean;
O'er heath-bells shall trace you the maids to embrace you,
And deck your blue bonnet with flowers of the brae;
And the loveliest Mari in all Glen M'Quarry
Shall lie in your bosom till break of the day.

Come o'er the stream, Charlie, dear Charlie, brave Charlie;
Come o'er the stream, Charlie, and dine with McLean;
If aught will invite you, or more will delight you,
'Tis ready, a troop of our bold Highlandmen,
All ranged on the heather, with bonnet and feather,
Strong arms and broad claymores, three hundred and ten!

James Hogg
1770-1835

Stirling Castle.

Scots, Wha Hae

Scots, wha hae wi'[1] Wallace bled,
Scots, wham Bruce has aften[2] led,
Welcome to your gory bed
    Or to victorie!

Now's the day, and now's the hour:
See the front o' battle lour,[3]
See approach proud Edward's power -
    Chains and slaverie!

Wha will be a traitor knave?
Wha can fill a coward's grave?
Wha sae base as be a slave?
    Let him turn and flee!

Wha for Scotland's King and Law
Freedom's sword will strongly draw,
Freeman stand, or freeman fa',
    Let him follow me!

By Oppression's woes and pains,
By your sons in servile chains,
We will drain our dearest veins
    But they shall be free!

Lay the proud usurpers low!
Tyrants fall in every foe!
Liberty's in every blow!
    Let us do, or die!

1 who have with
2 often
3 loom up

Robert Burns 1759-1796

The Lament of the Deer
(Cumha nam Fiadh)

O for my strength! once more to see the hills!
The wilds of Strath-Farar of stags,
The blue streams, and winding vales,
Where the flowering tree sends forth its sweet perfume.

My thoughts are sad and dark! -
I lament the forest where I loved to roam,
The secret corries, the haunt of hinds,
Where often I watched them on the hill!

Corrie-Garave! O that I was within thy bosom
Scuir-na-Lapàich of steeps, with thy shelter,
Where feed the herds which never seek for stalls,
But whose skin gleams red in the sunshine of the hills.

Great was my love in youth, and strong my desire,
Towards the bounding herds;
But now, broken, and weak, and hopeless,
Their remembrance wounds my heart.

To linger in the laich[1] I mourn,
My thoughts are ever in the hills;
For there my childhood and my youth was nursed -
The moss and the craig in the morning breeze was my delight.

Then was I happy in my life,
When the voices of the hill sung sweetly;
More sweet to me, than any string,
It soothed my sorrow or rejoiced my heart.

My thoughts wandered to no other land
Beyond the hill of the forest, the shealings of the deer,
Where the nimble herds ascended the hill, -
As I lay in my plaid on the dewy bed.

The sheltering hollows, where I crept towards the hart,
On the pastures of the glen, or in the forest wilds -
And if once more I may see them as of old,
How will my heart bound to watch again the pass!

Red deer, Glen Muick, Deeside.

1 Low country

Great was my joy to ascend the hills
In the cause of the noble chief,
Mac Shimé of the piercing eye - never to fail at need,
With all his brave Frasers, gathered beneath his banner.

When they told of his approach, with all his ready arms,
My heart bounded for the chase -
On the rugged steep, on the broken hill,
By hollow, and ridge, many were the red stags which he laid low.

He is the pride of hunters; my trust was in his gun,
When the sound of its shot rung in my ear,
The great ball launched in flashing fire,
And the dun stag fell in the rushing speed of his course.

When evening came down on the hill,
The time for return to the star of the glen,
The kindly lodge where the noble gathered,
The sons of the tartan and the plaid,

With joy and triumph they returned
To the dwelling of plenty and repose;
The bright blazing hearth - the circling wine -
The welcome of the noble chief!

Angus MacKenzie
published 1848

The Hind is the Forest

The hind is in the forest
as she ought to be,
where she may have sweet grass,
clean, fine-bladed;
    heath-rush and deer's hair grass
    herbs in which strength resides,
    and which would make her flanks
    plump and fat-covered;
    a spring in which there is
    abundant water-cress,
    she deems more sweet than wine
    and would drink of it;
    sorrel and rye grass
    which flourish on the moor,
    she prefers as food
    to rank field grass.

Of her fare she deemed
these the delicacies:
primrose, St John's wort
and tormentil flowers;
    tender spotted orchis,
    forked, spiked and glossy,
    on meadows where, in clusters,
    it flourishes.
    Such was the dietary

that would increase their strength,
that would pull them through
in the stormy days;
that would upon their back
amass the roll of fat,
which, over their spare frame,
was not cumbersome.

That was a comely fellowship
at eventide,
when they would assemble
in the gloaming:
    though long the night might be
    no harm would come to you;
    the lee base of the knoll
    was your dwelling place.
    Here are the beds of deer,
    where they have ever been,
    on a spacious, bounteous moor,
    and on mountain range.
    Delightful was their hue,
    when vivid was their hide;
    'twas no mean portion they desired,
    it was Ben Dobhrain.

Duncan Ban MacIntyre
1724-1808

O my luve's like a red, red rose

Dog rose.

O my luve's like a red, red rose,
    That's newly sprung in June:
O my luve's like the melodie
    That's sweetly play'd in tune.

As fair art thou, my bonnie lass,
    So deep in luve am I;
And I will luve thee still, my dear,
    Till a' the seas gang dry.

Till a' the seas gang dry, my dear,
    And the rocks will melt wi' the sun;
And I will luve thee still, my dear,
    While the sands o' life shall run.

And fare thee weel, my only luve!
    And fare thee weel a while!
And I will come again, my luve,
    Tho' it were ten thousand mile.

Robert Burns
1759-1796

Rest and Be Thankful, Strathclyde.

Durisdeer

We'll meet nae mair at sunset when the weary day is dune,
Nor wander hame thegither by the lee licht o' the mune.
I'll hear your steps nea langer amang the dewy corn,
For we'll meet nae mair, my bonniest, either at e'en or morn.

The yellow broom is waving abune the sunny brae,
And the rowan berries dancing where the sparkling waters play;
Tho' a' is bright and bonnie it's an eerie place to me,
For we'll meet nae mair, my dearest, either by burn or tree.

Far up into the wild hills there's a kirkyard lone and still,
Where the frosts lie ilka morning and the mists hang low and chill.
And there ye sleep in silence while I wander here my lane
Till we meet ance mair in Heaven never to part again!

Lady John Scott
19th Century

Thomas the Rhymer

Weed on the River Array,
Inverary.

True Thomas lay on Huntlie bank;
A ferlie he speid wi' his e'e;
And there he saw a ladye bright
Come riding down by the Eildon Tree.

Her skirt was o' the grass-green silk,
Her mantle o' the velvet fyne;
At ilka tert o' her horse's mane
Hung fifty siller bells and nine.

True Thomas he pu'd aff his cap,
And louted low down on his knee:
'Hail to thee, Mary, Queen of Heaven!
For thy peer on earth could never be.'

'O no, O no, Thomas,' she said
'That name does not belang to me;
I'm but Queen o' fair Elfland,
That am hither come to visit thee.

'Harp and carp, Thomas,' she said;
'Harp and carp along wi' me;
And if ye dare to kiss my lips,
Sure of your bodie I will be.'

'Betide me weal, betide me woe,
That weird shall never daunten me.'
Syne he has kiss'd her rosy lips,
All underneath the Eildon Tree.

'Now ye maun go wi' me,' she said,
'True Thomas, ye maun go wi' me;
And ye maun serve me seven years,

Thro' weal or woe as may chance to be.'

She's mounted on her milk-white steed,
She's ta'en true Thomas up behind;
And aye, whene'er her bridle rang,
The steed gaed swifter that the wind.

O they rade on, and farther on,
The steed gaed swifter than the wind;
Until they reach'd a desert wide,
And living land was left behind.

'Light down, light down now, true Thomas,
And lean your head upon my knee;
Abide ye there a little space,
And I will show you ferlies three.

'O see ye not yon narrow road,
So thick beset wi' thorns and briers?
That is the Path of Righteousness,
Though after it but few inquires.

'And see ye not yon braid, braid road,
That lies across the lily leven?
That is the Path of Wickedness,
Though some call it the Road to Heaven.

'And see ye not yon bonny road
That winds about the fernie brae?
That is the road to fair Elfland,
Where thou and I this night might maun gae.
'But, Thomas, ye sall haud your tongue,
Whatever ye may hear or see;

For speak ye word in Elfyn-land,
Ye'll ne'er win back to your ain countrie.'

O they rade on, and farther on,
And they waded river abune the knee;
And they saw neither sun or moon,
But they heard the roaring of the sea.

It was mirk, mirk night, there was nae starlight,
They waded thro' red blude to the knee;
For a' the blude that's shed on the earth
Rins through the springs o' that countrie

Syne they came to a garden green,
And she pu'd an apple frae a tree:
'Take this for thy wages, true Thomas;
It will give thee the tongue that can never lee.'

'My tongue us my ain,' true Thomas he said;
'A gudely gift ye wad gie to me!
I neither dought to buy or sell
At fair or tryst where I might be.

'I dought neither speak to prince or peer,
Nor ask of grace from fair ladye!'
'Now haud thy peace, Thomas, 'she said,
"For as I say, so must it be'.

He has gotten a coat of even cloth,
And a pair o' shoon of the velvet green;
And till seven years were gane and past,
True Thomas on earth was never seen.

Anonymous

To S. R. Crockett

(On receiving a Dedication)

Blows the wind today, and the sun and the rain are flying,
Blows the wind on the moors today and now,
Where about the graves of the martyrs the whaups1 are crying,
My heart remembers how!

Grey recumbent tombs of the dead in desert places,
Standing-stones on the vacant wine-red moor,
Hills of sheep, and the howes2 of the silent vanished races,
And winds, austere and pure.

Be it granted me to behold you again in dying,
Hills of home! and to hear again the call;
Hear about the graves of the martyrs the peewees3 crying,
And hear no more at all.

Robert Louis Stevenson
1850-1894

1 curlews. 2 hollows, glens. 3 lapwings.

Clatteringshaws Loch, Galloway.

The Highland Crofter

Frae Kenmore tae Ben More
The land is a' the Marquis's;
The mossy howes, the heathery knowes
An' ilka bonnie park is his;
The bearded goats, the towsie stots,
An' a' the braxie carcases;
Ilk crofter's rent, ilk tinkler's tent,
An ilka collie's bark is his;
The muir-cock's craw, the piper's blaw,
The ghillie's hard day's wark is his;
Frae Kenmore tae Ben More
The warld is a 'the Maruis's.

The fish that swim, the birds that skim,
The fir, the ash, the birk is his;
The Castle ha'sae big and braw,
Yon diamond-crusted dirk is his;
The roofless hame, a burning shame,
The factor's dirty wark is his;

The poor folk vexed, the lawyer's text,
Yon smirking legal shark is his;
Frae Kenmore tae Ben More
The warld is a' the Marquis's.
But near, mair near, God's voice we hear —
The dawn as weel's the dark is His;
The poet's dream, the patriot's theme,
The fire that lights the mirk is His.

They clearly show God's mills are slow
But sure the handiwork is His;
And in His grace our hope we Place;
Fair Freedom's sheltering ark is His.
The men that toil should own the soil —

A note as clear's the lark is this —
Breadalbane's land - fair, the grand —
Will no' be aye the Marquis's.

Anonymous

My Own, my Native Land!

Breathes there the man with soul so dead,
Who never to himself hath said,
This is my own, my native land!
Whose heart ne'er within him burn'd
As home his footsteps he hath turn'd,
From wandering on a foreign strand!
If such there breathe, go, mark him well;
For him no minstrel raptures swell;
High though his titles, proud his name,
Boundless his wealth as wish can claim;
Despite these titles, power, and pelf,
The wretch, concentred all in self,
Living, shall forfeit fair renown,
And, doubly dying, shall go down
To the vile dust, from whence he sprung,
Unwept, unhonour'd, and unsung.

O Caledonia! stern and wild,
Meet a nurse for a poetic child!
Land of the mountain and the flood,
Land of my sires! what mortal hand
Can e'er untie the filial band
That knits me to thy rugged strand?
Still, as I view each well-known scene,
Think of what is now, and what hath been,
Seems as, to me, of all bereft,
Sole friends thy woods and streams were left;
And this I love them better still,
Even in extremity of ill.

Sir Walter Scott
1771-1832

Rannoch Moor and the head of Glencoe.

The Tryst

O luely, luely, cam she in
And luely she lay doun:
I kent her be her caller lips
And her briests-sae sma' and roun'.

A' thru the nicht we spak nae word
Nor sinder'd bane frae bane:
A' thru the nicht I heard her hert
Gang soundin' wi' my ain.

It was about the waukrife hour
Whan cocks begin to craw
That she smool'd saftly thru the mirk
Afore the day wud daw.

Sae luely, luely, cam she in
Sae luely was the gaen;
And wi' her a' my simmer days
Like they had never been.

William Soutar
1898-1943

Bonny Kilmeny gaed up the Glen

Bonny Kilmeny gaed up the glen,
But it wasna to meet Duneira's men,
Nor the rosy monk on the isle to see,
For Kilmeny was pure as pure could be.
It was only to hear the yorlin sing,
And pu' the cress-flower round the spring;
The scarlet hypp and the hindberrye,
And the nut that hung frae the hazel tree;
For Kilmeny was as pure as pure could be.
But lang may her minny look o'er the wa',
And lang may she seek i' the green-wood shaw;
Lang the laird of Funeira blame,
And lang, lang greet or Kilmeny come hame?

When many a day had come and fled,
When grief grew calm, and hope was dead,
When mass for Kilmeny's soul had been sung,
When the beedes-man had prayed, and the dead
bell rung,
Late, late in a gloamin'when all was still,
When the fringe was red on the westlin hill,
The wood was sere, the moon i' the wane,
The reek o' the cot hung over the plain,

Like a little wee cloud in the world its lane;
When the ingle lowed with an eiry leme,
Late, late in the gloamin' Kilmeny came hame!
'Kilmeny, Kilmeny, where have you been?
Lang hae we sought baith holt and dean;
By linn, by ford, and green-wood tree,
Yet you are halesome and fair to see.
Where gat you that joup o' the lily schene?
That bonny snood of the birk sae green?
And these roses, the fairest that ever were seen?
Kilmeny, Kilmeny, where have you been?

Kilmeny looked up with a lovely grace,
But nae smile was seen on Kilmeny's face;
As still was her look, and as still was her ee,
As the stillness that lay on the emerant lea,
Or the mist that sleeps on a waveless sea.
For Kilmeny had been she knew not where,
And Kilmeny had seen what she could not declare;
Kilmeny had been where the cock never crew,
Where the rain never fell, and the wind never blew;
But it seemed as the harp of the sky had rung,
And the airs of heaven played round her tongue,

When she spake of the lovely forms she had seen,
And a land where sin had never been;
A land of love, and a land of light,
Withouten sun, or moon, or night;
Where the river swa'd a living stream,
And the light a pure celestial beam:
The land of vision it would seem,
A still, and everlasting dream . . .
When seven lang years had come and fled;
When grief was calm, and hope was dead;
When scarce was remembered Kilmeny's name,
Late, late in a gloamin' Kilmeny came hame!

James Hogg
1770-1835

Loch Sween, Knapdale.

A Kiss of the King's Hand

It was na from a golden throne,
Or a bower with milk-white roses blown,
But mid the kelp on northern sand
that I got a kiss of the King's hand.

I durstna raise my een to see
If he even cared to glance at me;
His princely brow with care was crossed
For his true men slain and kingdom lost.

Think not his hand was soft and white,
Or his fingers a' with jewels dight,
Or round his wrists were ruffles grand
When I got a kiss of the King's hand.

But dearer far to my twa een
Was the ragged sleeve of red and green
O'er that young weary hand that fain,
With the guid broadsword, had found its ain.

Farewell for ever, the distance grey
And the lapping ocean seemed to say —
For him a home in a foreign land.
And for me one kiss of the King's hand.

Sarah Robertson Matheson
poem appeared 1894

Glenfinnan Monument, Loch Shiel.

Gin I was God

The Thistle Chapel, St Giles, Edinburgh.

Gin I was God, sittin' up there abeen,1
Weariet nae doot noo a' ma darg2 was deen,3
Deaved4 wie' the harps an' hymns oonendin' ringing,
Tired o' the flockin'angles hairse5 wi' singin',
To some clood-edge I'd daunder6 furth an', feth,
Look owner an' watch hoo things were gyaun7 aneth.8
Syne,9 gin10 I saw hoo men I'd made mysel'
Had startit in to pooshan,11 sheet12 an' fell,
To reive13 an' rape, and' fairly mak' a hell
O' my braw birlin' Earth, - a hale week's wark -
I'd cast my coat again, rowe up my sark,14
An', or they'd time to lench15 a second ark,
Tak' bak my word an' sen' anither spate,
Droon oot the hale hypothec,16 dicht17 the sklate,18
Own my mistak', an' aince I'd cleared the brod,19
Start a' thing ower20 again, gin I was God.

Charles Murray
1864-1941
1 above. 2 work. 3 done. 4 deafened. 5 hoarse. 6 wander.

7 going. 8 beneath. 9 then. 10 if, given.
11 poison. 12 shoot. 13 harry. 14 shirtsleeves. 15 launch. 16 thing. 17 wipe. 18 slate. 19 board. 20 over.

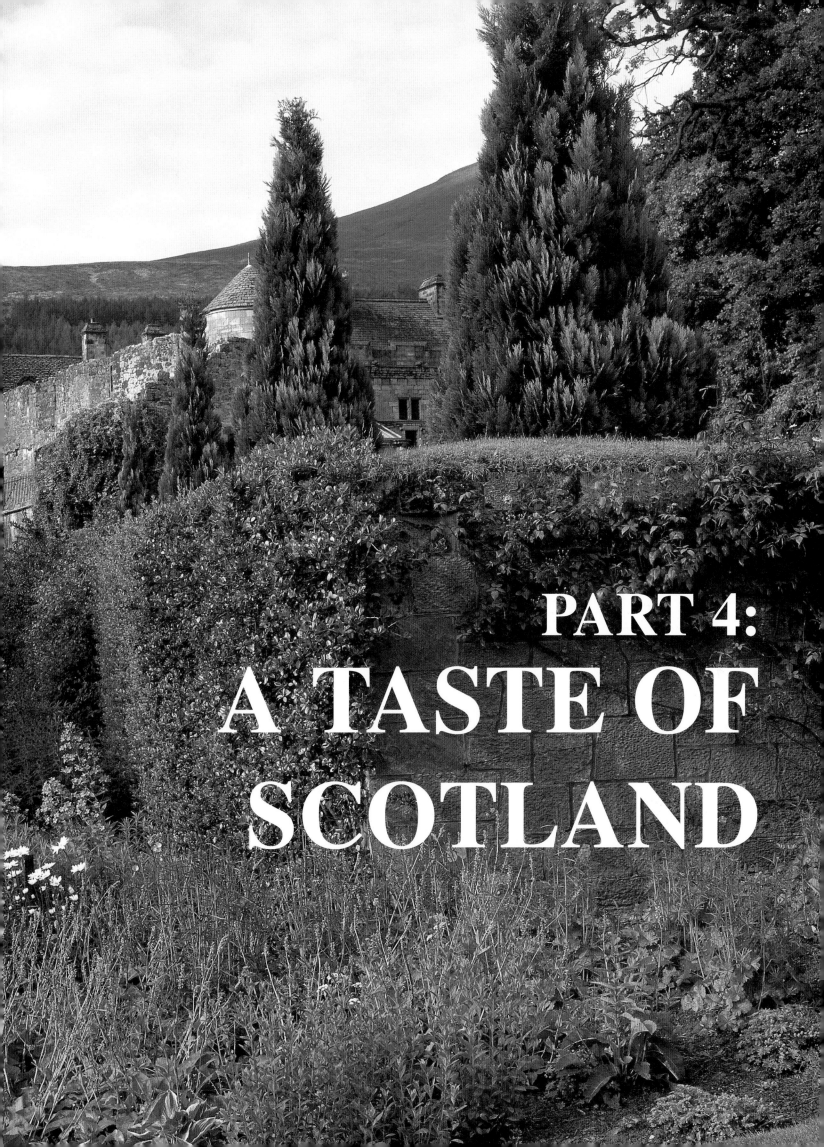

PART 4:
A TASTE OF SCOTLAND

22 Music and Festivals

Think of the music of Scotland and the sound of the bagpipes immediately springs to mind. It is impossible to be ambivalent about the 'skirl' of the pipes — you either love it or hate it. Personally the sound of a massed pipe band makes the hairs on the back of my neck stand up. On frequent holidays to Scotland as a small boy my uncles in Aberdeen used to take me to the Union Terrace Gardens where, on long summer evenings, there were invariably pipe bands marching and playing. To me, then, the thrill of watching and hearing the swaggering massed pipe bands of the Gordon Highlanders and the Seaforth Highlanders was incomparable. The sight of the proud pipe major hurling his mace skywards and the kettle drummers spinning and twirling their padded drum sticks, accompanied by the skirling pipes, was indeed wondrous to a young lad.

When, in Scottish history, the bagpipes replaced the harp as a call to arms is uncertain. What is not uncertain is that a bard twanging away while singing an exhortation in the frosty dawn to hundreds of Highland warriors — most of them out of earshot — had nothing of the effect of the skirl of the pipes shrieking through the glens. The courage of pipers in battle — who were inevitably a prime target — is legendary through the centuries. The sight and sounds of the Highland regiments, in their kilts and with their pipers, who fought in the First World War were so terrifying to the enemy in their opposing trenches that they nicknamed them the 'Ladies from Hell'. There are memorials all over Scotland to brave lone pipers. At the Haughs of Cromdale, near Grantown on Spey, there's the Piper's Stone onto which a badly wounded piper in the Jacobite army climbed and continued to play till he died, though the battle was lost. In the border country the Piper's Pool is still remembered where an intrepid piper played *Whurry Whigs Awa' Man*, to rally Montrose's troops in 1645, till a bullet knocked him into the Ettrick river, where he drowned.

In the 17th century the Highlander pipers reached classic peaks of beauty and power-achievement in pipe music. On the Isle of Skye, not far from Dunvegan Castle (still the seat of the Clan Macleod after 700 years) is Borreraig, where the famous MacCrimmon's School of Piping existed for 250 years and where the great pipers Donald Mor and Patrick Mor MacCrimmon transformed the rigid patterns of the piobaireachd, and raised it to new heights. The legendary MacCrimmons were hereditary pipers to the Macleod chiefs from 1500 to 1800 and their history and folklore is recorded in an excellent museum near the discernible ruins of the original college. The origins of this establishment can no doubt be historically authenticated but there is one fanciful story concerning a piping contest, called the Piper's Cave.

A legend tells of a colorful Macleod chieftain arranging a contest between the pipers of 11 other clan chieftains and his own brilliant player, a MacCrimmon. Macleod fully expected his man to 'blow the opposition away' but, on the day of the great competition, his champion reported sick with a severe respiratory problem. The furious Macleod declared that MacCrimmon's son should take his place. The lad considered himself only a moderate performer and, scared stiff he would make an ass of himself in front of the other accomplished pipers, he ran off and hid out on the castle battlements in tears.

Touched by the boy's cries of woe, a passing fairy sat down and listened to his sorry tale whereupon she offered him a tantalising choice; he could either be a bad piper and be widely acclaimed or be a great one who remained unknown. When he chose to be a great piper she handed him a silver chanter and told him he had every chance of winning the contest. The chanter was given to him on the condition that whenever she bade him he must obey the call. He returned to the hall and to everyone's surprise, including his own, he easily won the contest and this was the inspiration for the founding of the MacCrimmon's School of Piping.

One day, as the young piper was teaching at the school, the fairy appeared at his shoulder and bade him follow her. They walked along the shore, him playing his silver chanter, until they came upon what is known today as MacCrimmon's cave. He disappeared into the cave with the fairy and was never seen again. Various caves have been claimed as the one into which they disappeared but the new Piping Centre assert that the Piper's Cave at Borreraig is indeed the correct one. On the cliffs above the cave stands the beehive-shaped MacCrimmon Memorial which is the focal point of an annual pilgrimage of MacCrimmons to Skye.

Since the days of Sir Walter Scott, the Scots have liked to the remember their great romantic figures like Rob Roy or Bonnie Prince Charlie and historically, in self promotion, the Scots have always been their own worst enemy. Scott's historical novels enriched the world of literature but did the Scottish people a great harm and more recently they have only themselves to blame for their image. The Glasgow music halls, at the turn of this century with entertainers like Sir Harry Lauder and Will Fyffe, created the bizarre image of a Scotsman — the little man with a dram and a song, dressed in a kilt with a Lowlands shepherd's stick and canny to the point of meanness — which has stuck. In reality no indigenous Highlander would carry a Lowland shepherd's crook as he

Right: *The piping competition at the Glenfinnan Games. At some time in the past the bagpipes replaced the harp as the traditional Scottish call to arms. Since then the piper leads Scots into battle, his purpose is twofold: the skirl of the pipes is strong enough and loud enough to cut through the clamour of fighting; the pipes also make a terrifying sound which invariably unnerves the enemy.*

Previous page: *Still belonging to the crown, Falkland Palace in Fife was built between 1501 and 1541 as a royal palace for the Stewarts, and was the place where Mary Queen of Scots spent much time. The grounds contain the oldest Royal Tennis court in Britain, dating from 1539.*

would not want to associate himself with the animal that had displaced so many of his kith and kin in the notorious 'Clearances.'

The sad truth is the Scot's love this image and they still invent the best jokes about themselves as exemplified by the TV character Rab C. Nesbit today. Television was invented by the Scot, John Logie Baird, and the medium perpetuated the stereotypical Scot with programmes like the White Heather Club and the late Andy Stewart. Scottish country dancing, accompanied by the accordion band—both fairly recent inventions—have reduced the once proud culture of the Highlander to the level of the barn dance.

The most extraordinary expansion of any British custom must surely be the Highland Games with the kilts, pipes, feather bonnets and all the stereotypical trappings of the tourist trade's 'Bonnie Scotland'. Once confined to the Gaelic-speaking parts of the Highlands and, viewed elsewhere as an expression of the uncouth culture of a barbarian race, the phenomena spread inexorably southwards then world-wide. It started its migration early in the 19th century and first colonised the Lowlands and Borders, increasingly overshadowing their quite distinct customs and traditions. Tourists expect to see pipes and tartan the minute they cross the border and are rarely disappointed.

One of the first Highland games was the Braemar Gathering which was established in 1817 by officers and men who had fought at Waterloo. This probably would have taken a form unrecognisable to modern eyes although Putting the Stone, throwing the 56lb Weight, Throwing the Hammer — an iron ball on a chain; cross-country races and, of course, Tossing the Caber were included as competitive sports from the start and pipers from all over Scotland went to Braemar to contest their skills.

Tossing the caber had its origins in foresters heaving tree trunks across burns and streams. This event involves tossing a long and unwieldy pole (the Braemar Caber is 19ft long and weighs 120lbs) so that it revolves through a vertical semi-circle in as straight a line as possible: the direction of the 'toss' is therefore more important than the distance covered, and a perfectly tossed caber should lie in an exact '12 o'clock' line directly in front of the thrower, with its base facing directly away from him. Of the athletic events at all the Games easily the most demanding is the gruelling 13-mile marathon up and down the 4,406ft of Ben Nevis which takes part at the Fort William Games. The origins of this race, which has been held since 1899, lie in a wager made by a local Fort William hairdresser who bet that he could run to the top of the Ben and back without stopping.

The great popularity of Highland Games really dates from Queen Victoria's patronage which began in 1848, when the queen and her family for the first time attended the Braemar Gathering; this became an annual tradition and an occasion which the current royal family uphold today. At Braemar, as at most other large gatherings, the most spectacular event is the great opening march-past of kilted, bonneted clansmen wielding claymores, led by the local 'clan of the land' and preceded by a brave show of pipers. The games at Cowal in Argyllshire feature as many as a thousand pipers

Left: *Highland dancing at the Glenfinnan Games. There are now more than 70 annual games held in Scotland alone and Highland dancing is always one of the principal events.*

taking part in a hard fought contest to establish the finest solo piper. Highland dancing also features strongly at most Games with displays of the 'Gille Callum' — the Highland sword dance, the Highland Fling and the Sean Triuthas (Old Trousers), whose name is supposedly a scornful reference to the garments worn during the ban on the kilt after Culloden.

In Scotland more than 70 sets of Highland games are held annually, generally between June and mid-September, and though the majority take place in the Highlands they have become popular throughout the country penetrating even the Borders. Around the world there are some 5,000 Scottish societies where at least some of the 25 million people of Scottish extraction maintain the traditions of their forebears. At Grandfather Mountain at Linville, North Carolina, over a hundred Scottish clans have attended a Highland gathering each year since 1956. Most of the 15,000 who attend this event have been Americans for several generations, yet their displays of the tartan and their enthusiasm for Highland sport remains undiminished. The oldest Games in North America, established in 1861, are at Antigonish, Nova Scotia and are taken very seriously despite the fact that many of Nova Scotia's inhabitants have to go back six or seven generations to find ancestors born in Scotland.

Burns Night

Like the Highland Gatherings, Burns Night is celebrated all over the globe by expatriate Scots in their societies and clubs dedicated to the birth of their national poet on January 25, 1759. Whoever and wherever they are, be it in Delhi or Durban, Wellington or Washington, Scots will gather to hold their Burns supper and remember that lad born in Kyle over 200 years ago. The Burns supper does have its critics and certainly no one can deny that there is a great deal of gibberish spouted in 'Rabbie's' name at some of these events. The well-meaning disciples of this cult — for that is what it is — do, however, concur to 'Rabbie's' ideals to be happily content in a simple way. The essence of a good Burns Supper is the ability of the guests to behave informally and show the friendliness and 'guid' neighbourliness which 'Rabbie' himself seemed to carry with him permanently, and this alone renders much of the criticism churlish and ill-conceived. The undeniable fact is that Robert Burns is the only poet in the history of world literature who has been honoured in this strange and somewhat bizarre way.

The history of the Burns supper goes back to the poet's birthplace in Alloway where, five years after his death, nine of his friends gathered in a cottage to pay tribute to his memory. They continued to meet annually, usually in the summer, and it was not until 1809 that they referred to their meetings as a club. By now Burns's official biographer had established the correct date of the poet's birth and it was not long before the practice of meeting on this date was being observed throughout the country.

Today's Burns suppers are generally divided into three parts — the supper, the speeches and the songs. Tradition demands that the supper should be limited to homely cooking— 'hamerly farin' —a typical menu for a Burns supper is set out here with the traditional names. The bill of fare would not normally offer so many choices but they are included to show possible variations.

Besides listing the menu items, toasts, speakers, song and recitations the bill of fare is usually adorned with tributes in rhyme to special dishes or rhymed messages. The bill of fare may start with:

BILL O' FARE

HET KAIL
Cock-a-Leekie (soup made with fowl and leeks)
Feather Fowlie
Bawd Bree (hare soup)

CALLER FISH
Herrin Fillets (Fishwives style, fried in oatmeal)
Crabbie Claw (wind-dried codfish with
horseradish and egg sauce)
Boiled Turbot wi' Ou Sass

THE HAGGIS
Wi' champit Tatties, neeps and nips (champit means mashed) or
wi' Clapshot (potatoes and turnips mashed together with butter)

HET JOINTS
Roastit Bubblyjock wi' Cheston Crappin
(roast turkey with chestnut stuffing)
Wee Grumphie wi' Apple Purry (suckling pig with apple sauce)
Roastit Sirloin o' Aiberdeen-Angus Beef
Wi' Ayrshire Tatties, Champit an' Roastit, wee Sprouts

ITHER ORRA EATOCKS
Tipsy laird (trifle with generous alcoholic content)
Hattit Kit (Highland dish made from buttermilk, new milk,
sugar, and nutmeg)
Drambuie Cream
Scot's Trifle
Curds and Cream

RAREBIT
Finnan Toasties
Saft Herrin' Roes on toast
Kipper Creams
Highland Crowdie (type of home-made cheese)
wi' Bannocks (round oatcakes)
A Tassie o' Coffee

Happy we be a' the gither; happy we be ane and a'
Time shall see us a' the blither ere we rise to gang awa'.

After Cock-a-Leekie, the soup course may follow:

God bless your Honours, a' your days,
Wi' sowps o' kail an' brats o claes.

Then before the entry of the haggis:

Wheesht! Here it comes!
And on our boards the king o' foods,
A guid Scot's haggis.

The grace at the beginning of the meal is traditionally the Selkirk Grace which was used by Rabbie himself at a dinner given in his honour by the Earl of Selkirk and Kirkcudbright:

Some hae meat, and canna eat,
And some wad eat that want it;
But we hae meat and we can eat,
And sae the Lord be thankit.

The supper is then usually brought to an end with:

O Lord, since we hae feated thus
Which we sae little merit
Let Meg noo tak awa' the flesh
And Jock bring in the Spirit!

'The king o' foods', the haggis, is the most important part of the bill of fare and usually enters the room with great ceremony. Purists don't employ a piper, but it is now usual for the haggis to be piped into the dining room borne aloft by the chef, who marches behind the piper, accompanied by one or more waiters carrying a bottle of whisky and glasses. The pipes will begin before the haggis enters the room and that is the signal for the chairman and guests to stand. The procession with the steaming pudding goes around the room and comes to a halt by the chairman. The piper then stands to the chairman's right with the chef opposite, and the waiters, who have placed the bottle and glasses in front of the chairman, take up a position on his left. The glasses are charged and the chairman calls upon one of his guests to give the 'Address to the Haggis'.

If the guest speaker is particularly good the whole address might be given, but it is quite usual for it to be shortened to a couple or so verses, the opening verse, verse three and the last verse are perfectly adequate. At the words in the third verse 'An' cut you up wi' ready slight, Trenching your gushing entrails bright', the speaker — often accompanied by fierce grimacing and growling — stabs the 'chieftain' with his Sgian Dubh (black knife — dirk). It is advisable not to get too enthusiastic in the attack, which is usually restricted to making a St. Andrew's Cross-shaped incision in the 'paunch' and turning back the flaps.

The haggis was regarded for many years as an uncivilized dish for the uncivilized Scots by 'foreigners' who 'Look down wi' sneering, scornfu' view on sic a dinner' but has, today, become something for the connoisseur and gourmet.

Address to the Haggis

Fair fa' your honest, sonsie [1] face,
Great chieftain o' the puddin' race!
Aboon them a' ye tak' your place,
Painch, tripe, or thairm [2]:
Weel are ye wordy of a grace
As lang's my arm.

The groaning trencher there ye fill,
Your hurdies like a distant hill,
Your pin [3] wad help to mend a mill
In time o' need,
While through your pores the dews distil
Like amber bead.

His knife see rustic Labour dight [4],
An' cut you up wi' ready slight,

Trenching your gushing entrails bright,
Like onie ditch;
And then, oh, what a glorious sight,
Warm-reekin', rich.
Then horn for horn they stretch an' strive,
De'il tak' the hindmost! on they drive,
Till a' their weel swalled kytes [5] belyve [6]
Are bent like drums
Then auld guidman, maist like to ryve [7],
Bethankit hums.

Is there that o'er his French ragoût
Or olio that wad staw a sow,
Or fricassée wad mak her spew
Wi' perfect sconner [8],
Looks down wi' sneering, scornfu' view
On sic a dinner?

Poor devil! see him owre his trash,
As feckless [9] as a withered rash [10],
His spindle-shank a guid whip-lash,
His nieve [11] a nit;
Through bloody flood or field to dash,
Oh, how unfit!

But mark the rustic, haggis-fed,
The trembling earth resounds his tread,
Clap in his walie nieve [12] a blade,
He'll mak' it whissle;
An' legs, an' arms, an' heads will sned [13],
Like taps o' thristle [14].

Ye powers, wha' mak' mankind you care,
And dish them out their bill o' fare,
Auld Scotland wants nae skinking ware [15]
That jaups in luggies [16];
But, if ye wish her gratefu' prayer,
Gi'er her a Haggis!

Key
[1] jolly: [2] small intestines: [3] skewer: [4] wipe: [5] stomachs: [6] by and by: [7] burst: [8] loathing: [9] pithless: [10] rush: [11] fist: [12 large fist: [13] cut off: [14] tops of thistles: [15] thin stuff: [16] that splashes in bowls:

Recipe and Preparation of the Haggis
There are a number of recipes for haggis, all basically the same, but this is a very traditional one, in fact, my mother's!:

The Haggis
The large stomach bag of a sheep, the pluck (including heart, lights, and liver)
½lb fresh beef suet
1 breakfast cup coarse (pinhead) oatmeal
2 or 3 onions
salt and black pepper
pinch of cayenne pepper
1 breakfast cup stock or gravy

Method

Preparation of the bag

Brown and birstle (dry or toast) a breakfast cupful of oatmeal before the fire or in the oven. Clean the stomach bag thoroughly, washing it first in cold water and then, after turning it inside out, scald and scrap it with a knife; then let it soak overnight in cold, salted water and in the morning put it aside with the rough side turned out. Wash the pluck well and put it on to boil covered with cold water, letting the windpipe hang over the side of the pot to let out any impurities. Let it boil for a 1½ hours, then take it out and cut away the pipes and any superfluous gristle.

The stuffing

Mince the lights and heart and grate half the liver. Put them into a basin with ¼lb of minced suet, two medium sized onions finely chopped, and the toasted oatmeal, and season highly with black pepper, salt, and a pinch of cayenne pepper. Pour in, when cold, as much of the liquid in which the pluck was boiled (or better still good stock) as will make the mixture sappy.

Filling and boiling the haggis

Fill the stomach bag rather more than half full as it requires plenty of room to swell. Sew it up securely and place it on an enamel plate in a pot of boiling water to which half a pint of milk should be added, or better still boil it in stock. As soon as it begins to swell, prick it all over with a large needle to prevent it from bursting. Boil steadily without the lid, for three hours, adding boiling water as necessary to keep the haggis covered. Serve very hot.

Burns Supper Toasts

The toasts at the supper may vary to fit the occasion but generally include the 'Immortal Memory', the 'Lasses', and the 'Guests' with the appropriate replies. The 'Immortal Memory' is given by the principal speaker and, depending on the individual, this can be short and to the point, or it may drag on if the speaker has a particular bee in his bonnet. The bard must be mentioned of course, and the speech winds up with a toast to the 'Immortal Memory of Robert Burns.'

The second most important toast is the one to the 'Lasses'. This will usually involve a certain amount of poking fun at the opposite gender from the person who gives the toast and, even more so, from the lassie who replies. The traditional toast ends with this tribute:

Eve's bonnie squad priests wyte them sheerly,
For our grand fa'
But still, but still, I like them dearly,
God bless them a'!
Gentlemen, I give you — The Lassies.

If the haggis was piped into the room, it is normal to have a little ceremony and toast by way of a thank you to the piper. The piper pipes himself round the room coming to a halt in front of the chairman, who expresses his appreciation. He pours a stiff dram into a silver quaich which he presents to the piper. The piper lifts the double-handled cup to his lips, quaffs the whisky, turns to the audience and, reversing the quaich, kisses its base to show that it is empty.

Hogmanay

The greatest annual festival in Scotland, celebrated more than Christmas, is the welcoming of the New Year — Hogmanay. The origins of the word Hogmanay are unclear though it has variously been derived from the Anglo-Saxon *Haleg Monath* (Holy Month), the Gaelic *Oge Maidne* (new morning) and, less likely, the French *Au Gui Mener* (lead to the mistletoe). The Scottish importance of Hogmany was partly gained at the expense of Christmas celebrations which were suppressed as 'Popish and superstitious' by the Kirk. The result was that these mid-winter festivities assumed a more secular and in some ways pagan character.

The New Year festivities in Scotland are much wilder and more communal than those of Christmas with vast public gatherings, notably at Edinburgh's Tron Kirk and Glasgow's George Square, greeting the New Year with the linked-arm singing of Robbie Burns's 'Auld Lang Syne'. Total strangers are kissed and hugged like long-lost friends to a cacophonous background of car horns and all manner of noise-making instruments. The churches toll out the Old with muffled bells and, at midnight, the muffles are removed and the New is rung in with joyous peals.

These celebrations are held in earnest with the firmly-held belief that the coming year must begin happily and optimistically with a clean break from the past. New Year resolutions which are made to establish a fresh start, are usually the result of excess during the festivities and traditionally don't last much longer than the recovery period. The general custom of giving and receiving New Year's gifts has now declined and the giving of 'hogmanays' to 'New Year's gifting' children survived until very recently. It is very important that the first visitor to your house in the New Year should be a propitious one and throughout Scotland, midnight on December 31, finds 'first footers' poised to bring New Year luck. Tall dark strangers are considered the best guests and a high instep "that water will run under" is particularly desirable. An empty-handed visitor is a terrible sign of bad luck and they will be suspected of deliberately bringing misfortune to the house.

The traditional gifts of the 'first footer' are a piece of coal (for warming the house), a loaf or black bun and a bottle of whisky. On entering he must put the coal on the fire, place the loaf on the table, and pour a glass of whisky for the head of the house. This is all done in silence until he wishes everyone a 'Happy New Year'. He must enter the house by the front door and leave by the rear — New Year is let in the front and the Old leaves by the back.

Should auld acquaintance be forgot
And never brought to min'?
Should auld acquaintance be forgot,
And days o' lang syne?

CHORUS

For auld lang syne, my dear,
For auld lang syne,
We'll tak' a cup o' kindness yet,
For Auld lang syne?

(NB: Not a "for the sake of" in sight!)

23 Water of Life - Scotch Whisky

Scotland's single malts have for too long been eclipsed by their more heavily marketed cousins, the blended whiskies. I am very partial to a Famous Grouse, a J&B or a Chivas Regal; in fact, I find the entire world of whiskies a fascinating and enjoyable subject.

Scotland has a unique geography and climate, ideally suited to whisky making; pretenders to the throne have tried to replicate her product but failed. The Japanese distillers eventually adopted an "if you can't match them, buy them" philosophy to Scottish distilleries when their own attempts fell short of expectations.

What makes single malts so special? Three words come to mind — quality, personality, and diversity — and a fuller story emerges as you experience each new style. Single malts have individuality; each has its own unique presence and is uncannily good at reflecting the environment in which it was distilled and matured. These factors, and the diversity of available flavors, make malt drinking immensely pleasurable.

Just as each malt tastes different, each distillery set up is different. Most have an exclusive water source; their owners have individual preferences for the type of barley they buy and the amount of peat smoke they allow to infuse the grain. But the most profound influence, determining the body and soul of a malt whisky, is the size and shape of the pot stills used to make it. As a rule, small stills give heavier, oily spirit and the larger types give lighter results.

MALT IN THE MAKING

Early illicit distillers who used crude, concealable stills or 'black pots' would wonder at the sophistication of modern techniques and machinery. Yet the principles of whisky-making have changed little, and many features of today's distilleries betray more primitive origins.

Malting

Barley is steeped in bins for around three days before being spread on a malting floor. The grain is turned either by hand or mechanically to maintain an even temperature which promotes germination and the release of natural sugars. Next the barley is kiln-dried to prevent over-germination. It is spread out on a mesh platform under which a peat fire burns, and smoke is allowed to permeate the grains to a specified degree. The resulting intensity of "peat reek" can be detected in the finished whisky.

Mashing

The malted barley is milled, the resulting 'grist' mixed with water in a mash tun (large tank), and stirred until the sugars break down to produce a sweet liquid called 'wort'.

Fermentation

Wort is transferred into washbacks (cylindrical tanks with lids) and

Above: *Casks maturing at Bunnahabhain Distillery.*

Right: *Ardbeg is a strongly peat-flavoured whisky from Islay.*

yeast is added as a catalyst to trigger fermentation. Some hours later, a light beer called 'wash' results.

Distillation

Wash is 'cleaned up' in the first (wash) still to produce stronger 'low wines', which are collected and passed through the spirit still for further refinement. The heated stills cause their liquid contents to vaporize upwards to the swan-shaped neck where condensation occurs, and spirit is drawn off. There are normally two stills working in tandem, and when they reach optimum temperature the best spirit is produced.

The stillman decides at which point the required spirit is flowing, and diverts it by remote means through a spirit safe to cask (only the exciseman has direct access to the spirit via padlock and key!). The unwanted first and last cuts of each run ('foreshots' and 'feints') are separated and returned to the wash still for reprocessing.

Maturation

After three years—warehoused in oak cask—the spirit can official-

ly be called Scotch whisky. Each cask differently flavors its contents: it may previously have held bourbon or sherry for example, and as it sleeps the spirit breathes surrounding air losing some volume and strength. This percentage is the "angels' share." Malts average 12 years in wood before they are considered mature enough to bottle.

THE PRODUCING REGIONS

Some regions have a recognizable style, but it is unwise to over-generalize for there are frequent exceptions.

Lowlands

Despite associations with grain whisky, this region retains a handful of singles, separated from their Highland cousins by an imaginary line which runs from Clydeside north-eastwards to Dundee. Lowland malts are light and dry compared to others, and can be enjoyed as aperitifs.

Southern Highlands

Fuller, mostly sweeter than Lowlanders, yet by no means the biggest Highlanders. Distilleries are easily reached from Glasgow and Edinburgh; a trail which takes in the beauty of Loch Lomond, the Trossachs and Perthshire.

Western Highlands

This area has only two surviving distilleries. The town of Oban is the gateway to the Western Isles and its distillery sits in the high street. Ben Nevis, which lies in the shadow of its famous namesake-mountain, is Japanese-owned and is Fort William's only remaining distillery.

Speyside

Scotland's "Golden Triangle" of concentrated production: Speyside's salmon rivers are lined by a host of famous distilleries—Glenlivet, Glenfiddich, and Macallan, to name just three of its legendary malts. The demand for The Glenlivet malt was such that several surrounding distillers adopted its name as a suffix to their own, though some are now confident enough of their whiskies to have discontinued this practice. Some outlying distilleries, which spread northward to Elgin or eastward to Keith and beyond, are included as Speysiders. The malts are capable of great subtlety and complexity, sometimes spicy, sweet and floral with restrained smoke.

Eastern Highlands

A scattering of distilleries lie to the south-east of Speyside and up the North Sea coast from Montrose to Banff. These East Highland malts include some great after-dinner drams, although there is no particular regional style.

Northern Highlands

A good tank of fuel and an abstemious driver would be helpful if you wish to enjoy the hospitality of these far-flung distilleries. The area stretches from Dalwhinnie in Strathspey, northward past Inverness, taking in amongst others the famous Glenmorangie distillery at Tain. The trail ends at Wick, where the mainland's most northerly malt, Old Pulteney, is produced. A wide variety of styles can be tried including some salty coastal examples.

Islands

There are five producing islands—not including Islay which has earned its own appellation. Arran has a new set-up at Lochranza and the whisky already promises to be good. Jura lies just north of Islay: its malt is light for an Islander. Mull and Skye each have a distillery, and even the remote Orkneys have a distilling heritage. Highland Park at Kirkwall is one of the greats and readily available, whereas. Scapa is now closed and harder to find in bottle. The Islanders fall between Highland and Islay in style.

Islay

Islay stands apart from other regions—its whiskies are much peatier in style, and because the distilleries all have coastal locations, there is an inbuilt marine quality about them. Seven distilleries are able to produce, there would be eight, but for the closure of Port Ellen in 1984. It is now a malting center, supplementing the requirements of other distilleries.

The south-shore malts are fuller-peated, medicinal and intense. The legendary Laphroaigs, Lagavulins and Ardbegs can be too much for some palates, so for a gentler introduction try Bunnahabhain or Bowmore.

Campbeltown

Campbeltown is situated on Scotland's famous south-western peninsula, the Mull of Kintyre. It was once an important hub of distilling with over 30 operations, but reputations suffered when some producers cut quality to satisfy high demand and many closures followed. Only two distilleries still survive to keep the flag flying.

TUNING IN TO SINGLE MALTS

I enjoy my dram most at the end of a hard day when the armchair beckons and, with glass in hand, I close my eyes and sip. Naturally, we all have our own rituals and occasions when a glass simply hits the spot. There is, however, a more analytical approach to appreciating the complexities of malt whisky and although you may not always wish to be thinking while drinking, it is useful to learn the method and can be great fun.

Our senses of smell and taste combine to tell us much about single malts. The taste buds perceive salt, sweet, bitter and sour flavors but our olfactory or nasal senses are more highly developed and capable of identifying over 30 primary aromas.

There exists, in addition to the single malt whisky, a single-single variety which is not only the product of one distillery, but has been selected from an individual cask. These are often bottled at "cask strength," and it is not unusual to find examples in excess of 57 percent alcohol, leaving the consumer to dilute the whisky to a preferred drinking strength.

Nosing and Tasting Procedure

Step 1: Use your eyes. Assess the color of the whisky. Is it light or dark? If dark, it may be sherried, or could be more mature than an average aged malt. Swirl the malt around a bit, and look for 'legs' — these appear like tears on the side of the glass. A malt which has good legs will be oilier in body.

Step 2: Nose the whisky lightly to ascertain the more prominent aromas. Add a little water and try again. The water should kill some alcohol and unlock the whisky's aromatics: it should now be easier to identify compounds and background nuances should show through.

Step 3: Take a mouthful. Different parts of the mouth detect different flavors so coat the whole mouth before swallowing. Try to evaluate the   initial flavors, the mouth-feel of the whisky, and finally, assess the finish—is it long, short, dry, sweet, and so on, and which other flavors accompany it?

Some Do's and Don'ts

- Do use a fluted glass, preferably tulip-shaped so that the aromatics or "volatiles" can be concentrated around the nose.
- Do add good quality spring water (still) but reduce the whisky carefully so as not to drown it. Some sherried whiskies cannot take much water. Avoid using tap water which is hard or heavily treated with chlorine/fluoride.
- Do drink water between whiskies to refresh the palate.
- Don't add ice to malt whisky. This will destroy the aromatics.
- Don't sniff the whisky repeatedly. Your sense of smell will soon anaesthetize, especially with high proof malts, and furthermore, it can be unpleasant.
- Don't be afraid of tasting jargon: we are all different—we perceive things differently and express things differently.

Over the next few pages are the stories behind the best known of the single malts, whiskies of character and a depth of taste that have gained a steadfast and loyal following.

Key to map - opposite

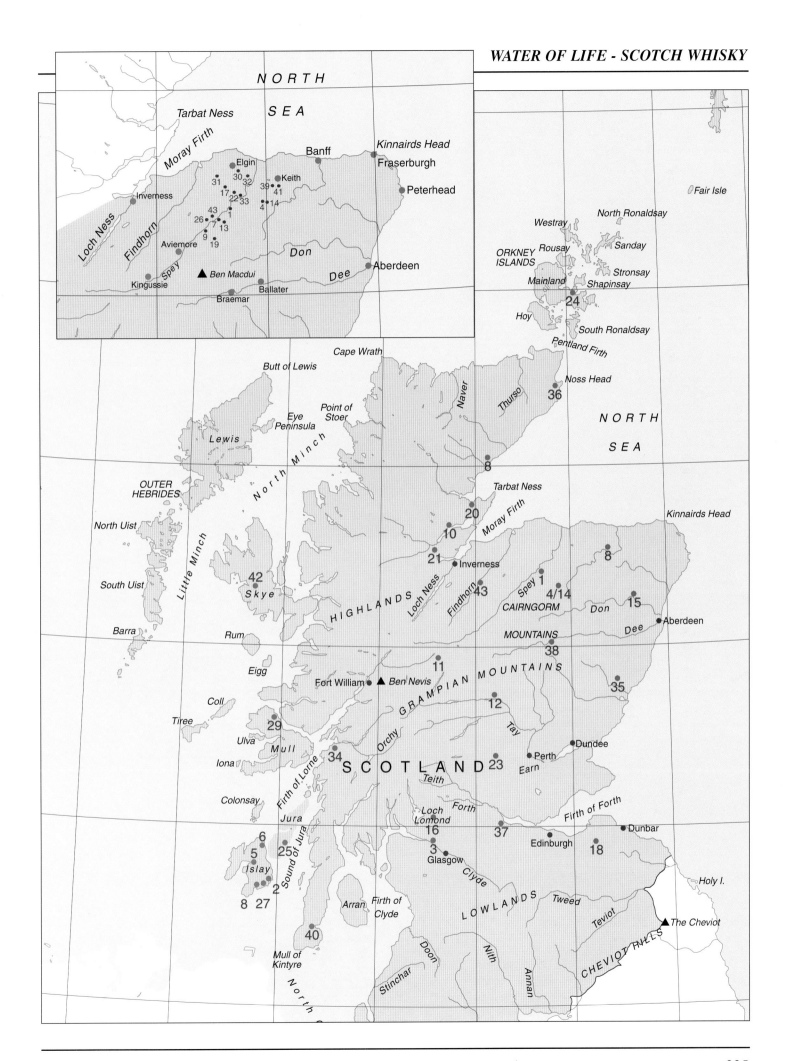

Aberlour

Region: Speyside
Owners: Campbell Distillers Ltd.

Aberlour is a whisky with a "French Connection," for it is owned by the giant Pernod Ricard Group. The brand is extremely popular in France and rates in the top ten selling malts worldwide.

The first distillery at Aberlour appeared in 1826 but was destroyed by fire and most of today's Victorian structure results from rebuilding in 1880. There have been further additions and modernization this century, and a major refit was undertaken in the 1970s when the current owners acquired it.

There is a well in the grounds where St. Dunstan is said to have held baptisms. Unfortunately its holy water is not abundant enough for modern distilling requirements, and springs on the slopes of nearby Ben Rinnes are now put to use.

Aberlour malt is a regular award winner, its style is such that it is considered one of the great all-rounder whiskies. Maturation takes place in a mixture of bourbon and sherry casks.

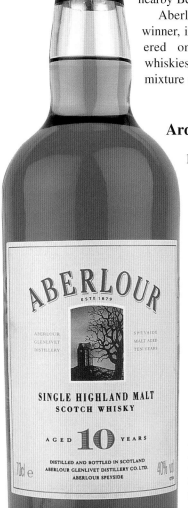
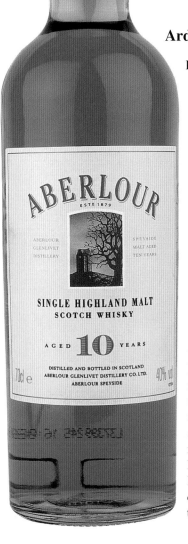

Ardbeg

Region: Islay
Owners: Glenmorangie Plc

Ardbeg is not a whisky for the unwary. This is one of Islay's emphatic south-shore malts and is legendary to those who have come to crave Scotland's big peat-flavored drams. Maturation in proximity to the sea adds a salty-seaweedy element to this very complex spirit. The distillery is remotely situated on a rocky stretch of coastline which was once the domain of smugglers.

Ardbeg has proved popular with blenders and was owned until recently by Allied Distillers who preferred to invest money in Laphroaig, their more famous operation nearby. As a result, production at Ardbeg has been sporadic in recent years and the buildings have a neglected and haunted look, sad to see when you consider its heritage dates from the early 1800s.

The new owners, McDonald & Muir, (who also own Glenmorangie) announced in 1997 that they were going to put things right and there is even talk of restoring the traditional maltings, which once supplied the distillery with its own strongly peated barley.

A 17-year old bottling was recently launched, complemented by a limited vintage release which is heavier in style.

Auchentoshan

Region: Lowland
Owners: Morrison-Bowmore Distillers Ltd.

Auchentoshan is one of only two working distilleries in the Scottish Lowlands and is currently the only one which continues to triple-distil its whisky—once a common practice in the region.

The distillery sits on the north bank of the River Clyde near the Erskine Bridge, just a few miles downstream from Glasgow. Despite being classically Lowland in style, the whisky is made with Highland water, drawn from the Kilpatrick Hills to the north.

Records show that Auchentoshan (from old Scots, meaning "corner of the field") was founded in the early 1800s, just as Glasgow prepared for its Victorian transformation and the growth of its shipyards. The Clyde was once the world's foremost waterway and past workers at Auchentoshan could have witnessed the maiden voyages of many famous ships as they sailed down from Govan. These same shipyards were targeted heavily by German bombers during World War II, unfortunately Auchentoshan was on the flight path, and suffered badly as a consequence.

Suntory the giant Japanese distillers now own the distillery whose whisky is pleasantly light in style.

Balvenie

Region: Speyside
Owners: Wm. Grant & Sons Ltd

Balvenie dates from 1892 and was the third distillery to be built in Dufftown; four more followed quickly and a local rhyme declares that "Rome was built on seven hills, Dufftown was built on seven stills."

William Grant resigned his position as manager at nearby Mortlach to start his own concern, which he named Glenfiddich; five years later he built Balvenie on adjoining farmland. His direct descendants still own both distilleries and much tradition has been maintained in the manufacture of their whiskies.

Balvenie was used primarily in the family's famous blends, and was not released as a single malt until 1973. It is fuller and richer than Glenfiddich although it shares water from the Robbie Dubh Spring along with coopering and coppersmithing facilities.

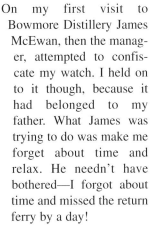

Balvenie has its own traditional floor maltings and exchanges a proportion of its grain in order to use Glenfiddich's in-house bottling services. The majority of casks used are ex-bourbon fills, and a proportion of sherrywood is used for finishing purposes. There are currently four pairs of stills in situ, which are heated by steam.

Bowmore Islay

Region: Islay
Owners: Morrison-Bowmore
Distillers Part of Suntory

On my first visit to Bowmore Distillery James McEwan, then the manager, attempted to confiscate my watch. I held on to it though, because it had belonged to my father. What James was trying to do was make me forget about time and relax. He needn't have bothered—I forgot about time and missed the return ferry by a day!

Islay is a pace or two behind the mainland, in fact the only thing which runs fast is the spirit off the stills. Bowmore is the island's capital and has a distinctive round church at the top of the main drag. It was constructed in such a fashion so that the devil had no corner to hide in. At the bottom of the town near the harbor lies Bowmore Distillery which is one of Scotland's oldest (1779). This is an excellent place to visit if you want to see how whisky is made in keeping with tradition.

Bowmore's malt is not the heaviest-peated of all the Islays; it is middle-weight and approachable to novice drinkers. Bourbon and sherry maturation is preferred, although there have recently been some limited edition "Black Bowmores" of rich, mature sherry character and huge complexity. These are now scarce and expensive.

Bunnahabhain

Region: Islay
Owners: Highland Distilleries Co. Plc

Bunnahabhain (pronounced Boonahavan) is Islay's most secluded distillery. The name translates from the Gaelic to "Mouth of the River," referring to the Margadale which enters the Sound of Islay nearby. The distillery water is drawn from streams in the hills behind, whence there is a spectacular view over the Isle of Jura and its famous mountains—"The Paps"—so named because they are said to resemble breasts.

The central buildings of Bunnahabhain form a courtyard. The distillery dates from 1883 when the Victorian whisky boom was in full swing, and the local landowners seized the opportunity to put their barley to lucrative use. Highland Distilleries have owned the operation since 1887 and the whisky is used in The Famous Grouse, their leading blend.

Bunnahabhain is light for an Islay, but still has peaty and salty traces, although latter-day bottlings were fuller, more distinctly Islay. Bourbon and sherry casks are used for maturation and there are two sets of large onion-shaped stills functioning.

Cardhu

Region: Speyside
Owners: United Distillers

I have tried to resist buying a bottle of Cardhu on occasions for I know it will "evaporate" very quickly in my house—nothing to do with central heating—it is just such an approachable whisky which slides down with impeccable manners.

The distillery occupies a site on the slopes of the Mannoch Hill, not far from Aberlour, and has an intriguing history, which predates its official licensing in 1824. John Cummings, a local farmer, took a lease on land surrounding Cardhu in 1811; he then set about making illicit whisky with the help of his wife, Helen, who acted as a look-out should the exciseman come snooping. Once legitimate, Cardhu grew to be highly regarded and eventually passed into the hands of Johnnie Walker and Sons, of whose blends it has long been a key ingredient.

The Cardhu single malt (sometimes known previously as Cardow), is now a leading brand for United Distillers and is widely available. The distillery is picturesque with traditional pagoda roofs and a dam alongside. There are three sets of stills in situ.

Clynelish

Region: Northern Highland
Owners: United Distillers

The town of Brora is situated on the eastern coast of Sutherland, a county which is often referred to as "Britain's last great wilderness." Brora's first distillery appeared in 1819 when the Marquis of Stafford (later to become Duke of Sutherland) built the Clynelish operation, drawing its water from the nearby Clynemilton Burn. In the 1960s a modern distillery was constructed across the road from Clynelish (pronounced Cline-Leesh). The new complex took the Clynelish name, the original became Brora Distillery and continued to produce alongside until fairly recently. Although the original set-up produced a heavier-peated whisky, there are similarities between the two styles, notably a pronounced coastal salt flavor which is unusually heavy for the region.

Clynelish (in either guise) is highly regarded as a connoisseurs' dram, often mistaken for an Islander, but distinctive in its own way. There are six sets of stills at the modern operation, and the old distillery is being considered for use as a museum in the future.

Cragganmore

Region: Speyside
Owners: United Distillers

Cragganmore features as one of United Distillers "Classic Six" malt range, representing the Speyside style with great panache. The label on each bottle depicts a steam train puffing its way from the distillery—recollecting the railroad which once carried casks off along the banks of the River Spey.

The founder of Cragganmore (in 1869), John Smith, was a large character (weighing about 300lb.) who had deep associations with distilling. His resumé was already impressive by the time he came to Cragganmore and his father (or so it is believed), George Smith, owned The Glenlivet Distillery just five miles away. The Cragganmore Distillery is thought to have been the first to be positioned to take advantage of the railroad and Smith made full use of the facility by building his own sidings. It is said that he was a great railway buff, although his bulk excluded him from using the carriages and he had to slum it in the guards van!

There are two sets of stills at Cragganmore, which have an unusual flat-topped appearance and it is thought that this helps bring about a lightness in the whisky. The malt is associated with White Horse blends and is a component of McCallum's bblended whisky which is prominent in Australasia.

Dalmore

Region: Northern Highland
Owners: Whyte & Mackay Group Plc

Dalmore is situated on a gentle stretch of shoreline on the Cromarty Firth, facing across the water to the Black Isle. The surrounding countryside is of rolling hills, woodland, charming Highland villages, and the nearby town of Alness, which gives its name to the river from which the distillery takes water. Dalmore Distillery was built in 1839 on farmland bought by Alexander Matheson, a wealthy tea and opium trader, and was let to the Mackenzie family who were his tenants. Eventually the Mackenzies were able to buy the distillery and retained ownership until 1960 when they joined forces with Whyte & Mackay. The stag's head, which appears on the Dalmore label, is the badge of the Mackenzie Clan and is a reminder of the malt's heritage.

The distillery is equipped with eight stills, four dating from 1966 when much work was carried out, and the spirit stills are cooled by rather unusual water jackets. Maturation is mainly in bourbon wood, although everything is vatted into sherry butts for finishing.

Dalwhinnie

Regional: Northern Highland
Owners: United Distillers

Dalwhinnie is not the sort of place you want to break down in winter: the wind howls, the roads are often blocked with snow, and the air is too pure for my London lungs. To get there, leave the A9, Perth to Inverness road, and climb up into the Grampian Mountains. By the Pass of Drumochter you will eventually reach a little transport café which once provided me with a good plate of sausage, egg, and chips. Just across the road lies Dalwhinnie

distillery, where I could have sampled an excellent aperitif malt whisky if the cooking smells had not got to me first. I tried a dram anyway. At over 1,000ft. above sea level this is one of Scotland's highest distilleries and the purity of air and water seem to translate into the whisky itself. The distillery was originally christened Strathspey; its modern name means "meeting place" in Gaelic, making reference to historical associations with the cattle drovers who would camp here before moving onto the lower market towns.

The blending firm Buchanan's has used Dalwhinnie malt over the years in its Black & White brand, although the single malt is now part of United Distillers' heavily promoted classic malts portfolio, and is deservedly reaching a larger audience. The distillery output is quite small as there is only a single set of stills in use.

The Edradour

Region: Southern Highland
Owners: Campbell Distillers Ltd.

Edradour and its big sister Aberlour (Speyside—see page 226) are French-owned by the giant drinks group Pernod Ricard. However, when you visit Edradour there is little evidence of global marketing. This distillery is Scotland's smallest, employing just three people at the last count, and it is a must to visit if you wish to see whisky being made in the original cottage craft fashion.

Distilling began in 1825 and there have been very few alterations to the formula in Edradour's history. The stills employed are the smallest the law permits. It is said that smaller stills are too easily concealed and might encourage some illicit DIY. The size of her stills, and the fact that there are but two, results in extremely limited output, just a dozen casks a week at Edradour, or about one-fiftieth of average annual output elsewhere.

Most of the malt is now bottled as a single and a little finds its way into Campbell Distillers' blends. Sherry casks are filled for maturation, the olorosse type being preferred, but the flavor does not overwhelm the whisky.

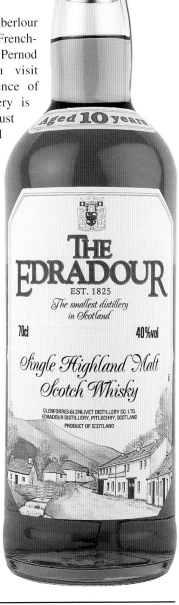

Glenfarclas

Region: Speyside
Owner: J. & G. Grant Ltd.

Glenfarclas is one of Scotland's "Rolls-Royce" malt whiskies and, fittingly enough, it is a regular stop-off for vintage car rallies. It is owned and operated by the Grant family, the present managing director, being John Grant, the great-great-grandson of his name-sake, who bought the distillery in 1865. The distillery was leased to John Smith (of Cragganmore fame) for five years until the Grant Association began properly in 1870.

Glenfarclas has the largest stills in Speyside, and for most of its long history made do with one set. Water for the distillery runs down from springs on the slopes of mighty Benrinnes, and its purity has much to do with the whisky's excellence. Much modernization has occurred in recent years, there now being six stills—two were added in 1960, two more in 1976—and all are exact replicas of the originals. The stills are gas-fired which is unusual today.

Glenfarclas single malt is available in a range of ages, with my personal favorite being the robust 15-year old, but having said that, I have never turned down a glass of any age or strength.

Glenfiddich

Region: Speyside
Owner: Wm. Grant & Sons Ltd.

Glenfiddich has won many friends since it became available as a single malt in the 1960s. Its owners, Wm. Grant & Sons, were the first to seriously attack the established blended whisky market, aiming their product at the de luxe sector. The brand has a unique position—able to mix with leading blends and yet respected as a malt by even experienced drinkers. Glenfiddich has a light style, which suits many palates and is regarded as a good introduction to single malts. I was once fortunate enough to try a 50-year old Glenfiddich and, I must admit, I found it an excellent introduction to 50-year olds.

Glenfiddich is a large distillery with 28 stills and its visitors can observe every function of whisky making, from barley to bottling. The first spirit ran from Glenfiddich's stills way back on Christmas Day 1887, after the founder, William Grant, had rescued much of the distilling apparatus from the newly refitted Cardhu Distillery. Grant soon found ready markets for his whisky, but was dealt a blow when his best customers, the Pattison Blending Company, failed in 1898. A determined individual, he nevertheless launched his own "Standfast" blend which helped to secure the success and independence of the family company to this day.

Glen Garioch

Region: Eastern Highland
Owner: Morrison-Bowmore Distillers Ltd.

Glen Garioch (pronounced Glen Geery) was founded 200 years ago. It is situated near the village of Old Meldrum, some 20 miles north-west of Aberdeen, in an area of rich farmland which is sometimes called "The Granary of Aberdeenshire." Just 10 miles from Glen Garioch lies the Pitsligo Moss from which the distillery cuts its peat. Glen Garioch operates its own maltings and peat-smoke is very evident in the whisky. Despite abundant peat and barley, the distillery once had a shortage of water, prompting The Distillers Company Ltd., (who acquired the operation in 1937) to close it in 1968. Two years later, however, Glasgow merchants Stanley P. Morrison bought Glen Garioch and created a fresh water supply by sinking a deep well in a near-by field.

The two-still set-up has now been increased to four, although the distillery is presently mothballed. Glen Garioch has two sisters— Auchentoshan (see page 226) and Bowmore (see page 227)—all three are now owned by a subsidiary of Suntory, the Japanese distilling giant.

Glengoyne

Region: Southern Highland
Owners: Lang Brothers Ltd.

First known as Burnfoot, later Glenguin, and nowadays Glengoyne, this pretty distillery has been around since 1833. It is set in a glen at the foot of the Campsie Fells, just to the north of Glasgow. The original Burnfoot name refers to a small stream which runs off the side of Dumgoyne Hill and cascades from a height of 59ft. (18m.) into a pool behind the distillery. Glengoyne is a small but neat and tidy distillery, producing a whisky which, although light for a Highlander, narrowly avoids Lowlander status, being situated just north of the dividing line. The distillery was remodeled in the late 1960s by longtime owners Lang Brothers, when a third still was added.

Much of the production process can be seen in one room, giving the visitor a nutshell explanation of distilling technique. There are three stills, one wash and two spirit, arranged to slowly produce a high quality spirit which, uniquely for scotch whisky, contains no peat traces. The younger versions of Glengoyne can be good pre-dinner drams, whereas more mature stocks have greater body and depth.

Glen Grant

Region: Speyside
Owner: The Seagram Company Ltd.

An image on every bottle of Glen Grant depicts its tartan-clad founders—the brothers James and John Grant—supporting a cask of their whisky (or vice versa). The Grants began their operation near Rothes in 1840 and soon found success. James, the elder, became Provost of Elgin before passing his business at Glen Grant to his son, Major James Grant. The major developed the distillery, later adding a No. 2 complex which became known as Caperdonich. In 1952 Glen Grant was merged with The Glenlivet Distillery and the association remains today, although both have been absorbed by the internationally famed Seagram empire.

Glen Grant has a whisky chateau feel, with extensive gardens which were landscaped by Major James Grant. He also took trouble to install a whisky safe in the garden wall so that he could dispense hospitality as he showed visitors around. The practice is kept up today and the guests' whisky can be cut with water from a handy burn which runs alongside. The malt can be found in mature bottlings from vintage distillations dating back to the 1930s, although the five-year old is Italy's No. 1 selling malt.

Glenkinchie

Region: Lowland
Owners: United Distillers

Glenkinchie is situated near the village of Pencaitland not far from the main A68 road, which skirts the east cost. The distillery nestles into the gentle farmland of East Lothian some 15 miles east of Edinburgh, and is the sole producer of malt whisky in the area. The distillery was once known as Milton, and adopted its current name in 1837. For a while Glenkinchie discontinued production, until the whisky boom of the late Victorian era helped revive its fortunes. It became one of the founder distilleries of D.C.L.—now United Distillers—and the company describes its 10-year old single as "The Edinburgh Malt."

There is much for the visitor to take in, including a museum, and the distillery even has its own bowling green. The malt is typically Lowland in character and represents the region in U.D.'s Classic Six malt whisky range. Odd bottles of a "Blonde" Glenkinchie called "Jackson's Row" may be found after a recent test-marketing exercise.

The Glenlivet

Region: Speyside
Owners: The Seagram Company Ltd.

The Glenlivet malt whisky barely needs an introduction, for its fame is global and its quality revered. The story started in 1823, when the Duke of Gordon, who owned land in Speyside, prompted Parliament to pass an Act which offered distillers an opportunity to become legitimate without the penalty of unfair taxation. One of the duke's tenants, a farmer and illicit distiller named George Smith, took up the offer, and bought a licence. His Glenlivet distillery—which opened a year later—was the first legitimate operation, though many soon followed suit.

Smith had more than a little trouble with threats from jealous rivals, so he bought a pair of pistols which he kept at hand for several years. They are now on display

at the distillery. With the Glenlivet distillery established and business going well, it became apparent that all and sundry were using its name as a marketing tool. The Smiths acted in 1880 and secured exclusive rights to the brand name, "The Glenlivet"—although some distillers in the area are still permitted to tag Glenlivet onto their own names.

The brand has done well in the U.S. market and remains the top-selling malt, assisted by the clout of its owners, The Seagram Company.

Glenmorangie

Region: Northern Highland
Owners: MacDonald Martin Distilleries Plc

It is my unerring habit, in whichever hostelry I find myself, to cast my eye along the whisky shelf. I will nearly always find a bottle of Glenfiddich, or The Glenlivet, but I am always pleased to find a Glenmorangie up there, vying for attention with the Super-Speys. This malt is one of Scotland's great successes, holding number one place in its domestic market and now exported to every corner of the world.

Glenmorangie hails from the town of Tain in Ross-shire, and this delightful pre-prandial dram is said by the marketeers to be crafted by 16 men from the town. The whisky is renowned for its aromatic bouquet, which shines through assisted by the overall lightness of the spirit. The stills at Glenmorangie are the tallest in the Highlands: they number eight today and are modeled meticulously on their predecessors. Glenmorangie's water is also an importantly different commodity, for it is hard when most distilleries prefer a soft supply. The springs employed rise in the Tarlogie Forest—which the owners have bought as a safeguard. The distillery has a sister operation at Glenmoray in Speyside, as well as the recently acquired Ardbeg set-up on Islay.

Glen Ord

Region: Northern Highland
Owners: United Distillers

Glen Ord single malt has been dangled temptingly in front of consumers under various guises. Initially it was known as "Ord" after the area in which it is produced, then changed for a spell to Glen Ordie, and is now being flashed before the TV watching population of the UK under its latest identity. This is a whisky with a bright future, not least because its label proclaims, "I shine, not burn."

The "Ord" referred to in the whisky's title is an expanse of land which stretches from the shores of the Beauly Firth inland towards the village of Muir of Ord. Even the distillery name has been changed: it was once called Muir of Ord after the nearby village, but now more logically shares the name of the product.

The region north of Inverness was once a smugglers' paradise and their illicit stills (or bothies) were numerous. Glen Ord stands on the site of one of these, and only gained legitimate status in 1838. The distillery operates its own maltings, converted in recent years to a saladin box mechanical system, although today it has been updated to a more efficient drum process. There are currently three pairs of stills in place; they can be viewed through a glass partition in the stillhouse wall. Glen Ord has been associated with Dewar's blends since the 1920s and current annual output is around 750,000 litres of spirit.

Glenrothes

Region: Speyside
Owners: The Highland Distilleries Co. Plc

Glenrothes Distillery in the town of Rothes produced its first spirit on Sunday, December 28, 1879. The very same night, amid howling storms, a train was blown from the bridge over the River Tay near Dundee and as Scots poet extraordinaire, William McGonagall, recounts "90 lives have been taken away." The distillery flourished despite the initial ill-omen, and extensions were added in 1896. In 1922 a fire caused one of the warehouses to burn down and large quantities of mature whisky poured into the Burn of Rothes, providing a drunken feast for the locals. It was reported that even a few cows overindulged themselves. Glenrothes is made using water from a spring in the nearby Glen of Dounie. The spring is known as "the Ladies Well," after the daughter of the Earl of Rothes, who was murdered there in the fourteenth century.

Glen Rothes malt whisky is lightly peated, matured mainly in American oak and partly in sherrywood casks. Much of the product goes into the famous Cutty Sark blend, which belongs to London wine merchants, Berry Brothers & Rudd Ltd., although it is highly regarded and widely used by other blenders.

Glenturret

Region: Southern Highland
Owners: The Highland Distilleries Co. Plc

The historic settlement of Creiff in Perthshire grew up as a cattle market town where the drovers would converge to sell their stocks. A different kind of stocks can be seen in the High Street where the less lawful or drunken folk were locked up in public view. There is evidence of distilling around the area since the early 1700s—the town's nearby Glenturret Distillery is said to have first opened in 1775, making it Scotland's oldest. For many years it was known as "the Hosh," there being another set-up in the vicinity using the Glenturret name. When this closed, the name was adopted by the existing distillery, although "the Hosh" is still referred to in its address.

Glenturret was stripped of its equipment in the lean years of the late 1920s and was not revived until 1957, when James Fairlie began to realize his dream of producing whisky in the traditional manner. Many of the procedures which are automated in modern operations are carried out by hand at Glenturret and there is a small, but much respected, output from its two stills. Glenturret is a showpiece distillery with brilliantly organised visitors' facilities, including its own bar and restaurant.

Highland Park

Region: Islands
Owners: The Highland Distilleries Co. Plc

The Orkney Isles have an ancient history of civilization, thought to have begun as long ago as 6,000 BC, although many of the Orcadian surnames betray the folk's Norse ancestry. The Danes and Norwegians ruled here for half a millennium before the islands were handed to King James III of Scotland in the fifteenth century.

Highland Park, at Kirkwall on the main island, is the world's most northerly distillery, with a history of legal production since 1825, although it was founded 27 years earlier by Magnus Eunson, a local smuggler-cum-preacher who is reputed to have hidden his casks in the church when the excisemen called by! Most of the equipment and processes used at Highland Park today are traditional. Peat is cut shallow from local beds and a heather-root character abides in the whisky. Occasionally sprigs of heather are thrown on the peat fire to augment the effect.

Highland Park whisky is highly regarded by blenders, having a fullness of body and a rounded enough character to help knit other whiskies together. It also has a broad appeal to the malt consumer, being one of the UK's top ten favourites and is now exported around the globe.

Isle of Jura

Region: Islands
Owners: Whyte & MacKay Group Plc

The Sound of Jura separates this Inner Hebridean Isle from the mainland. There is one distillery here and its produce is nowhere near as peaty as that of the neighbouring Islay malt whiskies. Jura has just over 2,000 inhabitants, who share the land with a much healthier population of sheep and deer (the island takes its name from the Norse for deer). The dominant feature on Jura is "The Paps," mountains which are said to resemble a pair of breasts from certain angles, the highest peak being over 2,500ft—hardly a ladylike measurement! The writer George Orwell came to Jura in the 1940s for a bit of solitude and it was in a cottage in the northern half of the island that he wrote 1984—his last work.

Jura Distillery has a chequered past, and was rescued and rebuilt in the 1950s and 1960s by Scottish and Newcastle Breweries distillery arm, now absorbed into the Whyte & MacKay empire. The stills at Jura are four—two wash and two spirit—and are unusually tall, a factor which is important to the lightness of the whisky. Stocks are matured in American oak casks and a smaller proportion in Olorosso sherrywood.

Knockando

Region: Speyside
Owners: International Distillers & Vintners Ltd.

Knockando Distillery was built by Ian Thompson in 1898, just as the whisky boom ended, and its owners soon had no choice but to halt production. They were eventually forced to sell out to Gilbeys in 1904. Gilbeys, now IDV Ltd, have retained the brand ever since, incorporating it in their popular J&B blends. Despite the negative sounding name, Knockando translates from the Gaelic for "small black hill," and because the whisky is a light style of Speyside, most palates find it will do very nicely.

Knockando is a true Speyside, situated literally a stone's throw from the river on a tree-clad bank, and although much rebuilding took place in 1969 there is still a Victorian charm about the structures. The distillery has its own pure water source at the nearby Cardnach spring. There are two sets of stills in place, and the spirit is run into American oak casks with a small amount maturing in sherrywood. The whisky is bottled when the distillery manager thinks the casks are mature, so a vintage appears on the label rather than a fixed age statement. Knockando has a sister operation, The Singleton of Auchroisk (see page 238), which is a recent distillery, situated down river near Mulben.

Lagavulin

Region: Islay
Owners: United Distillers

Islay was the stronghold of the Lords of the Isles and the ruins of their fourteenth century Dunyveg Castle overlook the entrance to Lagavulin Bay on the exposed south-eastern coast. Lagavulin means "the mill in the valley" in Gaelic, and the distillery occupies a hollow on the Kildalton shoreline. The area was a smugglers'

haven in the 1740s. There are reported to have been at least ten illicit operations on the site of the modern distillery, which gives its official birth year more conservatively as 1816.

In 1867 Lagavulin came into the hands of Peter Mackie, who used its produce as the base for his now famous White Horse blend. Mackie was one of the industry's great movers and shakers, nicknamed "Restless Peter" and later knighted for his achievements. Much of his energy was concentrated at Lagavulin where he experimented with production techniques and rebuilt the old "Malt Mill" distillery, which once shared the site. He aimed to produce a traditional smugglers' style whisky. Malt Mill finally closed in the early 1960s when more room was required by Lagavulin.

Lagavulin is a hugely complex and characterful malt, which is unmistakably Islay. The maturing casks breathe the salty, seaweedy, coastal air, giving a medicinal feel to this heavily peated spirit—a great dram on a cold night. It is one of United Distillers classic six range.

Laphroaig

Region: Islay
Owners: Allied Distillers Ltd.

I have included all three of the remaining south-shore, "Costa Del Peat and Seaweed," Islay Distilleries in this guide and, yes, I am a big fan of their whiskies. Lagavulin, Ardbeg, and this distinctive example, Laphroaig, are difficult to mistake as belonging to any other part of Scotland. If you cannot cope with their full-peated, medicinal flavors, then don't worry, they do take some getting use to. However, once bitten, you may be forever smitten! Laphroaig (pronounced Laffroyg) is a lighter-bodied malt whisky than its two neighbors, and as a result the peatiness shines through almost unhindered. Even the distillers confess that this is a malt you may either love or hate.

The distillery has its origins in the early 1800s and gained legal status in the hands of the Johnston family. Donald Johnston, son of the founder, gained control in 1836 and took such an interest in the distilling process that in 1847 he fell into a fermenting vat and drowned. The business continued to pass through family hands until 1954, when Mrs. Bessie Campbell took the reigns for a 16-year spell. Today, Laphroaig is owned by Allied Distillers, who have done much to promote the brand and it also features in many of their famous blends.

Ledaig

Region: Islands
Owners: Burn Stewart Distillers Plc

The Isle of Mull nestles close to the rugged west coast of Scotland, its south-eastern flank facing across the Firth of Lorn to the Port of Oban where the ferries set out for the scattered Western Isles. Tobermory is Mull's principal town and fishing port, tucked into a bay to the north-east of the island where it is sheltered from the extremes of the Atlantic Ocean. The town grew up around the harbor in the late 1700s and retains its period charm today, with many of its seafront buildings painted in an array of colors which contrast with the greenery rising behind them.

A distillery was introduced in 1798 by John Sinclair, who named it Ledaig, and this name stuck until the 1970s when it was rechristened Tobermory. However for much of this time—from 1930—Ledaig's doors remained closed and did not reopen until 1972, and then only for three years. The present owners have been able to do better and now market Tobermory as an unpeated, lightish malt together with some vintage releases of Ledaig, which retain much of its traditional peaty character. Both malts are well worth trying: Ledaig is the after dinner style, Tobermory is good at just about any time.

Linkwood

Region: Speyside
Owners: United Distillers

Linkwood is beginning to achieve better recognition as a single malt: for years only the independents bothered to bottle this Speyside gem. I recently tasted a 1954 distillation put out by Elgin specialists Gordon & MacPhail, and I have to say that it is one of the most beautifully balanced and complex whiskies I have tried. Peter Brown, a local land agent and agricultural improver, built the original distillery in 1824 and named it after Linkwood House, which once occupied the wooded site.

The distillery has a cooling dam, home to a number of swans which are depicted on the label of the official 12-year old. Linkwood was rebuilt by Brown's son during the early 1870s and the buildings have changed little in outward appearance since then, despite the addi-

tion of stills in the 1960s and 1970s. There are now three sets in operation. In the 1930s Linkwood's superstitious manager, Roddy MacKenzie, was firmly of the opinion that even minute changes in the still room could affect the quality of the spirit, and with this in mind he forbade the removal even of spiders' webs. United Distillers, who own the set-up today, would rather keep the swans—outside, of course.

Loch Dhu

Region: Speyside
Owners: United Distillers

This malt is a recent variation from a fairly recently built distillery called Mannochmore. Mannochmore malt whisky is normally unusually light in color, but the Loch Dhu version is black as sin. The color comes from double charring of the casks in which the whisky matures, a technique used in the production of bourbon, although I have never seen one this color. Charring casks was probably an accidental extension of the toasting technique used by coopers to warp the wooden staves into shape, and at some point in the mid-1800s the Americans discovered that charred wood improved the flavor of their whisky, giving it a sweeter, cleaner taste.

Loch Dhu is certainly not a normal malt whisky and it does have a background bourbon sweetness, almost liquorice-like in flavor. Mannochmore was built in 1970-71 and is classed as a River Lossie Distillery, falling into the general Speyside catchment. It is actually an annex of the Glen Lossie Distillery complex and produces only in times of heightened demand. This could mean that Mannochmore's black whisky is a fleeting experiment by United Distillers, so try it while you can.

Longmorn

Region: Speyside
Owners: The Seagram Company Ltd.

Longmorn is one of Speyside's great malt whiskies, golden in color, and winner of a recent gold medal in the 1994 International Wine and Spirit Challenge. It also claims the distinction of having been voted the best malt whisky in the world by the New York Times. They may soon have to make the warehouse doors bigger to get the ego-stricken casks out!

Production began at Longmorn in the 1890s on the site of an ancient abbey, and the name is said to be derived from "Lhanmorgund" meaning "place of the holy man." The distillery is located just south of Elgin and takes its spring water from the Mannoch Hills, which separate the Lossie and Spey Rivers. Floor maltings were suspended in 1970 but there is much of the traditional brewing and distilling equipment still in use. There are eight stills in situ today; much of their output is incorporated in the Chivas Brothers' blends which belong to Seagram, Longmorn's owners. Seagram own three additional distilleries in Speyside, which are marketed with Longmorn under the Heritage Selection banner, namely, Strathisla, Benriach, and Glen Keith.

Macallan

Region: Speyside
Owners: the Highland Distilleries Co. Plc

If malt whiskies could be likened to rare stamps, then Macallan is surely the "Penny Black," except it is harder to lick and infinitely more pleasant to the palate. This is a class act—a big Speyside of unending complexity and moreish flavor. I once tasted a 41-year old Macallan with John Milroy and writer Jim Murray. Eventually Jim and I sloped off to a football match and at halftime I was still enjoying the Macallan's rich finish.

The distillery was licensed in 1824—the same year that The Glenlivet got going—but Macallan took much longer to make the impact of its local rival. In 1892 Macallan was purchased by Roderick Kemp, whose family had connections with the business until recently. During the 1950s a series of expansions took place, the directors taking a decision to build more stills rather than enlarging the existing type. The demand for the whisky continued to grow and, because the stills are amongst the smallest in Scotland, output was increased by adding more a few years later. There are now seven wash stills feeding 14 spirit stills.

Part of The Macallan recipe for success in recent years has been the exclusive use of dry olorosso sherry casks for maturation. It is still possible to find at auction some bottlings aged for up to 50 or 60 years in cask, but expect to pay the price of a fully fitted kitchen.

Oban

Region: Western Highland
Owners: United Distillers

Oban is a pretty resort town and port, arranged around a busy harbor and climbing up into the hills behind. Above the town stands the coliseum-styled "McCaig's Folly," which never saw a chariot race but was commissioned as a kind of Victorian youth employment scheme to keep the local stone masons in work. Directly below it on the waterfront sits the distillery which is Scotland's only High Street operation.

Oban distillery was built by two brothers, the Stevensons, in 1794, although it took them a few years to secure a licence and it was not until the 1820s that production really got going. Towards the end of the century, new owners began to expand the distillery and while blasting into the cliff behind, the remains of Mesolithic bones were uncovered, believed to be around 4,000 years old. Dewars bought Oban in 1923, prior to the formation of the Distillers Company in 1930. Oban 14-year old is now an integral part of United Distillers' classic malts range, readily available around the world and winning many new admirers with its approachable style.

Old Fettercairn

Region: Eastern Highland
Owners: Whyte & Mackay Plc

This distillery lies just north of Brechin Town and a few miles inland of the North Sea. The eastern extremes of the Grampian Mountain range descend towards the village of Fettercairn, carrying pure Highland spring water to the distillery. Fettercairn was built on the Fasque Estate whose house and fertile lands once belonged to John Gladstone, father of British Liberal Prime Minster William Gladstone, who served four separate terms in office and was a useful ally of the distillers—in 1853 he abolished the malt tax, rejuvenating the industry.

Fettercairn's buildings were converted from an old corn mill in 1824 when the first licences for legal distilling were being granted. There was no shortage of local expertise as most of the farming population were well educated in the craft of whisky making. A fire destroyed the original distillery in 1887, but the demand for whisky was so great at the time, that the distillery was up and running again shortly afterwards.

The distillery fell silent in 1926 and remained so until the 1940s when Associated Scottish Distillers acquired it. Eventually Fettercairn was renovated and the number of stills doubled to four. Whyte & Mackay are the present owners and the malt is distributed by their subsidiary, Invergordon Distillers. Old Fettercairn was once filled into a tiny phial which is recorded in the Guinness Book of Records as the smallest bottle of whisky in the world.

Old Pulteney

Region: Northern Highland
Owners: Inverhouse Distillers Ltd.

Pulteney Distillery is situated in the fishing town of Wick, just a few miles south of John O'Groats on the north-east coast and has the distinction of being the northernmost operation on the Scottish mainland. The town grew up around the herring industry and for a time prohibition was imposed upon the unruly population, who must have been galled to see the distillery continuing to operate while they dried out.

Pulteney whisky was marketed under the Henderson name for many years. James Henderson opened the distillery in 1826 and his family retained control for over a century. The distillery was recently acquired by Inverhouse Distillers, who have released an official version, the first for many years.

Pulteney whisky is noted as one of the fastest maturing, making it useful to blenders. It has also earned the nickname "The Manzanilla of the North" due to its coastal, salty tang which is reminiscent of a particular style of

sherry. There is also a peaty element which translates from Pulteney's water source. The distillery has two small stills and has been much modernized in recent years.

Rosebank

Region: Lowland
Owners: United Distillers

Rosebank Distillery sits alongside the Forth-Clyde Canal at Camelon, near Falkirk. When Rosebank halted production in 1993, Dumbarton-based Auchentoshan (see page 226) became sole survivor of the triple-distilling process in Scotland. It can only be hoped that this great Lowland whisky does not suffer the same fate as its nearest neighbor, St. Magdalene (Linlithgow) which closed for good in 1983.

Rosebank was first produced in the 1840s by James Rankine—ironic that such a name should be shared with my childhood dentist near Glasgow, a man whose drilling first made me crave the soothing influence of whisky! In 1864 Rankine the distiller (not the driller) passed Rosebank to his son who rebuilt the operation and its produce increased in popularity during the boom years of the late 1800s.

Troubled times in the early 1900s forced an amalgamation with Scottish Malt Distillers who evolved to become today's United Distillers. U.D. still own the distillery but there is no certainty as to its future. The malt is highly regarded by connoisseurs and has long epitomized the Lowland style of single malt whisky. It would be a sad loss to the distilling heritage of the area if it were not to reopen.

Royal Lochnagar

Region: Eastern Highland
Owners: United Distillers

Queen Victoria may not have been amused when John Begg invited her to sample his Lochnagar whisky in 1848. His distillery near the Balmoral Estate on Deeside had only been going for three years, and yet Begg was confident enough that his whisky was fit for royalty. The Queen, Prince Albert, and entourage visited the distillery, sampled the wares and granted a royal warrant. John Brown, the Queen's confidant and security specialist, was also a great fan of this dram; on one occasion he is reported to have over-indulged and fell flat on is face in front of Victoria, who quipped that she too had felt an earth tremor.

Lochnagar is not a loch, but the mountain which provides water for the distillery. The first producer on the site was an illicit distiller named James Robertson, who incurred the wrath of his neighbors when he broke with convention and took out an official licence. His distillery was suspiciously burned down in 1841 but was rebuilt and operated for a few years adjacent to John Begg's newer set-up.

In 1880 Henry Begg inherited his father's company and it was retained by the family until 1916 when D.C.L bought it. Lochnagar is one of the smallest distilleries in the Highlands, but is beautifully kept and has an excellent reception center and restaurant.

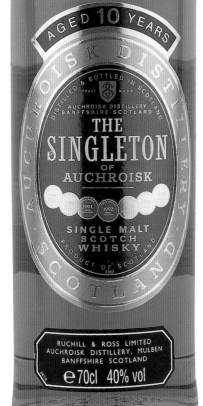

The Singleton of Auchroisk

Region: Speyside
Owners: I.D.V. Ltd.

During the 1960s Justerini & Brooks, owners of the famous J&B blended whisky, discovered a particularly good source of soft water emanating from a hillside spring near the Burn of Mulben. The source, known as Dorie's Well, was purchased by the company, along with surrounding land. A protective housing was built over the well and plans were laid for the building of a new distillery, which was finally completed in 1974.

Auchroisk is pronounced "Othrusk" from the Gaelic meaning "the forest of the red stream." The distillery buildings occupy a clearing in the forested hills between the towns of Aberlour and Keith. The bottled single malt became available only as recently as 1986, and has already won many awards gaining worldwide recognition. A decision to introduce

the whisky as The Singleton (meaning single malt) was wisely taken, although the Auchroisk part of the name gets easier after a couple of glasses.

Springbank

Region: Campbeltown
Owners: J. & A. Mitchell & Co. Ltd.

The Mitchell family were practising the illicit craft prior to 1828 when their Springbank Distillery was built. The operation remains in the ownership of direct descendants to this day, having survived the great Campbeltown slump which saw the closure of over 30 neighboring businesses between 1880 and 1930. Now only two exist, the second being Glen Scotia, although Springbank manages to keep alive the name of Longrow, meaning an "old distillery," the site of which forms part of the present warehouse accommodation. Longrow whisky is made in a separate process using Springbank's stills and is much peatier in character than its sister malt.

The stills at Springbank are unusual in set-up. There are three in place, two wash and one spirit, with some of the resulting spirit being triple- distilled. There is an antique feel about Springbank's equipment and all of the traditional whisky making processes are carried out by the staff, including peat cutting, malting, and even bottling. The end product is a whisky of outstanding quality and character—truly one of Scotland's greatest and a personal favorite.

Strathisla

Region: Speyside
Owners: The Seagram Company Ltd.

Strathisla, on the River Isla in Keith, began its life as a flax mill and was converted for distilling purposes as early as 1786, making it one of Scotland's oldest operations. It probably has also one of the prettiest set of buildings, with its ornate pagoda roofs and old watermill. The distillery was originally known as Milltown, later becoming Milton, a name which it kept until the 1950s when the current owners, Seagrams, gave it its present title. The whisky had been marketed locally as Strathisla since the late 1800s and Elgin merchants, Gordon & MacPhail, were given a concession to buy and mature stocks which they sold further afield.

Prior to the takeover by Chivas brothers in 1950, the company was in receivership, its owner at the time, Jay Pomeroy, was found to have been supplying non-existent companies in London with his wares. The whisky was actually sold to black marketeers and Pomeroy was eventually prosecuted for tax evasion amounting to over £110,000. Strathisla's sister distillery, Glen Keith, is situated on the opposite bank of the River Isla. Both whiskies contribute to Chivas brothers blends.

Talisker

Region: Islands
Owners: United Distillers

Skye is an island of legends, and indeed its single distillery at Carbost on the shore of Loch Harport, produces a legendary single malt. Talisker's fame is affirmed in numerous pieces of literature, including Robert Louis Stevenson's poem, from 1880, "The Scotsman's Return from Abroad," part of which runs, "The King of drinks as I conceive it, Talisker, Islay or Glenlivet."

The distillery was constructed by the Macaskill brothers in 1843, but only once they had cleared the land of crofters and profited from sheep farming. In 1892, Alexander Allan took control at Talisker and merged it with Dailuaine Distillery on Speyside. Both distilleries were absorbed by The Distillers Company in 1925.

Talisker was once triple-distilled, but is now produced in the more conventional manner. In 1960 the stillhouse caught fire, destroying all five stills. Exact copies were made and the quality of the whisky has not suffered.

Skye was once accessible only by ferry, but recently a bridge has been built to the mainland making distillery visits more feasible.

Tomatin

Region: Northern Highland
Owners: Takara Shuzo & Okura & Co. Ltd.

Fifteen miles or so up the main A9 road from Aviemore to Inverness is situated one of Scotland's largest distilling operations. Tomatin sits high up on exposed moorland close to the point where the River Findhorn meets the Allt-na-Frithe, the "Free Burn" which provides Tomatin's soft water. The burn runs off the Monadhliath Mountains, crossing peat and granite before reaching the distillery.

Tomatin was built 100 years ago with a two-still configuration, and this remained the case until 1956 when the first of many expansions took place. Much of Tomatin's output contributes to the blended market, a factor which was critical when the market slumped in the 1980s and the company failed. In 1986 the distillery was rescued by a Japanese partnership, which has continued to invest in modernization. Tomatin now has 23 stills and enough mechanical and electronic gadgetry to ensure that two people can oversee the entire distillation process.

Scotland's distillers are capable of diverse initiatives and experiments have taken place recently to utilize warm waste water from the plant to raise eels and trout in tanks. There is, however, nothing fishy about the quality of Tomatin malt whisky.

PART 5:
A SCOTTISH CHRONOLOGY

24 A Scottish Chronology

c.450 million BC The Grampian Mountains and the northern Highlands are formed by distinct geological sheets which slide in along lines of weakness like the Great Glen Fault, colliding and fusing together.

c.200 million BC A great shift in the earth's crust creates the Great Glen, a 60-mile long cleft cutting diagonally across the heart of Scotland.

c.18,000BC Glaciers scour and smooth the Great Glen creating the four great lochs along its length: Linnie, Lochy, Oich, and Ness.

c.7,000BC The first inhabitants — mesolithic hunter-gatherers almost certainly Celts, but some argument as to their origin. These people arrive at the end of the last glaciation.

c.4,000BC The first Neolithic farmers arrive. They construct burial chambers and stone circles which still stand today.

c.2,000BC The arrival of the more sophisticated Bronze Age man. They build the splendid stone circles at Brodgar and Stennes in Orkney and Callanish in Lewis.

c.500BC The Iron Age tribes of the Northern Isles begin building their famous stone towers, the brochs.

80AD Gnaeus Julius Agricola, governor of the Roman province of Britain, invades southern Scotland.

83AD Agricola vanquishes the local Caledonians in the battle of Mons Graupius.

123AD The Emperor Hadrian visits Britain and orders the building of his wall as a deterrent to the raiding parties of the Scottish lowland tribes.

138AD Roman Emperor Antoninus Pius reoccupies Lowland Scotland.

c.142-145AD The Antonine Wall built across the waist of Scotland formed by the Rivers Forth and Clyde.

397AD St. Ninian founds his mission at Whithorn

c.430AD Romans abandons Scotland and England to defend homelands from the Goths.

c.500AD Fergus Mor moves the seat of the kingdom of Dalriada from Ireland to Scotland.

563AD Columba and his followers arrive on Iona to spread the word of Christianity throughout Scotland.

597AD Death of St. Columba.

638AD Din Eidyn receives its English name of Edinburgh.

c.650AD St. Aidan of Lindisfarne establishes his monastery *Mailros*.

685AD 20 May, Picts crush the Angles at the Battle of Nechtansmere.

795AD Vikings sacked Iona.

797AD A Viking raid on Kintyre leads to Norse control of the Northern and Western Isles, also the Isle of Man and much of Ireland.

830-860AD Kenneth MacAlpin unites the Picts and Scots and creates the kingdom the Irish Scots called Alba.

c.872AD A Viking earldom established at Jarlshof in Orkney.

c.1018 Kingdom of the Britons of Strathclyde merges into the Kingdom of Scotland.

1018 King Malcolm II defeats the English at the Battle of Carham.

1030 Beginning of the rule of Duncan, King of Strathclyde, who begins to bring the Scottish people together under one rule.

c.1035 Kirkwall in Orkney founded by Earl Rognvald Bruason.

1040 Macbeth killed Duncan, King of Strathclyde.

1057 Macbeth killed in battle by Malcolm Canmore, who became Malcolm III.

1072 William the Conqueror invades Scotland.

1093 King Malcolm III killed by the English at the Battle of Alnwick.

1097 Edgar became king.

1107 Edgar's brother Alexander became king.

1124 Alexander died and was succeeded by his brother David.

1136 Cistercian monks start building Melrose Abbey.

1137 St. Magnus's Cathedral founded in Kirkwall, Orkney, by Earl Rognvald Kolson.

c.1138 King David I founds Kelso and Jedburgh Abbeys.

1138 Battle of the Standard at Cowton Moor, Yorkshire, where David I's army is defeated by the English.

1150 The Viking earl, Rognvald Kali, gathers Crusaders together in Orkney.

1153 Death of David, King of Scotland, succeeded by Malcolm IV. Earl of Atholl attempts a surprise attack on Orkney.

1156 The chieftain, Somerled, establishes his breakaway kingdom in the Western Isles.

1174 Stirling castle handed over to Henry II of England to help pay for the release of Scottish King William the Lion after his capture at the battle of Alnwick.

1189 Scottish control of Stirling Castle regained.

1214 Death of King William, the 'Lion of Justice'.

1266 Under the Treaty of Perth, after the battle of Largs, Norway hands the Western Isles over to the Kingdom of Scotland.

c.1270 William Wallace born.

1286 Death of Alexander III.

1291 Edward I of England takes control of all Scottish royal castles while he adjudicates on who is the rightful king of Scotland.

1297 September 11, William Wallace overthrows the English at Stirling Bridge and occupied Stirling Castle.

1298 July 22, Edward I defeats Wallace at the Battle of Falkirk.

1303 Edward I's sixth invasion of Scotland begins.

1304 April 21, Edward I begins his three-month siege of Stirling Castle.

1305 William Wallace captured and put to death in London after a trial on August 5.

1306 March 25, Robert the Bruce crowned King of the Scots at Scone. June 19, Robert the Bruce defeated by an English army at Methven.

1307 April, an English army slaughtered by Bruce's men at Glentrool. May 10, Bruce beats the Earl of Pembroke at Loudon Hill. July 7, death of Edward I of England.

1308 Battle of the Pass of Brander where the rival Campbell and MacDonald clans fight side by side against the MacDougalls.

1314 June 23 and 24, Robert the Bruce defeats Edward II of England at the Battle of Bannockburn.

1320 The Declaration of Arbroath, asserting Scotland's independence from England, i s made in the town's cathedral.

1326 Robert the Bruce's first parliament.

1327 Murder of Edward II of England.

1328 Treaty of Northampton finally formally recognizes Scotland's independence under Robert the Bruce.

1329 June, the death of Robert the Bruce.

1331 Robert the Bruce's son David crowned king at the age of six.

1332 Scottish nobles siding with the English landed at Fife.

1333 July 19, at the battle of Halidon Hill Edward III of England defeats the Scots and recaptures parts of the Scottish Lowlands.

1335 Young King David sent to France and the regency entrusted to Robert Stewart. Edinburgh Castle taken by the English.

1339 Robert Stewart captures Perth.

1340 Robert Stewart clears the English out of Scotland north of the Forth.

1341 King David returns from France to resume government of the country. Edinburgh Castle retaken by the Scots.

1346 October 17, King David captured by the English at Neville's Cross near Durham. Robert Stewart took regency again.

1349 Black Death first strikes Scotland.

1356 Burnt Candlemas, Edward III ravaged south-eastern counties of Scotland.

1357 Treaty of Berwick.

1371 Following the death of David, Robert Stewart takes the Scottish throne as Robert II, the first Stewart king.

1390 Death of Robert Stewart, succeeded by his son Robert III.

1410 St. Andrews, Scotland's oldest university founded.

1424 James I returns from captivity in England.

1430 Bishopric of the Isles formed on Iona.

1437 James I murdered.

1440 The 'Black Dinner' at Edinburgh Castle when the young Earl of Douglas and his brother are assassinated.

1452 William, 8th Earl of Douglas, murdered by James II in Stirling castle.

1460 Death of James II. Her is succeeded by James III.

1469 Marriage of James III to Margaret, daughter of the King of Norway, Sweden, and Denmark. Northern Isles falls to the Scottish crown as non-payment of wedding dowry.

1479 Duke of Albany, James III's brother, escaped from Edinburgh Castle.

1488 Death of James III, James IV succeeded to the throne.

1497 Forfeiture of the Lords of the Isles title to James IV.

1501 Glen Coe MacDonalds captured Innis Chonnell, the Campbells' island fortress on Loch Awe, and rescued Donald Dhu.

1512 James IV ordered Henry VIII of England to withdraw from France or be invaded from the north. Birth of John Knox the Protestant Reformer.

1513 September 9, the English defeat the Scots at the Battle of Flodden and kill their king, James IV.

1526 The young King James V held captive at Edinburgh Castle by the Earl of Angus.

1528 James V escapes from Edinburgh and took over direct rule.

1532 Foundation of the College of Justice to strengthen the powers of royal law.

1537 Marriage of James V to Mary of Guise.

1542 James V offered the crown of Ireland. November 24 the English defeats James V at Solway Moss. December 14 Scottish king dies shortly afterwards. December 7, the birth of Mary Queen of Scots.

1543 September 9, the Coronation of the infant, Mary, as Queen of Scotland at Stirling Castle.

1545	The 'Rough Wooing', under the Earl of Hertford; English troops ravage the Scottish countryside.
1547	September 10, 'Black Friday', Edward VI of England defeats the Scots at the Battle of Pinkie and occupies eastern Scotland.
1548	The infant Queen Mary leaves Scotland for France.
1549	Treaty of Boulogne allows the French to occupy the English-held territories in Scotland.
1553	July 6, death of Edward VI of England, succeeded by his sister Mary.
1557	The 'Lords of the Congregation' made a covenant to quit the Roman Church and make Scotland Protestant.
1558	April 24, marriage of Mary Queen of Scots to François, Dauphin of France. Death of Mary Tudor of England, who is succeeded by Elizabeth I.
1559	January 1, the Beggars' Summons demands that friars quit their houses for the poor by the 12 May. May 11, John Knox denounces the Roman Church as idolatry from the pulpit of St. John's Kirk in Perth. Birth of Oliver Cromwell.
1560	June 11, death of Mary of Guise. July 6, under the Treaty of Edinburgh the French recognise Elizabeth Tudor as Queen of England and withdrew their troops from Scotland. Death of François II, husband of Mary Queen of Scots.
1561	August 19, Mary Queen of Scots returns to Scotland from France.
1565	July 29, marriage of Mary Queen of Scots to Henry, Lord Darnley.
1566	June 19, the future James VI born in Edinburgh Castle.
1567	On June 15, Scottish confederate lords defeats the army of Mary Queen of Scots at Carberry Hill. June 16 the Queen is imprisoned in Loch Leven Castle. July 24, Mary Queen of Scots is forced to abdicate in favour of her son Charles James, who succeeds to the throne as James VI on July 29.
1568	May 2, Mary Queen of Scots escapes from Loch Leven Castle. May 13, The Queen and an army of 6,000 men are defeated at Langside. May 16, Mary Queen of Scots leaves Scotland for the last time.
1571-3	The 'Lang Siege' of Edinburgh Castle.
1572	November 24, death of John Knox.
1581	The Confession of the Faith signed by James VI.
1584	May, James VI passes the so-called 'Black Acts' which reaffirm Episcopal Church government.
1586	October 15, trial of Mary Queen of Scots for treason begins.
1587	February 1, Elizabeth I signs the death warrant of Mary Queen of Scots.
1587	February 8, execution of Mary Queen of Scots at Fotheringay Castle.

1589	Marriage of James VI to Anne of Denmark.
1603	March 24, death of Elizabeth I of England. Union of the Crowns as James VI of Scotland is proclaimed King James I of England, Scotland, France, and Ireland.
1604	James VI commissions the Authorised Version of the Bible.
1609	James VI makes the first formal invitation to Scots to participate in the plantation of Ulster.
1617	The 'hamecoming' of James VI.
1625	Death of James VI succeeded by Charles I. Act of Revocation passed by Charles I compelled the Scottish nobles to give up the ecclesiastical property they had taken at the Reformation.
1633	Charles I crowned King of Scotland.
1638	February 28, representatives of the Scottish people signed the National Covenant expressing resistance to the despotic aims of Charles I.
1639	Covenanting army under the Earl of Montrose defeated a Royalist army at the Battle of the Brig o' Dee, Aberdeen.
1641	June, Charles I signed a Treaty with the Covenanters at Ripon.
1643	Covenanting Scots signed a Solemn League with the English Parliamentarians.
1644	Charles I defeated by Cromwell at Marston Moor.
1645	Battle of Philiphaugh where Montrose's Highland army was defeated by General Leslie's Covenanters. Royalist defeat at the Battle of Naseby.
1646	May, Charles I surrendered to the Scottish army at Newark.
1647	December 27, Charles I signed a treaty called The Engagement, where he was promised Scottish military support from the Covenanters if he agreed to make England Presbyterian for a trial period.
1648	Trial of Charles I by the Parliament of England.
1649	January 30, execution of Charles I.
1650	April 27, Montrose's Royalist army routed at Carbisdale. 21 May, Montrose executed in Edinburgh. 3 September, Battle of Dunbar where Cromwell defeats a Scottish Royalist army under General Leslie. Charles II returns to Scotland.
1651	January 31, Coronation of Charles II at Scone. 3 September, Charles II forced into exile after defeat at Worcester.
1652	Scotland accept the rule of Cromwell.
1653	Cromwell abolishes the General Assembly.
1660	Charles II restored to the throne.

Right: *The great square tower of Drum Castle is one of the three oldest tower houses in Scotland — the turrets are just visible above the roof line on the right of the building. The castle had additions in 1619 and in Victorian times, but essentially remains a fine Jacobean mansion.*

1661	The Earl of Lauderdale made Secretary of State for Scotland.
1666	November 28, 900 Covenanters defeated by General Tam Dalyell at Rullion Green outside Edinburgh.
1671	Birth of Rob Roy Macgregor.
1673	Marriage of James VII to Mary of Modena.
1680	Last major pitched battle between two clan armies — the Sinclairs and the Breadalbane Campbells — at Altimarch. The Covenanter Richard Cameron openly declares war on Charles II.
1681	Viscount Stair's Institutions of the Law of Scotland published.
1685	February 6, death of Charles II. James II of England and VII of Scotland comes to the throne.
1687	Declaration of Indulgence by James VII concedes a general religious tolerance throughout Great Britain and puts an end to the 'Killing Time'.
1689	In February James VII was forced to quit England, and William of Orange and his British-born wife Mary Stewart, daughter of James VII, were offered the crown. July 27, battle at the Pass of Killiecrankie where the Jacobite Highlanders under Viscount Dundee defeat the government army led by General Hugh Mackay.
1690	The Westminster Confession, formulated in 1643, once again adopted. May, Jacobite army finally broke up after being defeated at Cromdale.
1691	August 27, Order issued for an oath of allegiance to King William. December 31, the MacDonalds of Glencoe refused to take the oath.
1692	February 13, the Massacre of the MacDonalds at Glencoe.
1694	Death of Queen Mary of England.
1695	Bank of Scotland founded, and the Scottish Africa and India Company established.
1697	Treaty of Ryswick which puts an end to Stewart political ambitions.
1699	Funded by the Scottish Africa and India Company, Scots settle in Darien on the isthmus of Panama.
1700	Spanish attack Scottish settlement at Darien. King William of England refuses help.
1701	King James dies and his son James Francis Stewart, the 'Old Pretender', is proclaimed King James VIII of Scotland and III of England by the French King Louis XIV. Act of Settlement proclaims the Hanoverian Sophia—grand daughter of James VI—and her children, heirs to the English throne on Queen Anne's death.
1702	March 7, death of William of Orange; by the 1689 Declaration of Right, Mary's sister Anne, becomes Queen.
1703	August 13, Act of Security passed which prevent the successor to the Crown of England from becoming the Scottish monarch, unless Scotland's conditions are met.
1705	March, 'Alien Act' passed where all Scots who are not resident in England, Ireland, and the English colonies, or serving in Queen Anne's army and navy, are to be declared aliens.
1707	January 16, the Act agreeing to the Articles of Union passed by the Scottish Estates. March 6, English parliament voted in favor. May 1, first official day of the Union uniting Scotland with England under a single parliament, with Scotland becoming North Britain.
1708	James Stewart's first abortive attempt for the crown when he sets sail from Dunkirk with 6,000 French troops. May, Scottish Privy Council abolished.
1711	The Society for Propagating Christian Knowledge founded to promote education north of the Highland Line.
1712	The Toleration Act allows the Scots' Episcopalian clergy to use 'the liturgy of England.' The patronage Act restores to Scottish landowners their right to choose and appoint parish ministers.
1713	British Parliament instigates the Malt Tax.
1714	Death of Queen Anne. December, Commission of Police set up to keep a strict watch on suspected Jacobites.
1715	September 6, at Braemar James Stewart is proclaimed King of Scotland, England, Ireland, and France. Indecisive battle at Sherrifmuir between a Jacobite army led by the Earl of Mar and George I's army under the Duke of Argyll. December 22, the Old Pretender lands at Peterhead.
1716	February 4, the Old Pretender leaves Scotland and returns to France, never to return.
1717	Act of Grace and Pardon frees imprisoned Jacobites.
1719	June 10, Jacobite force defeated at Glen Shiel.
1720	December 31, birth of Charles Edward Stewart, Bonnie Prince Charlie — the 'Young Pretender'.
1725	Westminster passes a second Disarming Act forbidding Highlanders to carry arms. The Glasgow Malt tax riots.
1736	Porteous Riot in Edinburgh.
1739	Black Watch Regiment formally constituted. Jacobite Association formed.
1742	The Bounty Act gives financial incentives to exporters in Glasgow.
1745	July 25, Prince Charles Edward Stuart — Bonnie Prince Charlie — arrives in mainland Scotland proclaiming himself king — the 'Young Pretender'. September 21, Charles Stuart victorious at the Battle of Prestonpans. December 4, the Jacobite army reaches Derby in England. December 6, 'Black Friday', Charles Stuart's decision to retreat.
1746	April 16, the Jacobite army defeated at Culloden Moor, the last battle fought on British soil. September 20, Charles Edward Stewart flees to France.

1747	Heritable Jurisdictions Act which removed from clan chiefs their hereditary powers. Jacobite rebel Lord Lovat the last peer executed in Britain.
1748	Treaty of Aix la Chapelle, Charles Edward Stewart banished from France.
1759	Robert Burns born on January 25.
1765	Steam Age began when James Watt patented his famous condenser.
1766	Death of the Old Pretender. Charles Stewart took the title King Charles III of Great Britain and Ireland.
1771	Birth of Sir Walter Scott.
1772	Marriage of Charles Stewart to Princess Louisa of Stolberg.
1788	January 31, death of Charles Edward Stewart, the Young Pretender. His brother took the title Henry IX.
1796	The death of Robert Burns.
1803	Thomas Telford begins work on the Caledonian Canal.
1807	Death of Henry, brother of Charles Edward Stewart, marks the end of the male line in the House of Stewart.
1813	March 29, birth of David Livingstone.
1817	The first Braemar Gathering established by officers and men who had fought at Waterloo.
1819	Factory Act which bans children under the age of nine working in cotton mills.
1820	April 1, Scottish Insurrection, national strike in Scotland.
1828	The patenting of J. B. Neilson's discovery of the hot-blast smelting process. Patrick Bell produces the world's first reaping-machine.
1832	The Great Reform Bill which took the first steps towards giving political representation to the middle classes. Death of Sir Walter Scott.
1835	Birth of Andrew Carnegie.
1842	Queen Victoria first visits Scotland.
1843	May 18, Free Church of Scotland born.
1846	Blight wipes out the entire west coast potato crop.
1850	Mines Act allows miners themselves to check how much coal they had produced.
1852	Prince Albert pays £31,000 for Balmoral Castle.
1855	United Coal and Iron Miners' Association of Scotland founded.
1856	August, birth of James Keir Hardie.
1858	Glasgow United Trades Council formed.
1865	William Usher of Edinburgh pioneers whisky blending and is the first to sell the drink under a 'propriety' label which guarantees its quality.

1873	May, death of the explorer David Livingstone in Northern Rhodesia.
1882	April, Highland Land League formed to obtain security of tenure and fair rents.
1884	Third Reform Act extends franchise.
1866	City Improvement Trust set up in Glasgow to alleviate the city's overcrowding and ill-health.
1871-1901	A quarter of Scotland's total natural increase in population— 483,000 — emigrates to Canada, America, and Australia.
1872	Education Act passed which discourages the use of Gaelic.
1873	Scottish Football Association formed.
1879	The infamous Tay Bridge disaster when a train plunges off the bridge into the water below with the loss of over 100 lives.
1888	The rebuilt Tay rail bridge opens.
1890s	The uncovering of the Iron Age village Jarlshof near the southern tip of Shetland. This is one of the most important archaeological sites in Britain, as it shows the development of civilisation from the earliest times through to the medieval age.
1890	The Forth Rail Bridge is opened.
1892	Keir Hardie becomes an MP and goes on to form the Labour Party.
1883	October 4, Boys Brigade founded.
1897	Scottish Trades Union Congress formed.
1914	August 4, First World War breaks out.
1918	November 11, armistice with Germany ends the First World War.
1930	Population of Hirta, the main island in the St. Kilda archipelago, evacuated at their own request.
1934	September 26, the *Queen Mary* launched on Clydeside.
1939	September, Second World War breaks out.
1940	February 28, *Queen Elizabeth* launched on Clydeside.
1941	March 13, Clydeside blitzed by upwards of 200 German bombers.
1944	November, battleship *Vanguard* launched on Clydeside.
1964	September, the Forth Road Bridge opened.
1965	Highlands and Islands Development Board set up to create work north of the Highland Line.
1970	British Petroleum discover oil off Aberdeen.
1979	March 1, Not enough Scots vote in favour in a referendum for a Scottish Assembly.
1997	Referendum held by Blair's New Labour government returns an overwhelming 'Yes' vote for the founding of a Scottish Parliament, with its own tax-raising powers.

25 Index of Historic Buildings

NATIONAL TRUST FOR SCOTLAND INDEX
Scenes and sites of Ancient Scotland administered by the National Trust For Scotland 95 Charlotte Square, Edinburgh EH24DU

Antonine Wall, three sections of Roman wall and ditches, near Falkirk (under guardianship of Historic Scotland).

Balmerino Abbey, 13th century Cistercain, near Newport-on-Tay.

Bannockburn, an important historic sites in Scotland, scene of the 1314 battle when Robert the Bruce routed the English, Stirling.

Ben Lawers, Perthshire mountain reserve with views over towards the North Sea.

Ben Lomond, rising to 3,200 ft from east shore of Loch Lomond.

Blackhill, Iron Age hill fort, near Lanark.

Boath Dovecot, site of ancient motte, Nairn.

Brodick Castle, 13th century castle on ancient Viking fortress isle, Isle of Arran.

Goatfell, highest peak on Arran.

Brodie Castle, family home since 1160, Forres, near Inverness.

Bruce's Stone, granite boulder marks where Bruce defeated English in 1307, near New Galloway.

Bucinch and Ceardach, uninhabited islands in Loch Lomond. Burg, cliffs known as 'The Wilderness', Isle of Mull.

Caiy Stone, site of battle between Picts and Romans, Edinburgh.

Canna, most westerly of the so-called Small isles, Hebrides.

Castle Campbell, imposing 15th century chief's home, in Dollar. Glen, Clackmannanshire (under the guardianship of Historic Scotland).

Clava Cairns, 2000BC, near Inverness (under guardianship of Historic Scotland).

Castle Fraser, magnificent 16th century turrets, Inverurie, near Aberdeen.

Corrieshalloch Torge, box canyon near Ullapool.

Craigievar Castle, 17th century "fairytale" castle, Alford, near Aberdeen.

Craigower, beacon hill near Pitlochry.

Crathes Castle, lands granted by the Bruce surround 16th century castle, Banchory, near Aberdeen.

Crookston Castle, 15th century, Glasgow (under guardianship of Historic Scotland).

Culloden, site of last battle on British soil, Jacobite Rebellion ended here in 1746, east of Inverness.

Culross Palace, 16th century, Fife.

Dirleton Castle, beautiful ruins dating from 1225, near North Berwick, Lothain (under guardianship of Historic Scotland).

Drum Castle, one of the three oldest tower houses in Scotland, begun 13th century, near Aberdeen.

Dunkeld, large areas of old village, Perth & Kinross.

Fair Isle, isolated inhabited island, Shetland.

Falkland Palace, country residence of Stewart Kings, Fife.

Falls of Glomach, Kyle of Lochalsh.

Finovon Dovecot, largest dovecot in Scotland, 2,400 nesting boxes, 16th century, Forfar.

Fyvie Castle, grandest example of Scottish baronial architecture, 13th century, Aberdeenshire.

Gladstone's Land, 17th century tenement, Edinburgh.

Glencoe and Dalness, historic glen and scene of 1692 massacre, Highlands.

Glenfinnan Monument, Loch Shiel, near Fort William.

Glenluce Abbey, 12th century Cistercian, Dumfries & Calloway (under guardianship of Historic Scotland).

Grey Mare's Tail, spectacular waterfall near Moffat, Dumfries & Galloway.

Hamilton House, 17th century home of prosperous Edinburgh merchant, and adjacent 15th century Preston Tower, Prestonpans, Lothian.

House of the Binns, 17th century mansion, Linlithgow, Lothian.

Hugh Miller's Cottage, 17th century, Cromarty.

Iona, 1,800 acres of the island where St Columba arrived in 563AD.

Kellie Castle, 14th and 16th century, Pittenweem & Fife.

Killiecrankie, pastoral reserve close to 1689 battle site, Pitlochry.

Kintail and Morvich, magnificent stretch of West Highland scenery, near Kyle of Lochalsh.

Lamb's House, 16th century home of prosperous Edinburgh merchant, Leith.

Leith Hall, family estate since 1650, Huntly, north of Aberdeen.

Linn of Tummel, characteristic beauty of Perthshire Highlands, near Pitlochry.

Mar Lodge Estate, 77,500 acres containing four of the ten highest mountains in the Britsh Isles, Ballater, Aberdeenshire.

Pitmedden Garden, laid out in 1675, Ellon, Aberdeenshire.

Provan Hall, 15th century, the most perfect pre-Reformation mansion house in Scotland, Glasgow.

Provost Ross's House, 16th century, overlooking harbour, is one of oldest houses in Aberdeen.

St Abb's Head, spectacular headland, Borders.

St Kilda, remote, dramatic and now uninhabited archipelago 110 miles out into the Atlantic Ocean.

Scotstarvit Tower, fine 16th century tower house, Cupar, Fife (under guardianship of Historic Scotland).

Staffa, island of Fingal's Cave, immortalised by Mendelssohn, west of Mull.

Strome Castle, 15th century stronghold of the Lords of the Isles, Loch Carron, Highlands.

Threave Castle, 14th century stronghold in island in River Dee,

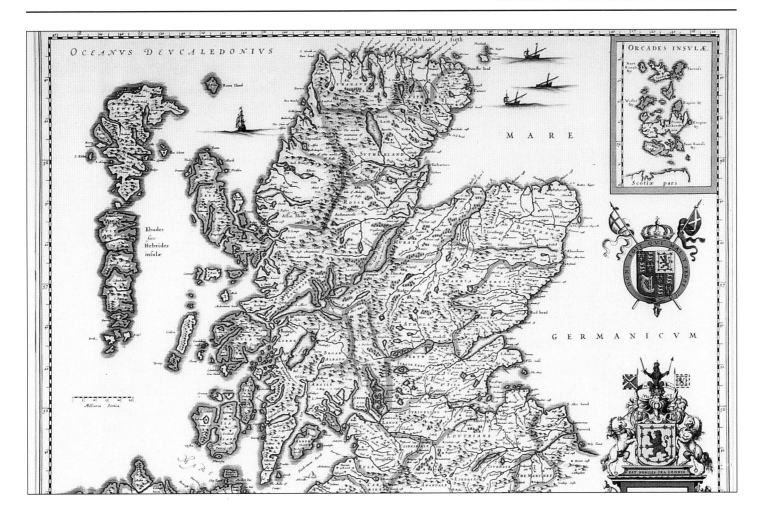

Dumfries & Galloway (under gardianship of Historic Scotland).
Torridon, 16,00 acres of Scotland's finest mountain scenery (including Shieldaig Island, in Loch Torridon), Highlands.
Turret House, opposite Kelso Abbey, Borders.
West Affric, 9,000 acres of wild landscapes, near Cannich, Highlands.

By joining the National Trust For Scotland, you will help preserve the fine examples of Scotland's rich , architectural, scenic and historic heritage which are in its care. You can join Scotland's leading conservation organisation at its headquarters at 5 Charlotte Square, Edinburgh EH2 4DU or at any of its properties. Ordinary membership is £25, family membership is £42.

HISTORIC SCOTLAND INDEX
Scenes and sites of Ancient Scotland cared for by Historic Scotland (Longmore House, Salisbury Place, Edinburgh EH 9ISH)

Aberdour Castle, 14th century fortified residence, Fife.
Aberlemno Sculptured Stones, in churchyards near Forfar, Tayside.
Abernethy Round Tower, 11th century, Tayside.
Achnabreck Cup and Ring Marks, Bronze Age, at Poltalloch, near Lochgilphead, Argyll & Bute.

Arbroath Abbey, 12th century ruins, Tayside.
Ardchattan Priory, 13th century, near Oban.
Ardclach Bell Tower, 17th century, near Nairn, Inverness.
Ardestie Earth-house, Iron Age, near Arbroath.
Ardunie Roman signal Station, near Auchterarder.
Argyll Lodging, 17th century Stirling.
Auchagallon Stone Circle, Bronze Age burial cairn, Isle of Arran.
Ballygowan, Cup and Ring marks and Balluachraig Cup & Ring marks, Bronze Age, near Poltalloch, Highlands.
Balvaird Castle, 15th century, Bridge of Earn.
Balvenie Castle, 13th century, Dufftown.
Bar Hill Fort, on the Antonine Wall.
Barochan Cross, Celtic cross in Paisley Abbey.
Barsalloch Fort, Iron age hill fort, Dumfries and Galloway.
Bearsden Roman Bathhouse, 2nd century AD.
Beauly Priory, 13th century.
Bishop's and Earl's palaces, 13th century-plus, Kirkwall, Orkney.
Blackfriars Chapel, Dominican friar's church, St Andrews.
Blackhall Roman Camps, Tayside.
Blackhammer Chambered Cairn, Neolithic, Orkney.

Blackhouse, thatched house, Arnol, Isle of Lewis.
Blackness Castle, 15th century, Linlithgow.
Bothwell Castle, largest 13th century stone castle in Scotland, overlooking the Clyde.
Brandsbutt Symbol Stone, Pictish stone, near Inverurie.
Brechin Cathedral Round Tower, 11th century, Tayside.
Brough to Birsay, Norse church and village ruins, Orkney.
Broch of Gurness, Orkney.
Broughty Castle, 16th century tower, Dundee.
Burghead Well, early Christian baptistry, Grampian.
Burleigh Castle, roofless ruin c1500, Tayside.
Caerlaverock Castle, splendid Renaissance castle, near Dumfries.
Cairnbaan Cup and Ring Marks, near Lochgilphead.
Cairn Holy Chambered Cairns, Neolithic burial chambers, Dumfries and Galloway.
Cairn o'Get, burial chamber, Lybster.
Cairnpapple Hill, burial site from 3000 to 1400BC, Lothian.
Callanish Standing Stones, near Stornoway, Lewis.
Cambuskenneth Abbey, in 1326 Robert Bruce's parliament, Stirling.
Cardoness Castle, 15th century, Gatehouse-of-Fleet.
Carlungie Earth-house, Iron Age, Tayside.
Carnasserie Castle, 16th century, Dumfries & Galloway.
Castle Campbell, 15th century, near Dollar, Tayside (National Trust for Scotland property under the guardianship of Historic Scotland).
Castlecary, Earthworks, Fife & Central.
Castlelaw Hill Fort, Iron Age, Lothian.
Castle of Old Wick, Norse Tower House, Caithness.
Castle Sween, 12th century, Argyll & Bute.
Caterthurns, hill forts near Brechin, Tayside.
Chapel Finian, c1000AD, Dumfries & Galloway.
Chesters Hill Fort, Iron Age fort and ramparts, Lothian.
Church of St Magnus, 12th century, Orkney.
Clackmannan Tower, 14th century.
Clava Cairns, Stone Age-Bronze Age stone circles, Inverness (National Trust for Scotland property under the guardianship of Historic Scotland).
Claypotts Castle, 16th century, Tayside.
Clickhimin Broch, Iron Age tower, Lerwick.
Cnoc Freiceadain Long Cairns, Neolithic, Thurso.
Corgarff Castle, 16th century tower house, Grampian.
Corrimony Chambered Cairn, Glen Urquhart, near Drumnadrochit.
Coulter Motte, Norman castle mound, south Strathclyde.
Craigmillar Castle, 15th century, Edinburgh.
Craignethan Castle, 16th century, near Lanark.
Crichton Castle, built by the Earl of Bothwell, 16th century, Lothian.
Crookston Castle, 15th century, Glasgow (National Trust for Scotland property under the guardianship of Historic Scotland).
Cross Kirk, Peebles, 13th century,
Crossraguel Abbey, 13th century, South Strathclyde.
Cubbie Row's Castle, built by Norsemen around 1145, Wyre, Orkney.
Cullerlie Stone Circle, 2000BC, Aberdeen.
Culross Abbey, 13th century, Firth of Forth.

Clush Earth-house, 2,000 years old, Grampian.
Cuween Hill Chambered Cairn, Neolithic, near Kirkwall.
Deer Abbey, Cistercian ruins, near Peterhead.
Deskford Church, late-medieval, near Cullen, Grampian.
Dirleton Castle, beautiful 13th century ruins, Lothian (National Trust for Scotland property under the guardianship of Historic Scotland).
Doonhill Homestead, site of hall of a 6th century chief, near Dunbar.
Doune Castle, 14th century.
Druchtag Motte, 12th century castle, Dumfries & Galloway.
DrumcoltranTower, 16th century, Dumfries & Galloway.
Drumtroddan Cup and Ring Marks and Standing Stones, Bronze Age carvings and stones, Dumfries & Galloway.
Dryburgh Abbey, magnificent 12th century, Borders.
Duffus Castle, fine motte castle, near Elgin.
Dumbarton Castle, ancient capital of Strathclyde.
Dunadd Fort, spectacular stronghold of Scots kingdom of Dalriada, Argyll & Bute.
Dun Beag Broch, occupied until 18th century, Skye.
Dunblane Cathedral, noble medieval church.
Dun Carloway Broch, beautifully preserved, Lewis.
Dunchraigaig Cairn, Bronze Age, Argyll & Bute.
Dundonald Castle, large structure on site of prehistoric hill fort, South Strarthclyde.
Dun Dornaigil Broch, Sutherland.
Dundrennan Abbey, Cistercain founded 12th century, near Kirkcudbright.
Dunfermline Abbey and Palace, 11th century Benedictine abbey and palace birthplace of Charles I.
Dunfallandy Stone, Pictish sculpture, Pitlochry.
Dunglass Collegiate Church, 15th century, Lothian.
Dunkeld Cathedral, 15th cenury, on banks of Tay.
Dunstaffnage Castle and Chapel, 13th century, Oban.
Dwarfie Stane, Neolithic burial chamber, Orkney.
Dyce Symbol Stones, Pictish carvings in ruined parish church of Dyce, Grampian.
Earl's Palace, Birsay, 16th century palace of Earl of Orkney.
Eassie Sculptured Stone, in Eassie church, near Glamis, Tayside.
Easter Aquhorthies Stone Circle, 2000AD, near Inverurie, Grampian.
Eileach an Naoimh, island associated with St. Columba, north of Jura.
Eilean Mor, island with 12th century chapel, in sound of Jura.
Edinburgh Castle, the most famous in Scotland.
Edin's Hall Broch, Iron Age, near Granthouse, Borders.
Edrom Church, Norman doorway, near Duns.
Edzell Castle, 16th century, near Brechin, Tayside.
Elcho Castle, complete 16th century, mansion, on Tay.
Elgin Cathedral, 13th century superb ruin.
Eynhallow Church, 12th centruy, Orkney.
Fort Charlotte, 1665 artillery fort, Lerwick, Shetland
Fortrose Cathedral, 13th century, near Inverness.
Glasgow Cathedral, only medieval mainland cathedral to have

Right: *St. Clement's church, Rodel, Isle of Harris.*

survived the Reformation complete.

Glebe Cairn, Bronze Age burial chambers, Argyll & Bute.

Glenbuchat Castle, 16th century, Grampian.

Glenelg Brochs, two towers in beautiful setting, Kyle of Lochalsh.

Glenluce Abbey, 1192, Cistercian, Dumfries & Galloway, (National Trust for Scotland property under the guardianship of Historic Scotland).

Grain Earth-house, near Kirkwall, Orkney.

Greenknowe Tower, 16th century, near Gordon, Borders.

Greay Cairns of Camster, Neolithic burial chambers, Lybster, Caithness.

Hailes Castle, 13th century, Lothain.

Hermitage Castle, 14th century ruin, near Hawick, Borders.

Holm of Papa Westray Chambered Cairn, massive tomb, Orkney.

Holyrood Abbey and Park, 12th century, of Augustinian order, adjacent to Palace of Holyrood.

Huntingtower Castle, 15th century, Perth.

Huntly Castle, 12th century motte, beautiful setting, Grampian.

Inchcolm Abbey, 1123, best preserved monastic buildings in Scotland, on isle in Firth of Firth.

Inchkenneth Chapel, medieval, off Mull.

Inchmahome Priory, 13th century Augustinian, in Lake Menteith, Fife & Central.

Innerpeffray Chapel, 16th century, near Crieff, Tayside.

Inverlochy Castle, finely preserved 13th century, near Fort William.

Jarlshof, amazing Prehistoric and Norse settlement, Shetland.

Jedburgh Abbey, magnificent ruins from 1138, Borders.

Kelso Abbey, 1128, beautiful but less well preserved, Borders.

Kilchurn Castle, 16th century with spectaculaar views of Loch Awe.

Kildalton Cross, 9th century finest high cross in Scotland, Isle of Islay.

Kildrummyn Castle, 13th century, Grampian.

Kilmartin Sculptured Stones, grave slabs in parish church, Argyll & Bute.

Kilwinning Abbey, 13th century ruins, South Strathclyde.

King's Knot, formal 17th century gardens, beneath Stirling.

Kinkell Church, 16th century ruins, Inverurie, Grampian.

Kinneil House, 15th century tower, Bo'ness, Fife & Central.

Kirkmadrine Early Christian Stones, 5th century, earliest Christian memorial stones, Sandhead, Dumfries & Galloway.

Knap of Howar, Neolithic, oldest standing stone houses in north-west Europe, Orkney.

Knowe of Yarso Chambered Cairn, Neolithic, Rousay, Orkney.

Largs Old Kirk, elaborate 17th century monument.

Lauderdale Aisle, St. Mary's , remains of great 15th century church, Haddington, Lothian.

Lincluden Collegiate Church, 14th century, Dumfries.

Linlithgow Place, magnificent ruin, birthplace of Mary Queen of Scots and James V, Lothian.

Loanhead Stone Circle, 2000BC-plus, Grampian.

Loch Doon Castle, 700-years-old masonary amazingly transplanted from original island site in the 1930s, south Strathclyde.

Loch Leven Castle, 14th century jail of Mary Queen of Scots on island in Loch Leven, Tayside.

Lochmaben Castle, 14th century, Dumfries & Galloway.

Lochranza Castle, 16th century, Isle of Arran.

Machrie Moor Stone Circles, Bronze Age, Isle of Arran.

Maclean's Cross, 15th century, Kirkcudbright.

Maes Howe Chambered Cairn, finest Megalithic tomb in the British Isles, near Kirkwall, Orkney.

Maiden Stone, 9th century Pictish carved slab, Garioch, Grampian.

Maison Dieu Chapel, medieval hospital, Brechin Tayside.

Mar's Wark, 1570 Renaissance mansion, Stirling.

Meigle Sculptured Stone Museum, 25 monuments, Tayside.

Melrose Abbey, 1136 Cistercian abbey, most famed ruin in Scotland, Borders.

Memsie Cairn, Bronze Age, near Rathen, Grampian.

Midhowe Broch and Chambered Cairn, huge and impressive. Megalithic monument, on Rousay island, Orkney.

Morton Castle, 13th century hall house, Dumfries & Galloway.

Mousa Broch, superb surviving Iron Age broch tower, Shetland.

Muir o'Fauld Roman Signal Station, watch tower site, Ardunie, Tayside.

Muness Castle, 16th century tower house, Unst, Shetland.

Muthill Old Church and Tower, 15th century, Crieff, Tayside.

Ness of Burgi, Iron Age block house, Scatness, Shetland.

Nether Largie Cairns, Neolithic and Bronze Age, Argyll & Bute.

Newark Castle, 15th century, Port Glasgow.

Noltland Castle, 15th century unfinished, Westray, Orkney.

Ordhardton Tower, unique circular 15th century tower, Dumfries & Galloway.

Ormiston Market Cross, 15th century, Lothian.

Orphir-Earl's Bu and Church, 12th century and earlier Viking ruins, near Kirkwall, Orkney.

Peel Ring of Lumphanan, 13th century defensive earthwork, Grampian.

Picardy Symbol Stone, one of oldest Pictish stones, perhaps 7th century, near Mireton, Grampian.

Pierowall Church, medieval, Westray, Orkney.

Preston Market Cross, elaborate 17th century monument, Lothian.

Quoyness Chambered Cairn, Megalithic and Neolithic, Sanday, Orkney.

Ravenscraig Castle, royal artillery fort, Kirkcaldy, Fife.

Rennibister Earth-house, near Kirkwall, Orkney.

Restenneth Priory, Augustinian, near Forfar, Tayside.

Ring of Brogar Stone Circle and Henge, magnificent circle of standing stones with ditches, Stromness, Orkney.

Rothesay Castle, 13th century residence of Stewart kings, Isle of Bute.

Rough Castle, best preserved ramparts of Antonine Wall, near Bonnybridge, Fife & Central (this and two other sections of the Antonine Wall are National Trust for Scotland properties under the guardianship of Historic Scotland).

Ruthven Barracks, burned by Jacobites in 1746, near Kingussie.

Ruthwell Cross, 7th century Anglican cross, one of major Dark

Right: *Edinburgh Castle.*

Age monuments in Europe, near Dumfries.

St. Andrews Castle, ruins from 13th century, Fife & Central.

St. Andrews Cathedral and St. Rule's Tower, remains of largest cathedral in Scotland, early 12th century.

St. Blane's Church, Kingart, site of Celtic monastery, isle of Bute.

St. Bride's Church, Douglas, 14th century, South Strathclyde.

St. Bridget's Church, Dalgety, medieval churuch on banks of Forth.

St. Clement's Church, Rodel, 16th centruy, Isle of Harris.

St. Machar's Cathedral Transepts, 16th century ruins, Aberdeen.

St. Martn's Church, Haddington, 13th century ruins, Lothian.

St. Mary's Chapel, Crosskirk, simple 12th century chapel, near Thurso, Caithness.

St. Mary's Chapel, Rothesay, late-medieval remains, Argyll & Bute.

St. Mary's Church, Grandtully, 16th century, near Aberfeldy, Tayside.

St. Mary's Kirk, Auchindoir, one of finest medieval parish churches in Scotland, near Lumsden, Grampian.

St. Ninian's Cave, early crosses founded here, near Whithorn, Dumfries & Galloway.

St. Ninian's Chapel, 13th century pilgrim's chapel, Isle of Whitorn, Dumfries & Galloway.

St. Peter's Kirk and Parish Cross, Duffus, 14th century, Grampian.

St. Triduiana's Chapel, James III's unique shrine to Pictish saint, in Restalrig Collegiate Church, Edinburgh.

St. Vigean's Sculptured Stones, 32 early Pictish and Christian Stones, Arbroath, Tayside.

Scalloway Castle, built 1600, Shetland.

Scotstarvit Tower, 16th century, Cupar, Fife (National Trust for Scotland property under the guardianship of Historic Scotland).

Seton Collegiate Church, 15th century, Lothian.

Skara Brae Prehistoric Village, best preserved Stone Age houses in Western Europe, Shetland.

Skipness Castle and Chapel, 13th century, Kintyre.

Smailholm Tower, impressive rectangular tower near Kelso, Borders.

Spynie Palace, 14th century, Elgin, Grampian.

Staneydale 'Temple', Neolithic hall, near Walls, Shetland.

Steinacleit Cairn and Stone Circle, enigmatic prehistoric ruins, near Stornaway, isle of Lewis.

Stirling Castle, second most famous castle in Scotland and arguably the grandest.

Stirling Old Bridge, dating from 15th century, with Jacobite connections.

Stones of Stenness Circle and Henge, Stromness, Orkney.

Sueno's Stone, 20ft high, claimed to be one of the most remarkable sculptured monuments in Britain, Forres, Grampian.

Sweetheart Abbey, ruin in 30 acres, 13th century monument by Lady of Galloway in memory of her husband, near Dumfries.

Tentallon Castle, remarkable 14th century fortification dramatically situated on promontory near North Berwich.

Tarves Medieval Tomb, near Aberdeen.

Taversoe Tuick Chambered Cairn, megalithic and Neolithic, Stromness, Orkney.

Tealing Dovecot and Earth-house, Iron Age earth-house and elegant 16th century dovecot, near Dundee.

Threave Castle, 14th century tower on island, near Castle Douglas, Dumfries & Galloway (National Trust for Scotland property under the guardianship of Historic Scotland).

Tolquhon Castle, 15th century, near Aberdeen.

Tomnaverie Stone Circle, 2000BC Abouyne, Grampian.

Torhouse Stone Circle, Bronze Age, Wigtown, Dumfries & Galloway.

Torr a'Chaisteal Fort, Iron Age fort, near Blackwaterfoot, Arran.

Torrylin Cairn, Neolithic, near Lagg, Arran.

Tullibardine Chapel, complete and unaltered medieval church, near Crieff, Tayside.

Unstan Chambered Cairn, Neolithic, Stromness, Orkney.

Urquhart Castle, beautiful ruins from several ages, dramatically sited on a promontory overlooking Loch Ness.

Watling Lodge, best section of ditch of Antonine Wall, Falkirk.

West Port, 16th century city gate of St Andrews.

Westquarter Dovecot, 17th century, near Lauriston, Fife & Central.

Westside Church, Tuquoy, 12th century, Westray, O rkney.

Whithorn Priory and Museum, cradle of Christianity in Scotland, founded in the 5th centruy as St. Ninian's "Shining Light."

Wideford Hill Chambered Cairn, Neolithic, near Kirkwall, Orkney.

By becoming a 'Friend Of Scotland', you will be preserving the nation's heritage and helping to protect more than 300 buildings, monuments, and other priceless properties. Membership means free admission to them all — and the knowledge that you're supporting a team of archaeologists, historians, architects, and conservators in preserving these historical gems for future generations.

For membership details, write to Historic Scotland at: Longmore House, Salisbury Place, Edingurgh EH9 ISH.

Right: *Threave Castle, Dumfries & Galloway.*

INDEX